MIRACLE AT SING SING

ALSO BY RALPH BLUMENTHAL

Last Days of the Sicilians: At War with the Mafia:
The FBI Assault on the Pizza Connection

Once Through the Heart: A Police Detective's
Triumphant Struggle to Rescue His Daughter from Drugs

Stork Club: America's Most Famous Nightspot
and the Lost World of Café Society

MIRACLE AT SING SING

How One Man Transformed the Lives of
America's Most Dangerous Prisoners

RALPH BLUMENTHAL

St. Martin's Press
New York

www.stmartins.com

Book design by Michelle McMillian

Frontispiece photo: Prisoners in front of Sing Sing Prison. © Bettmann / Corbis.

Grateful acknowledgment is given for permission to reprint the song "Just One More Chance." Words by Sam Coslow. Music by Arthur Johnston. Copyright © 1931. Renewed 1958 by Famous Music Corporation. International copyright secured. All rights reserved.

Library of Congress Cataloging-in-Publication Data

Blumenthal, Ralph.
    Miracle at Sing Sing : how one man transformed the lives of America's most dangerous prisoners / Ralph Blumenthal.
        p. cm.
    Includes bibliographical references (p. 289) and index (p. 293)
    ISBN 0-312-30891-4
    EAN 978-0312-30891-9
    1. Prison administration—New York (State). 2. Sing Sing Correctional Facility. 3. Capital punishment—New York (State) 4. Death row inmates—New York (State). 5. Lawes, Lewis Edward, 1883–1947. I. Title.

HV9470.B58 2004
365'.9747277—dc22   2003070104

First Edition: June 2004

10 9 8 7 6 5 4 3 2 1

To *my* ever-faithful "boys"—
Debbie, Annie, Sophie . . . and Molly

Hell, the only law in Sing Sing is Lawes.
—Lewis E. Lawes, Invisible Stripes

PREFACE

In the end were all the beginnings, the brave starts and struggles of an eternity behind bars—twenty thousand years, he had once calculated, if you chalked up all his years and the years of all the men doing the time. He'd been there with them throughout, behind the walls, and when he tried to think which side of the walls the real world was found, he would have to say on his side—on their side—for he was, in the end, one of them, even though he had killed 303 of them, some as close as brothers. Theirs was a world apart, a world of cruelty and fear and evil and man-made death by electrocution, but also a world of faith and courage and humanity. This is how he saw it. A jail was a lockup, but a prison was a community. In the end, it would be said, he had taken a city of silent men and given it voice.

He had made Sing Sing sing.

He had made his beginning in the infancy of the bright new century, and a young guard's first posting to the harsh Siberia of New York State's remotest prison. He bore, to be sure, a comically perfect name for someone in his profession, but it was his inner gift, a telepathic understanding of the wants and needs of men—prisoners and their jailers—that propelled him upward through the walled archipelago of Clinton, Auburn, Elmira, and finally to the pinnacle of American penology: warden of Sing Sing, America's dread Bastille on the Hudson.

His name adorned books and countless articles and radio plays. He had grown up with the new wireless medium, and his deep and authoritative voice with its surprising touch of softness was among the first ever heard by families gathered in their living rooms to "listen in," as the wondrous saying then went. He dabbled on the stage and in motion pictures too, silent films and talkies, for there was little in the advance of civilization that did not enchant him with possibilities for promulgating his ideas and, yes, for a measure of fame. He did not mind the limelight. He liked a laugh and a good time too, so he brought football to Sing Sing, his Black Sheep eleven certain to outrage those who thought prisoners had no business having fun.

Running Sing Sing, where bruising political wars still raged, made him the nation's chief expert on crime and punishment, particularly capital punishment. On this he expounded tirelessly, denouncing the death penalty as worse than morally indefensible—it was ineffective and therefore useless. Killing had been punished by death since the days of the Bible, yet he knew better than anyone that men continued to kill, usually with no thought of the consequences. Good God, murders were committed within sight of the death house, and even a man who had himself worked on the first electric chair was sentenced to die in it. This was deterrence? Murderers, he had found, were not even criminals in the usual sense. For many it was their first, and last, brush with the law. What was punishment for, anyway? Revenge? Reformation? Protecting society? Whatever the reason, he thought, there had to be far wiser ways of restraining and reclaiming those who lived by choice or by chance outside the law. And who knew better than the man who had to fix the hour and minute of death and order the pulling of the switch?

Prison, he thought, was rather late to do much for a man. Prison was a confession of society's failure.

Now, two decades after he'd taken over Sing Sing's forbidding battlements and execution chamber, with the debased century engulfed in carnage and war lapping at the nation's shores, Lewis Edward Lawes was bidding farewell to his boys.

Work at Sing Sing halted early that July afternoon in 1941. The factories and workshops shut down, and 2,400 inmates crowded into the austere brick chapel where Lawes had so often rallied them at times of upheaval. He had been young and self-assured when he first arrived with a woman at his side who melted men like these. Now his long forehead was gaining on the thinning once-blond hair, and the woman was a sainted memory, dead by fate's mysterious hand.

"I am about to join the ranks of the unemployed," he began, and their roars of laughter and disbelief shook the roof. Earlier, he had received a retirement gift of a silver service from the guards and administrative staff and a painstakingly illuminated testimonial scroll from the prisoners; if asked to show which was dearer to him, he'd have returned the silver.

"Almost anybody likes to get out of prison," he continued, to an approving chorus of yeas, "and any one of you fellows would like to be in my place." He paused, professionally, for the cheers he knew would come, and they came. He could work a crowd, especially this crowd, and their raw energy stirred him. He spoke of the early days at Clinton and Auburn, where harshness ruled, and he contrasted them with Sing Sing and what was called its honor system. But really, he said, there was no honor system—how could there be when men with machine guns patrolled the walls? Yet they had understood each other, he and his boys. He had never preached to them, he said, and they had never whined to him. He hadn't given sympathy, and they had never asked for it. But, he said, there was an unspoken bond between them that would outlast his departure.

The ceremony had been set to occur months earlier. But just as Lawes had prepared to leave in April, three convicts in the hospital ward shot their way out in the most violent breakout in Sing Sing's history. A guard was killed, and outside, at the train depot, an Ossining police officer was gunned down as his partner shot one of the escapees. The surviving two commandeered a boat at the Hudson and made it across the river to the Palisades, where they were hunted down and beaten and hauled back to Sing Sing.

Was this, then, how it was to end—the grim-faced warden saying little as he donned a mourning band and grieved for the families of the slain officers? Was that his farewell? No, he would force himself to stay, to do things his way, as he always had, and leave when he was ready. He postponed his departure until the pair's quick trial, conviction, and inevitable end in the chair, the chair that Lawes had spent his career denouncing. And then he faced his men a final time.

In the chapel, the farewell speeches droned on and the boys cheered. . . .

MIRACLE AT SING SING

1

From the water it looked like an old New England factory, maybe a knitting mill, red brick with neat rows of white-framed windows, tall gray smokestacks, a railroad track, and a flagpole with a flapping American flag.

From the water you couldn't see the bars.

In summer the greenery almost swallowed the sharp-peaked turrets that poked up like deadly mushrooms along the snaking walls. Behind the factory buildings and just visible between them was a long building the color of bleached bones. This had no windows to speak of, just little vertical lines, the way a child might draw windows if he had to draw a lot of them. Even up close they were only slits that called up visions of medieval archers bending cocked bows pregnant with showers of arrows. But the slits concealed only prisoners, more than a thousand of them, crammed into cubes of weeping stone cells so small they might have been carved out of dice. From the water, you could not see these, either.

But few viewed the place from the water, only the crews of rusty tankers heading up the river—which wasn't a river at all, really, but an estuary, an arm of the sea complete with tides—and pleasure boaters bound for Bear Mountain or West Point, or Albany or Troy beyond the Catskills. Most saw Sing Sing prison from the land, as did the big, fastidiously dressed visitor and honey-haired woman who drove up to a guardhouse at dusk one Sunday not long before Christmas, 1919.

A soft rain had fallen earlier in the weekend but then the mercury had plunged, sending frigid gusts knifing across the choppy gray waters. Across the ocean, the great guns had been silent for more than a year, but the

Senate was still deadlocked on a peace treaty with Germany. Rampaging Bolsheviks were taking Poltava in the Ukraine. And thirty-one miles down the Hudson, New York hotels were wondering what they were supposed to do with five million dollars' worth of liquor that Prohibition would render illegal in less than three weeks.

At the gate, the man boomed out his name, given in the papers the next day as Major Louis Lawes, which suited him fine, since he had long believed that you could safely discount 75 percent of what you read in the press. Major Lewis Lawes said he was there to see Warden Edward V. Brophy.

The guard's welcome was cool, almost disdainful. Clearly he dismissed Lawes as just another short-timer. But Warden Brophy, Lawes felt certain, would be glad to see him. After eight months at Sing Sing, Brophy—the ninth warden in the last eight years—was like a condemned man hoping for a reprieve. Fed up with the meddling of state officials, particularly prison superintendent Charles F. Rattigan, Brophy had put in his retirement papers a month ago. He had already lost forty pounds at Sing Sing.

Lawes, sure enough, held the keys to Brophy's fate. To the guard at the gate who asked his business he said, "I have been offered the wardenship." The guard shrugged. The wardens changed so fast at Sing Sing that the staff never knew who would greet them in the morning. The gate swung open.

Earlier that afternoon, Lawes and his wife, Kathryn, had motored down from New Hampton, New York, in the wilds of Orange County across the river, where Lawes was running a New York City prison farm for delinquent boys. An audacious experiment, a reformatory without walls on six hundred rural acres, it had proved, as Lawes had somehow known it would, more impervious to escape than institutions with the most hermetic security, even when Lawes, in a caper that left state officials gasping with incredulity, armed 150 of his boys with rifles, revolvers, and blank cartridges to shoot a movie about the Mexican-American War.

Lawes remained deeply attached to the place, to the point where he still wasn't sure he should trade it for Sing Sing, glory and his word be damned. He had told Governor Al Smith he would take it, but he continued to waver, keeping Brophy and everyone else guessing. He was thirty-six years old. None of the previous thirty-eight wardens who had tried to run Sing Sing in its nearly ninety-five years had ever been that young. He knew that Sing Sing was America's greatest prison and its warden the nation's penologist in chief, but he couldn't help wondering if he had gone crazy. The last great reform warden, Thomas Mott Osborne, had been driven out barely four years before, charged with sodomy.

Kathryn too had her doubts. She was an independent sort, one of the determined turn-of-the-century young women who put off marriage and domesticity for the raffish allure of office work as a "typewriter" in a robustly male environment. Now that she had settled down with a family, she did not relish bringing up their two young daughters in a prison.

But privately Lawes knew what he wanted to do. Sing Sing wasn't a posting. It was a career.

After meeting with Brophy, Lawes and Kathryn were treated to a tour of the yard. From somewhere the prison band belted out a refrain from *The Pirates of Penzance*. Lawes was tone-deaf, but that much he could recognize. Then he alone was escorted inside. No one thought it advisable to bring a woman into the cellblock, and certainly not a woman who looked like Kathryn. For a while she sat on a bench in the reception area and crossed her legs and waited. But then she grew curious and got up to peek around, entering the ward of the prison clinic.

Lawes meanwhile had entered the slit-windowed cellblock, which seemed little changed since convicts from Auburn had been barged across the Erie Canal and down the Hudson to quarry the rock for the first eight hundred cells in 1825. Small wonder they called it the Bastille on the Hudson.

Five years earlier, on an errand here from his hometown of Elmira, New York, Lawes had been revolted by the debris in the yard and the zombielike shuffling of the prisoners. Now he saw it was still filthy. The cells, piled four tiers high, hadn't changed either. They were still seven feet deep, three feet three inches wide, and six feet seven inches high. On cold winter nights like this, the stone wept with cold. But at least now there was only one man to a cell. Until a few years ago there had been two, guaranteeing God only knew what perversions. The doors, interwoven strips of steel that barred almost all the air and light that managed to penetrate the dismal outer shell of the building, were locked and unlocked, fifty at a time, by a 150-foot-long sliding steel bar invented by an inmate. There was no plumbing. The prisoners used slop buckets that they emptied in the river on their way to breakfast and picked up again at night. Warden Osborne had been as repulsed as Lawes was by conditions. The cells were "unspeakably bad," Osborne said.

Undated photo, probably predating Lawes's arrival, of old Sing Sing cellblock. (COLLECTION OF RALPH BLUMENTHAL)

"To call them unfit for human habitation is to give them undeserved dignity. They are unfit for pigs." But Osborne, with all his humanity and splendid intentions, was ultimately broken, hounded out of Sing Sing for his trouble, and branded a pervert. Osborne's fate didn't augur well for Lawes.

From the cellblock, Lawes was led into the adjoining death cells, viewing them with little inkling how they would come to overshadow his life. He was surprised to find them overflowing with twenty-three condemned prisoners, waiting to keep their date with the chair that had claimed the lives of 156 men and one woman since 1891. Five others sentenced to die had to be housed elsewhere. He walked through quickly, resolving to come back when he had the job. If he took the job.

Outside in the dark, lighting up a fresh panatela to rid his nostrils of what he couldn't stop thinking was the stench of death, his foot caught in a rabbit hole and he nearly went down, swearing, "Goddamn it!" The creatures had the run of the place and were obviously being kept as pets. They would have to go if he took the job, along with those pineboard shacks where the boys had to be brewing their hooch. He hadn't missed the brazen hand-lettered sign by the mess hall: "Please Don't Stand Up While Room Is in Motion." The potato-water stills would go too.

Kathryn was making her way through the hospital ward, gazing with moist eyes at the poor souls stretched out on rickety cots. It was unutterably sad. She stopped by the side of a cadaverous figure with the face of a paving block, granite gray hair, a straight slash of a mouth, and the remnants of a permanent scowl, as if someone had just snatched away his pince-nez. He lay listlessly, but there was something aristocratic in his bearing, and his eyes, which had followed her around the room, were obsidian-hard, like a snake's, and grayish blue. Before she could catch herself, she blurted, "Oh, you are such a nice-looking man. What are you doing here?"

He didn't answer, perhaps in fear that he was hallucinating this beatific vision. In turn he barely managed to croak out his own question. What was she doing there?

"My husband may be the next warden," she said.

He was silent at first, then said, "I hope to God he is."

Lawes, his tour finished, found Kathryn at the old man's bedside. Lawes asked how he was doing and the man smiled for the first time. "You are the first man who gave me a kindly nod since I came here," he said.

Old warden's house at Sing Sing, probably 1920s. (OSSINING HISTORICAL SOCIETY MUSEUM)

Outside the ward Lawes and Kathryn found out about him, prisoner no. 69690. He was Sing Sing's most famous, or infamous, denizen: Charles E. Chapin, for two decades the tyrannical editor of Joseph Pulitzer's *New York Evening World* and undoubtedly the ablest and meanest son of a bitch ever to run a newsroom. When New York mayor William J. Gaynor was shot in full view of a *World* photographer in 1910, Chapin, who had been prescient enough to dispatch his man well beforehand, was exultant. "Blood all over him, and an exclusive too!" Now sixty-one, he had come to Sing Sing eleven months earlier for a stay of twenty years to life. He had murdered his wife.

Before leaving the prison, Lawes and Kathryn were invited to dine with Brophy in the warden's house, a rambling gingerbread stone-and-wood mansion with twenty bedrooms, three tiers of verandas, and a cupola. Kathryn was appalled to see that it not only stood within the prison walls but also abutted the cellblock.

They left at 9 P.M. Brophy still didn't know if he was reprieved.

But if Lawes hadn't yet shown his hand, others felt sure they knew what he would do. The day before Lawes ventured to Sing Sing, a Brooklyn boys club director wrote to congratulate him on becoming warden of Sing Sing. He thanked Lawes too, for "helping me out of my trouble in Albany, N.Y.," and closed, "I am getting along fine now."

Reading the letter, Lawes had to smile. Leave it to one of his ex-boys to sniff out the real story.

A week later, a letter arrived from the editor of the *Star Bulletin,* Sing Sing's illustrated monthly. It requested a halftone cut or recent photograph for the next issue. The prison press was on the story.

Word was spreading. The inspections director of the New York City Health Department offered congratulations, although Lawes had yet to formally accept the appointment and was still torn by doubts. "I am leaving a hopeful, cheerful and congenial place to accept a position which has been the graveyard of many ambitious institutional executives," he wrote back, adding, "all my friends think that I am either looney or that I have laid in a supply of wet goods and imbibed too freely."

But privately he had made up his mind, confiding to a pal from his days at the Elmira Reformatory, "This position is a life job and I have it on my fingers end and of course most of my friends think I am foolish in making the move. However, I have reasons of my own."

With the shuffle of a thousand pairs of feet and the rattle of tinware, the prisoners of Sing Sing arranged themselves in facing rows at the long mess-hall tables for New Year's Day dinner. The night before, they had been treated to a half hour's celebratory concert by the prison band. Between numbers, the inmates banged their cell doors, shouted, whistled, and offered three cheers for Warden Grant, who had succeeded the finally reprieved Brophy and was the shortest-lived of their many masters. If the babble in the austere hall was more raucous than usual, it was in good riddance to another year chalked up, one more long and dreary slog through the seasons in discharge of a supposed debt to society, a debt that somehow kept running up interest. But now a fresh new decade beckoned, the twenties, which held, for those who still harbored hope, the promise of release. Suddenly the band burst into "Auld Lang Syne," and a phalanx of blue-uniformed keepers and officials in suits surged through the entranceway.

Moments earlier, Lawes, this time alone, had arrived in a taxi from New Hampton. Waved through the gate, he was greeted inside by his new boss, Charles Rattigan, the battle-scarred superintendent.

Lawes had heard from him less than a month before, in a telegram to New Hampton on December 5, 1919: "Can you arrange to meet the Governor and me at the Biltmore Hotel on Tuesday, December 9, at 11 o'clock?"

Lawes guessed it was about Sing Sing. The prison was a mess and administrators were always looking for a new warden. But he was an independent Republican, not an enrolled Democrat, and he wondered if the governor knew that. Lawes went to New York, telling himself he would turn the job down.

Al Smith offered a jovial welcome and plunged right in. "How about going up to Sing Sing to take charge? They need a man with experience."

Lawes gave his prepared speech. Smith let him finish, then, eyes atwinkle, drawled, "Young fella, it's all right with me. It's a tough spot. I don't blame you for being scared. It'll take a big man to go up there and stay."

Lawes saw what Smith was up to, but now he knew he would take the position. Although he had decided to accept the job, he still asked for a week to think it over. He also told the governor he wanted a free hand with no political interference, and the post of warden had to be put under civil service protection. Smith scowled but nodded. "It's yours, son."

Lawes took the further precaution of visiting Bill Ward, the Westchester Republican boss. If he took the job, Lawes said, Sing Sing had to be free of patronage. "Do you think you can run it?" Ward asked.

Lawes said he could.

Then run it, Ward said, "but don't let those reformers run it for you."

Lawes also saw Ward's counterpart, Democratic boss Mike Walsh. He, too, promised hands off.

Lawes had gotten what he wanted. Now he had to live with it.

With the first notes of "Auld Lang Syne," the prisoners in the mess hall looked up to see Rattigan with a husky man with receding sandy hair, a strong jawline, and, even from a distance, striking blue eyes. He could have been a priest. He could have been a cop. He could have been almost anything. He was big, but somehow not as big as he seemed. He was immaculately dressed, almost dandyish, in a dark suit and white shirt with a crisp, high, rounded collar nestling a subdued silk necktie. The prisoners saw his attire as a bad sign. He'd also come up from the ranks as a guard—another bad omen—and at Clinton, the Siberia of New York. Once a guard, always a guard, the men figured. They looked on silently.

Warden had followed warden in rapid succession at Sing Sing. Brophy hadn't lasted three-quarters of a year. His successor, Daniel J. Grant, a career criminologist from Auburn, had served all of sixteen days. Now another warden was stepping in. For how long? the men wondered.

Rattigan stood on a makeshift platform atop a table and called for their attention. This, he announced to a swelling chorus of applause and jeers, was their new warden, Major Lewis E. Lawes. "I think he is capable of handling you fellows," he said. "Some I know are a little tough, some all right, some all wrong. I want you to give him every possible consideration. He was represented to me as a 'regular fellow' who will give you a chance—every possible chance that can be given to you under the laws of the state of New York."

There were catcalls as Lawes approached the platform. Then, hesitating, he chose to remain on the floor, standing among them. "I'd rather talk to you men on the level," he began in a clear and sonorous voice. "I hope to stay here. I can't tell you what I'm going to do here, for I don't know. I have received from you resolutions of cooperation and loyalty. That's all I want. I am going to be warden."

This was greeted by scattered applause and whistles. He went on: "If I wasn't, I wouldn't be here. I am going to be around the yard and want you to feel that you may approach me and talk to me." The men were stamping their feet now and yelling, whether in support or dismissal of Lawes was not clear.

He would meet them halfway, he pledged, but they had to get one thing straight: there would be no "You be a good boy and I'll be a good warden." There was no equality. He was the boss. What privileges they got they would have to earn. The room turned quiet.

He then delivered his best line, swiped from a joke making the rounds. "If you want to get out of this place quickly," he said, "you have to come in as a warden."

There was a split second's pause and then a ripple of welcome laughter.

2

Lawes had resolved to revisit the death house since his first exploratory visit in December 1919, less than two weeks before returning as Sing Sing's thirty-ninth warden. Many had already trudged its hopeless corridor with none of Lawes's prospects of freely walking out again.

The small stone building grew like a tumor on the cellblock annex of the skeleton-white main prison. The addition had been put up in 1889, a year after the state superseded its localities in the power to execute its citizens and voted to employ a modern instrument, the electric chair.

Inside were the condemned cells off a corridor ending at a brown door. It had once been green and was still widely known as the green door. Lawes passed through the portal, and there was the chair itself, a bizarre contraption of oak and brass fittings, leather straps, and wires. Strictly speaking, it wasn't really an electric chair, because the chair wasn't electric. It was just a wooden device for holding down a person to be shocked to death by electric current. It was, Lawes had heard, surprisingly comfortable, with rubber pads on the seat and on the headrest. The oiled straps were soft and pliable, and two round holes in the crosspiece between the chair's legs provided a convenient and secure resting place for the feet.

Amazingly, the guard who had led the building's construction project in 1889—and had then already been there ten years—was still there to greet Lawes. Keeper Alfred Conyes had done forty years at Sing Sing. Ruddy and severe-looking, Conyes was then almost seventy and remembered well the days of discipline at the end of a hickory club. While no one was still alive

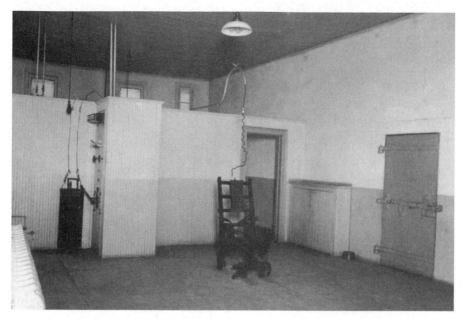

Early photo of Sing Sing electric chair. (OSSINING HISTORICAL SOCIETY MUSEUM)

who remembered the founding of Sing Sing more than a century before, Conyes came close.

In 1824 a legislative commission had voted to replace Newgate, the state's first prison, built on the Hudson in Greenwich Village in 1797. The early, unbridled years of the new American republic had proved hard on the jails. A second prison had been built at Auburn in the Finger Lakes region west of Syracuse in 1816, but it was too remote for New York City prisoners.

Auburn's authoritarian warden, Elam Lynds, was commissioned to plan a new prison. In 1825 he and the state selected the site, a former silver mine and marble quarry some thirty miles up the river from New York City, on the east bank of the Hudson. The water made travel easy, and rock would be plentiful, as the Native Americans had recognized when they named the place Sint Sinck, meaning stone upon stone. The state bought 130 acres for just over twenty thousand dollars.

Lynds arrived with a hundred Auburn convicts that May, and in little more than three years, by November 1828, the first eight hundred prisoners of the new Sing Sing, as both the prison and the town would be known, were locked in their cells. The block, modeled after Auburn's north wing, was a double-shelled structure, the cells catacombed within an outside building that allowed little light and air to seep through narrow-slitted windows. Its location on the banks of the Hudson ensured a miasmic dampness, excellent for the proliferation of vermin and diseases like tuberculosis but savage on human life. The brutal Auburn system of discipline also prevailed: enforced silence and liberal use of the "cat." Prisons were filled with "coarse beings," Lynds told the visiting Alexis de Tocqueville, and would be ungovernable "were it not for the continual use of the whip."

By the time Conyes arrived, two hundred more cells had been added, along with a women's section that took almost forty years to be declared a failure and closed. A library had been established, two part-time teachers had been hired, and the rules had been relaxed to allow prisoners two visits a year. A railroad line had stitched an iron hem along the prison's eastern edge, and the lash was history, replaced, paradoxically, by more fiendish punishments: yokes, balls and chains, and the shower bath, a restraining chair placed below a barrel that loosed a torrent of icy water on the hapless victim, nearly drowning him.

Conyes, then almost twenty-eight and a stonecutter from Kingston up the Hudson, had been to a fortune-teller who had prophesied success, seeing Conyes's destiny as a boss with power over men. That, Conyes decided, had to mean a career at Sing Sing. He had friends talk to the governor, which was the way such positions were awarded, and won appointment as a guard.

Sing Sing had loosened since the harsh rule of Lynds, but the old penology still prevailed. The prisoners were still garbed in stripes. Their heads were shaved. They walked everywhere in lockstep. They were consigned to silence. The only thing a guard could say to a prisoner was yes or no, and yes was a rare answer.

Conyes was tested with a work strike in one of the shops where prisoners made goods for private industry. He ended it quickly, with his hickory club, and afterward, the inmates who could still stand went back to work. Others went to the hospital. The ringleaders went to the dungeon, strung up by their wrists until they bled. The dungeon was completely dark, with hard stone for beds and two padded cells for those who went insane.

He was a young guard there in 1885 when Sing Sing welcomed its first celebrity, the Wall Street embezzler Ferdinand Ward, who had ruined ex-president Ulysses S. Grant. Four years later, Conyes was in charge of the prison crew that built the first death house, a wooden shack housing eight cells and the electric chair. One of the prisoners on the construction job, Thomas Pallister, was later convicted of murder and ordered to die in his own creation, leaving Conyes to wonder how much of a deterrent the death penalty really was. But Pallister never did suffer that poetic justice. He and a crony broke out of the death block and were later found floating in the Hudson, each with a mysterious bullet hole in the head.

Conyes had guarded the first inmate ever sentenced to die by electric shock, Charles McElvaine, a twenty-year-old driver and printer from Brooklyn who had fatally stabbed a grocer during a botched burglary and entered Sing Sing's new death cells in October 1889. But McElvaine won a new trial. By the time he was reconvicted in October 1890, he had lost his preeminent place in the lineup and the dubious distinction of making execution history. Instead, in July 1891, four other men would inaugurate Sing Sing's chair.

Sensation seekers thronged the hill overlooking the prison, pressing to witness the spectacle, but Warden W. R. Brown would have none of it. He drew a line in the earth—forever establishing his nickname, "Deadline" Brown—and posted Conyes on the prison wall with a rifle.

"You keep them back," he told the keeper. "Shoot to kill if you have to, but keep them back."

As dusk fell, the crowd surged forward. "Halt!" yelled Conyes, enlisting three large men below to help him stem the invasion. Folks could follow events from outside the walls, he said. With each execution, a flag would be run up the halyard.

Inside, at the death cells, keepers had set up iron screens to block the view through the bars so none of the four would know the order of their summoning. James J. Slocum, a husky twenty-two-year-old manslayer, was called first. He submitted meekly, putting his arms and legs where ordered. The guards had practiced and were quick. One took a can and poured cold salt water on the electrode sponges, ensuring better conductivity. Slocum winced at the touch of the damp electrodes. When all was ready, one of the doctors standing behind the chair with a stopwatch in one hand and a white handkerchief in the other let his handkerchief drop. The prison electrician turned a lever shunting current to a line connected to the chair. Then the executioner, hidden from view, threw the switch, sending fifteen hundred volts into Slocum.

The leather straps creaked under the strain of the large body lunging forward as if to spring out of the chair. Twenty seconds later, the current was switched off. The body collapsed, limp and flaccid, as doctors gathered around for their examination. They stood back as a second jolt was administered, for certainty's sake. The body stiffened and lurched, and a wheezing rush of air escaped the lips. Slocum was irrevocably dead. His body was wheeled out to the autopsy room.

Outside, the crowd watched as a white flag slowly mounted the pole and unfurled in the breeze.

"There's one gone," Conyes announced to cheers.

Next to go was Harris A. Smiler, a thirty-two-year-old Salvation Army worker and bigamist who had murdered one of his wives.

A blue flag climbed the pole.

Then came Joseph Wood, a twenty-one-year-old "colored" man, as the papers made sure to mention. For some reason, perhaps to enforce the racial distinction, the wires were reversed in his case. The negative electrode was attached to his left leg instead of the right.

For him, a black flag was raised.

Last was Shibuya Jugiro, a thick-bearded Japanese. Despite his fierce appearance, he had proved the most disciplined of prisoners, dispensing with a bed and preferring to sleep on naked stone. He was exceptionally docile. His flag was red.

"That's all," Conyes bellowed. "You can go home now." The crowd dispersed peacefully.

The experiment was a great success, witnesses agreed. "The system is now absolutely perfect, and has come to stay," said one expert, Dr. A. P. Southwick, proud to be called "the father of electrical executions."

Sing Sing's warden—"Deadline" Brown—was certain this would ease all qualms. "If any fanatic on the subject of electrocution had been present he would have been more than pleased with everything he saw."

The Reverend Dr. Law, chaplain at New York City's Tombs, where hangings had been carried out before the state took over capital punishment, gave his blessing. "A success. I came here opposed to electrical execution. Now I am converted." The Reverend Father Hogan of Peekskill was similarly impressed. "I have examined the heads of all four of the men, and not the slightest trace of scorching exists."

But a reporter who examined Smiler's body at the undertaker's on 125th Street found that "the eyes had been burned away, the cheeks and the lower part of the face were covered with blood-red scars which the electric fluid had left, the bridge of the nose had been burned clear to the bone and the eyebrows had been singed till there was nothing left to show where they had been."

Smiler's wife claimed his disfigured remains. The other three were sprinkled with quicklime and disposed of in the prison graveyard opposite the north wall. There were no religious services.

McElvaine got his turn the following year. He became the Sing Sing chair's sixth victim.

In 1899, with a new twelve-cell death house replacing the original shack, Conyes attended the first woman to die in the chair. Martha Place, its twenty-sixth victim, was a dour forty-four-year-old Brooklynite who had slain her stepdaughter in a fit of jealousy. Officials were afraid she might try to cheat the state by taking her own life before they could execute her, and assigned Conyes to watch her. She was belligerent at first, but he won her over. She ended up asking Conyes to escort her to the chair, and he chivalrously agreed. A matron and a woman physician were drafted to stand in front of the chair and block the view of male witnesses in the event the bolt of current made Place's skirt ride up, revealing her ankles.

3

A week after taking over Sing Sing, Lawes had to kill his first man. He had never given the chair or capital punishment much thought. When he did think about the death penalty, he, like most people, instinctively supported it. How else could society protect itself from killers? As for harnessing electricity to replace the hangman's rope, it was logical enough. Lawes and electric power had grown up together, and its mysteries were as widely feared as its miracles were hailed. Thomas Alva Edison had hooked up his first power plant for electrical distribution in New York City in 1882, a year before Lawes was born, and Lawes was a schoolboy in Elmira when Edison and his archrival George Westinghouse feuded over competing electrical delivery systems.

Edison deviously backed experiments with the electric chair using Westinghouse's alternating current in order to brand it as far more dangerous than his own direct current. By 1890 the new device using Westinghouse's system was installed at Auburn, ready for its debut with a first human subject, the black-bearded William Kemmler of Buffalo, who had murdered a woman. If anything, Kemmler seemed awed by the distinction. "Well, I wish everyone good luck in this world and I think I am going to a good place." The guards, fumbling with the straps, were more nervous than he. "Don't hurry," he joshed, "we got plenty of time." At the first bolt, Kemmler's body stiffened, lurched violently against the restraints, then went limp. After seventeen seconds, the doctors pronounced him dead. They were preparing to unbuckle the body when the chest began to heave. He was breathing. The switch was thrown again, long enough to fill the chamber with the stench of burning flesh, and this time the body lay still. To make sure, it was quickly autopsied.

With that record of success, the following year the chair came to Sing Sing.

The man Lawes had to kill was Vincenzo E. Esposito, inmate no. 69645. At thirty, six years younger than Lawes himself, Esposito was a semiliterate Italian from upstate Schenectady who, befuddled by drink, had shot dead a couple during a four-hundred-dollar robbery in November 1917. He had been on death row for more than two years.

The witnesses and the morbidly curious, prosecutors and lawyers and newsmen from Schenectady, converged on Ossining, eager to see justice done. Some stopped at A.W. Curry's Home Restaurant on Main Street, where a local paper, the *Democratic Register*, was quick to record their patronage and plug the eatery.

Lawes sought the counsel of the Catholic chaplain, Father William J. Cashin, a tall, long-faced priest with cheerless spectacles but a kindly manner. He had seen thousands of prisoners come and go and was no longer as certain of his pieties as when he had arrived. Unraveling the causes of crime seemed more difficult every day, and he no longer knew where misfortune ended and culpability began.

"He'll be all right," Father Cashin assured Lawes. "He's made his peace with God." Esposito had a good heart, he went on, and he had been waiting for this for a long time. It would come as a relief. The warden would take it harder than Esposito himself, the priest felt. After all, he said, "It's your first one."

Alone in his study, Lawes wondered for the first time what he had signed on to. The state had set the sentence of death. Easy enough. But he had to fix the moment and carry it out. It was suppertime. Kathryn and the girls would be expecting him for dinner, but still he delayed. A sudden chime made him flinch. It was just the clock in the corner, red second hand sweeping the dial like death's own crimson scythe.

He left his office and walked to the death house, entering the realm of the doomed like a man on his own final journey. His legs seemed bound in iron chains; his heart raced.

Inside he heard a sweet voice singing.

The powers of death have done their worst
But Christ their legions hath dispersed
Alleluia!

Lawes walked quizzically down the corridor, peering into the barred cells. "It's all right," someone said. "He's not disturbing us. He goes tomorrow." Lawes followed the sound of the singing and stopped outside a shadowed cell.

The three sad days have quickly sped
He rises glorious from the dead
Alleluia!

Esposito was lying on his cot but leaped to his feet when he spotted his visitor. "What can I do for you, mister?"

Lawes was flustered. "I'm . . . the warden."

Esposito peered out and laughed. Lawes was quite a spectacle. Relax, Esposito said, Father Cashin had saved him. He'd be all right. He had a reservation in heaven and he couldn't wait to keep it.

Lawes, silenced, waved uncertainly and moved on, hearing the mellow baritone echo down the corridor.

Abide with me: fast falls the eventide;
The darkness deepens—

Lawes had been the last one out of the charnel house, tiptoeing past the darkened cells of those condemned to follow, Esposito for sure now blessedly cocooned in sleep.

Later, after the killing—for Lawes could call it nothing else—he sat in his office replaying the image of Esposito ecstatically kissing the crucifix before settling himself in the chair. Then the room had filled with the smell of burning flesh. He had returned to the death house afterward, seeing the condemned men all up on their cots, staring at him. One had beckoned him over, asking him to listen. Then he heard it, a high-pitched whine like a fine saw cutting through—he suddenly knew what it was cutting through. Esposito's skull. Everyone on death row could hear the autopsy. Some of the men started to scream. God, Lawes thought, couldn't they do that somewhere else?

He was hunched over his desk filling out the execution paperwork in a puddle of yellow lamplight when a noise made him jump. He whirled to find

Father Cashin, in his usual black cassock, with the prison's chief physician, Amos O. Squire, a mournful-eyed blue blood with silky plastered hair parted off-center atop his high, round forehead. They had seen his light and thought he might want company, unless he wanted to sleep.

Lawes waved off the thought. Sleep wouldn't be possible until he had written a letter to Governor Smith appealing for a new death house, one with the morgue away from the cells. They could use a new electric chair, too. One that didn't roast its victims. Esposito had taken thirteen minutes to die, and smoke had come out of his head.

They were working on it, Squire said. He'd seen some who died in as little as eight minutes, but still, they all burned. That was why the men called it frying. Someday, he said, they might get it down to four or five minutes. Squire admitted he hated it, especially the rushed autopsies. That, he confided, was to make sure the executed didn't come back to life.

Lawes was incredulous, but Squire simply smiled a sad indulgent smile. It was only Lawes's first. Wait till he had killed fifty-four, like Squire. "Wait till they pile up on you."

Father Cashin cleared his throat. It was his seventy-second, and he had started in 1912, only two years before Squire. In his first year, fifteen went.

"Do you always . . . count . . . them?" Lawes asked.

No, Squire said, you tried to forget them. But they always came back to you.

Squire, whose forebears had arrived in the colonies a dozen years after the *Mayflower*, had been chief physician since 1914—a year after the death house was expanded yet again—but his association with Sing Sing went back to 1900. As a young Ossining doctor out of Columbia's College of Physicians and Surgeons he had been invited into Sing Sing to see the annual show put on by the inmates. He was intrigued by the place, and when the regular doctor took a leave, Squire filled in, eagerly ministering to the prisoners' overwhelming health problems, physical and mental, and finally taking over as chief. One of the things he noticed was how often prisoners were brutalized by the police. Once he treated an accused forger who had tried to pass a bad check at a bank and arrived with black eyes and many facial bruises. Squire asked if he'd been hit by a train. No, he'd replied, not a train. "It was the bulls." They'd taken him into the bank vault and taken turns beating him. Squire was dubious until a friend at the bank produced the victim's glasses. The police had carefully removed them before punching him in the face. It was a pattern, Squire told Lawes. The police were often left free to impose their own rough "justice."

Until the year before Lawes arrived, Squire alone decided whether inmates on death row were sane enough to be executed. Finally in 1919 the decision was put in the hands of a commission of alienists, physicians who specialized in the treatment of mental illness. Along with hating the process of legal homicide, Squire had come to believe that crime was a social maladjustment, just as sickness was a biological maladjustment. You might as well, he said, execute someone for catching tuberculosis.

The killing process was hedged about by macabre conventions. For some reason, the usual time had long been Thursdays at 5 A.M., adjusted after Squire's arrival to an only slightly less inconvenient 11 P.M., affording the condemned man nearly full use of his last day on earth.

A routine preceded each electrocution. First, the condemned was led out for a bath, often to a chorus of well-wishes from the others on death row. "Hold tight!" "Chin up!" "Don't forget to smile!" He was given new clothes, his own if he wanted and could afford them, but usually white shirt, dark trousers, and felt slippers. He was shaved and given a haircut, although hair, contrary to lore, did not interfere with the electrodes and was, in fact, an excellent conductor. He was then relocked in a cell on a corridor leading to the green door, under close scrutiny.

Squire had been there in July 1916, when a death row inmate, twenty-four-year-old Oreste "John" Shillitoni, who had killed his crony and two policemen in New York, feigned insanity or genuinely cracked up, shedding all his clothes down to his underwear. Somehow he had gotten hold of a revolver and ammunition and shot his way out, killing a guard and making it over the wall to where a confederate was to have stashed clothes. But Shillitoni had become disoriented and, still in his underwear, flailed about until finding his way to Ossining Hospital, where an intrepid nurse, pretending to be searching for clothes for him, delayed him until he could be recaptured and, shortly afterward, made to keep his date with the chair. Was he truly insane? Squire was left to agonize. Who should have decided? And if he was insane, wasn't it even more insane to kill him?

On a doomed man's last afternoon and evening, about the time the visiting executioner arrived, he received visits from the doctor and chaplain and

relatives. By tradition he could order whatever he wanted for a last meal, although food was usually the last thing on his mind. Still, as a last assertion
of his humanity, he often played along, ordering up an elaborate repast of
hard-to-obtain delicacies, quail on toast with asparagus tips or out-of-season
strawberries, which prison officials, also playing along, did their best to ob-
tain. Often then he gave away the food to his fellow inmates, preferring instead to smoke to excess, with his cigarettes or cigars lit through the bars by
ever watchful guards.

As the invited witnesses assembled, twelve by law, and took their places
on the churchlike pews facing the chair, the condemned was retrieved from
his cell, a guard slitting his right trouser leg to the knee. Led by a chaplain
reciting Scripture, the prisoner, wobbly-kneed, was conducted down the corridor and through the notorious green door to the chair. Practiced guards
strapped him down in a minute or two. Through the slit trouser, one electrode was applied to the right leg. A leather mask was slipped over his face to
his mouth, with slits for his nostrils, and fastened to the back of the chair.
Then a skullcap with the second electrode was set atop his head. Occupants
of the chair were not asked for last words, but anyone who wanted to could
speak. Some talked a lot. Some were literally scared speechless. Most kept
their remarks brief, for fear of being cut off by the current. Some acted
drugged. The terror of death seemed to induce a narcotic reaction. But try as
he could later with his experiments in the autopsy room, Squire could never
isolate a chemical that induced the change.

His job was to stand close to the chair and signal the executioner, who, to
spare his own sensibilities, sat in a nearby booth. Squire watched for the
right moment, when the man in the chair took a breath, so that when the
current surged and his lungs collapsed there was less air inside to produce a
last hideous gasp. Then he gave the signal, pulling a string attached to the
executioner, who instantly threw the switch.

Squire saw his first man executed in 1900, a thirty-seven-year-old Italian
from Brooklyn named Antonio Ferrera, who, like Shillatoni later, stripped
to his underwear in his cell. It took seven throws of the switch to stop
his heart while his body smoked and burned. At fourteen hundred volts,
the electrical pressure, or voltage, hadn't produced sufficient amperage, the
amount of electricity forced through the body, to kill efficiently. Even one
ampere, the amount of electricity coursing through a hundred-watt bulb

each second, could kill, but the human body offered varying degrees of resistance. A big man could take longer than a small man to die. A lower voltage might suffice on a hot day, with the body perspiring, than on a day when the skin was dry. Men with tuberculosis and consequently less chloride in the blood could withstand a higher voltage. Eventually it was found that about two thousand volts and ten amperes, sufficient to light eight hundred bulbs, was effective.

The first jolt, Squire guessed, felt like a stunning blow to the top of the head. The electricity outraced sensation, so it was almost certainly painless. On the skin, the electrodes reached temperatures of close to 2000 degrees Fahrenheit, above the melting point of copper, searing the flesh and driving the body heat up to around 138, beyond survivability. From his autopsies he knew that the muscles contracted instantaneously, causing grotesque contortions of the face, limbs, fingers, and toes, and a bulging of the eyes. The blood turned dark brownish and granular, the red corpuscles destroyed.

And yet, he found, curiously, that an hour after death he could still produce fibrillations of the heart by touching it with an instrument.

The new day's sun on the window bars was already striping the office black and yellow before Squire and Father Cashin got up to leave Lawes alone with his thoughts. They had twenty-one days until the next one, Squire said, and if anything, that one would be harder. Esposito hadn't drawn much press interest. The next one would be a newspaper circus.

Was this, Lawes wondered, what Katharine Bement Davis had meant when she prophesied that one day he would be honored with the high responsibility of putting people to death? Davis, an early mentor and one of the pioneering women of penology, had often argued with him about capital punishment. She opposed it and he saw nothing wrong with it. He'd come around, she predicted. "The first one will change your mind."

4

In his first weeks on the job, Lawes got lots of free advice. "Treat 'em rough," some keepers urged, while others counseled him to go easy. One retiring keeper passed on his wisdom earned from a nearly thirty-year career as a guard. Early on, he had caught prisoners in adjoining cells conversing through the ventilators and ordered them to stop. One of the two climbed off his bunk and called over to the eager newcomer. Take a tip, he said, from an old-timer who had spent much of his life in prison: "Don't see too damn much."

Lawes agreed that was great advice. It was often wise to ignore small infractions. But he thought he knew what he wanted to do. What these boys needed, he figured, was a sympathetic ear, someone who would stretch humanitarianism to the limits while also keeping a good stiff punch in reserve.

To master the population of 1,096 inmates, Lawes had a principal keeper and an assistant keeper, one guard sergeant, one night captain, and 150 guards. The Bertillon Department, which handled the physical identification of prisoners according to a system of marks and measurements, was manned by inmates led by a one-eyed receiving officer. In the absence of a cook, the food was prepared by kitchen helpers. There was no painter or plumber. The school had one teacher. There was no psychologist or psychiatrist, just Squire and his deputy. The chief clerks were political appointees. Shacks and huts dotted the prison's fourteen acres, and Lawes could only imagine what went on inside them. The grounds were filigreed with rabbit holes.

Lawes also soon discovered that some of his prisoners were playing the horses through cronies on the switchboard who were calling bookies. A small

Old cellblock around time of Lawes's arrival. (OSSINING HISTORICAL SOCIETY MUSEUM)

exception to the rules, the right to wear a few personal items, had become a giant loophole that made a mockery of Sing Sing's gray uniform, with privileged prisoners garbed in rainbows of silk shirts. Haphazard business practices shredded the prison budget, Lawes could see from reading the prison reports. No normal person ever read them; indeed, he thought, they were produced to be filed away, never to be seen again. But what revelations lay therein. Crooked clerks in the supply office had swindled the state out of a thousand dollars by sending payments to confederates for nonexistent woolens. Earlier, a similar scam, this one involving nonexistent coal, had stung the state for more than eight thousand dollars. Clerks tossed a coin whether to send goods by freight or more expensive express.

The Mutual Welfare League, begun six years before as the Golden Rule Brotherhood, was a laudable experiment in prisoner self-government, administering discipline for minor infractions and organizing entertainment and sporting events, but it had run amok, Lawes could see. Feuding factions replicated the worst of ward politics, with the victor reaping the spoils. League officials ran a lucrative visitors service, touring outsiders through the prison in throngs that the Statue of Liberty might envy. The league ran its own store and bank and minted its own scrip; league tokens were inscribed on one side, "Do Good," and on the other, "Make Good." The leadership of the league handpicked a sergeant at arms who designated deputies to monitor the sports field, the chapel, entertainment events, and the mess hall. The league also administered its own justice. Violators of the rules appeared before seven judges of the League Court, who were hardly blind to favoritism. Worse, executives of the league had easy access to the visiting room, where prisoners mingled with wives, molls, and ex-confederates. Who knew what contraband passed back and forth? Drugs, booze, and weapons for sure. The league also passed liberally on the movies and plays to be shown the inmates. Lawes looked over the script of his regime's first big stage production, the Annual Show, and shrank with disapproval. He called for several deletions.

The league's man was indignant. "That line is in the book," he protested, "and went big on Broadway."

Lawes sighed. "There's a lot goes on Broadway," he said, "that won't get over in Sing Sing."

He set up a meeting with the league's leaders in his office.

One, grandstanding for his cronies, said, "Warden, there are only two classes of people in the world."

Lawes played along. "What do you mean?"

"Those who are in jail—and those who ought to be."

His buddies roared.

Lawes waited for the ruckus to subside. "You're wrong," he said. "There are three classes of people. Those who are in jail. Those who are on the way. And those who will never get there."

These clowns didn't represent the prisoners, Lawes decided. He had to connect with the others, so he took a risky step. He abolished the League Court. He also abolished the political system. Ward politics was fine in Hell's Kitchen, but it had no place in Sing Sing. Even self-government didn't belong. Self-government worked fine on the outside, but these men were behind bars because they couldn't govern themselves. The league could remain, but its purview would shrink. It would regulate the leisure hours of the men, subject always to the censorship of the warden.

Lawes's moves against the league infuriated prisoners. They had fought hard for their perks, abused or not. They seethed and waited for their moment.

It came one night during one of the fierce thunderstorms for which the Hudson Valley was renowned, cataclysms of water and earthshaking blasts between sizzling bolts of lightning. The prisoners especially hated the lightning. They already had all the electricity they wanted.

They had been herded into the chapel to hear Lawes explain his views on the league when the mood turned ugly. The men encircling Lawes pressed in closer, some hiding sharpened spoons.

Lawes had dressed especially formally for the occasion, suit and vest and tie to convey authority. But the airless room damp with rain and the throng of menacing bodies made him realize his mistake. He was sweating through his clothes.

There was another explosive crash and a phosphorescent jag of lightning, and the lights went out.

Now Lawes was alone with the men in the dark. He couldn't see, but he imagined them stepping closer.

He kept talking, trying to keep his voice level. "Well, I must say," he muttered, "I know how Moses must have thought and felt when the lights went out for him." Then he did the only thing he could think of: he told the filthiest joke he knew.

A few men laughed, and it was enough to break the tension. When the lights came on again, the men could be moved back to their cells. Lawes tried not to look too relieved.

He continued to meet with dissident leaders. One was a Bolshevik, an ex-doctor convicted for an illegal operation that had killed a patient. He presented his pleas on behalf of his inmate constituents along with discourses on Lenin's sublime cause in revolutionary Russia. "It's an experiment, Warden," he proclaimed. "A lesson in self-control. Could the proletariat measure up to it? Time will tell. It may be all wrong but it's worth the try."

Another would-be leader was little more than a messenger boy who indifferently carried all prisoners' requests to Lawes. His philosophy, he told the warden, was that of the customer in the barbershop who was asked: "Wet or dry?" His answer: "Comb my hair, I don't want to start no argument."

Two weeks after his arrival at Sing Sing, Lawes tried to codify his thoughts for a reporter from the *New York Evening Post* who voyaged up to the prison to follow the new warden around for a day. His immediate policy was not to have a policy, said Lawes, dressed for his first interview in an especially elegant dark suit, patterned tie, and white shirt that encircled his neck with acreage of dazzling collar. "My desire is to be humane and just, but

I believe in order. I think the rule of good horse sense is about the best rule I can use, and I shall meet each situation as I come to it." There were twelve hundred men there and not a one was average, he said. They were all different and had to be handled accordingly. "I believe thoroughly in rational prison reform. It's here and here to stay."

At the same time, he saw room for improvement. Prison regulations, in case no one noticed, were not yet perfect. And, he pledged, there would be no political interference. But the days of inmates running the institution were over, he said, deriding the "extremes" of his flamboyant predecessor Warden Osborne. Prisoners would no longer be allowed to escorts guests, male or female, through the institution. The Mutual Welfare League could remain and offer advice, but he alone would administer discipline. He was bidding farewell to an era of "excitement and change," he said. "I want to begin a calm, business-like administration which the prisoners will understand."

Finally, he vowed, as business agent as well as warden, to personally review all the invoices so there would be no scandals on his watch. And he would be the first warden to read all incoming mail, including every letter to every prisoner.

In Portsmouth, New Hampshire, the commander of the U.S. Naval Prison read the *Evening Post* story and snickered. He sat down at his typewriter and tapped out a reply to Lawes.

Dear Sir:

You will not take it amiss, I hope, that I do not congratulate you on becoming warden of Sing Sing. In my judgment, it is, under existing conditions, what Mr. Rattigan once called it, "an impossible job." If you can succeed in making it a possible one you will deserve the highest credit and no one will be more pleased than I.

It was signed Lieut. Cmdr. Thomas Mott Osborne.

5

Surrounded by hapless felons and dull-witted bureaucrats, Lawes found himself thinking again and again about the cryptic Charles Chapin, the once mighty press lord he and Kathryn had found sprawled on a grim hospital cot. What had landed him of all people in Sing Sing? More than a week after their first encounter, Lawes sought him out again. The prison barber had shorn off his clipped military mustache, exposing a weak nakedness in his long pallid face. Even his Sing Sing number, 69690, carried a sad message. The digits added up to a fateful thirty, which, by a newspaper tradition so old no one could say how it started, signed off the end of a story, hence farewell.

"Charlie," he said, "how would you like to get out of bed?"

"No."

"Charlie," Lawes persisted, "I have something that might interest you." Had Chapin ever heard of the *Star Bulletin?*

What had started as the twice-monthly *Star of Hope* in 1899 had merged with the Mutual Welfare League's two-year-old *Bulletin* in 1917 to become Sing Sing's monthly, the oldest continuously published prison paper in the state, distributed free to prisoners, penologists, and interested citizens. Founded by an imprisoned banker, broker, and embezzler, it was being run, when Lawes arrived, by a convicted lawyer. Chapin, with his expertise, would be a perfect replacement. It was as close to newspapering as he could get inside the walls.

Chapin lay still. Was it an order? he asked. As warden, Chapin said, Lawes could issue orders as commandingly as any publisher or managing editor. No, Lawes said, it wasn't an order, simply something that Chapin might want to do for himself and others. But Chapin would have to get well fast, Lawes said. It was a limited-time offer.

Lawes was increasingly intrigued by Chapin. What interested Lawes was not just the mystery of how the tyrant had been laid low, but the possibilities inherent in having a renowned editor as his involuntary guest, as a letter Lawes received within days of arriving at Sing Sing spelled out.

"I knew Mr. Chapin long and from a certain angle intimately in the years he was at the *New York World*," it began. "He was the worst curse our reportorial craft ever enjoyed. I used to think him a sort of a devil sitting on enthroned power in the *World* office and making Park Row gutters flow red with the blood of ambitious young men. If you enjoy him I hope you keep him long and carefully."

Indeed, Lawes soon learned that Chapin had been as renowned for his cruelty as for his lofty competence.

A descendant of Deacon Samuel Chapin, a Pilgrim who came over on the *Mayflower*, Charles Chapin had been born in Watertown in western New York in 1858 and practically began life as a newspaperman. Though small for his age, he won a job at fourteen as a news delivery boy. He had to be in the pressroom at 3:30 A.M. to grab papers from the press as fast as they rolled off and then package them for his five-mile route. He earned four dollars a week with free lodging, bedding down on rolls of newsprint in the pressroom. His privations could have been avoided, for there was a potential legacy in the family. His grandmother was the only sister of the financier Russell Sage, one of the richest men in the country, but the eccentric and miserly Sage, preaching self-sufficiency, withheld his largesse from his relatives.

An editor at the paper took Chapin under his wing, giving him access to a library of Aristotle and Epictetus, Emerson and Carlyle, Balzac, Dumas, Hugo, Dickens, Scott, and the Bible. Chapin, who had added telegraph messenger to his job titles and quickly mastered the Morse code, filled in one night at the paper when the telegraph operator was too drunk to transcribe the Associated Press report.

At seventeen, following in the footsteps of a grandfather who had joined the rush to the California goldfields, he set out for the west, finding himself in Dodge City, Kansas, when Bat Masterson and his outlaw gang of brothers donned lawmen's badges to cheat justice. Chapin saw Bat Masterson shoot a man in cold blood and kick his girlfriend into insensibility until she took poison, and Chapin was standing with Eddie Masterson in front of the Skinner Dance Hall when four gunmen with a grudge put a bullet through Eddie's belly, sending Bat and his gang in vengeful pursuit.

Back east, he started a printing business and then moved to Chicago to dabble on the stage, taking the role of Simon Legree in a stage version of *Uncle Tom's Cabin*. He also played Romeo and, at twenty-one in 1879, wed his Juliet, Nellie Beebie, a few years his senior.

They had met when a card he was sending to another actress was mistakenly put in her hands. They laughed it off, but when their touring paths crossed later in a little western town, he carried Nellie's bag to her hotel and made a date for breakfast. She did not show up, and he found her ill and bedridden. He brought her medicine and that very afternoon decided to make her his wife. He called for her at the hotel and invited her for a walk that ended in a minister's rectory. He had still not asked for her hand. But she too was smitten and offered no objection, though the unprepared bride wore black—"an evil omen," she feared.

When the troupe suffered some setbacks, he went back to his first and only love, newspapering, landing a job on the bare-knuckle *Chicago Tribune*, which once headlined a story about a hanging JERKED TO JESUS! Chapin knew he had found his calling. He settled Nellie in a hotel room and went to work.

By twenty-nine he had become city editor, first at the *Chicago Times*, then at the *Chicago Herald*, and finally, in 1898, at Joseph Pulitzer's vaunted *New York Evening World*, which was bringing a brash new view of the news to a million New Yorkers a day from its gilded dome tower that was the wonder of Park Row. It was a New York before subways and automobiles, with steam-drawn elevated lines crisscrossing the city, a single electric el along Amsterdam Avenue, and horse-drawn trolleys on Broadway.

Chapin, who took over from Ernest Chamberlain, literally driven mad with martial fever on the eve of the Spanish-American War, wasted no time in whipping—for that was the operative word—his staff into shape. If the *Morning World* was well mannered, as befitted a newspaper carried to the breakfast table, its afternoon twin, Chapin's *Evening World*, had a sassier mission: "Give 'em what they want."

He lived, some said, at the furious pace of those destined to end their lives in tragedy. He was a bully and brute. He was a cold-blooded machine.

And he was a fop, favoring double-breasted wasp-waisted suits, lavender or orange cravats with pearl stickpins, and tortoiseshell pince-nez attached to his buttonhole with a black ribbon.

He woke each morning at five for a canter through Central Park in the saddle of one of his several steeds, which included a fifteen-hundred-dollar stallion given him by Joseph Pulitzer after Chapin predicted the political tides in Great Britain and scooped the world with an interview of the new prime minister, Lloyd George. Chapin named the gift horse after the PM. Pulitzer adored Chapin, who had counseled the publisher, shortly after he bought the bankrupt *World*, to throw its weight behind a drive to raise public funds for a pedestal for the Statue of Liberty. Chapin, it was said, even edited the words of Emma Lazarus inscribed on the base. The boss, in turn, did not stint on generosity. After one particularly admirable exclusive, Chapin found four thousand dollars in gold coins in his desk.

But Chapin offered no such largesse to his staff. He blithely sent a reporter to interview a betrayed husband whose wife had run off with her lover. The reporter had barely gotten the first question out when the enraged cuckold threw him down the stairs. The reporter limped back to report to Chapin, who was indignant. "You go back there," he ordered, "and tell that son of a bitch he can't intimidate me."

He delighted in firing reporters, especially those grown old in loyal service to the *World*. When one staffer complained that his paycheck was a day's wages behind, Chapin assured him he would fire him a day early. A reporter who came in late with a bandaged foot and an intricate tale of woe drew uncharacteristic silence until the following week, when Chapin sacked him, explaining, "I would have fired you earlier but I wanted to see how long you could keep on faking that limp."

When, one rare day, the managing editor announced that Chapin was out ill, the crack rewrite man Lindsey Dennison spoke for all when he said, "I trust it's nothing trivial."

And yet, the men recognized Chapin as a master with an incomparable nose for news. He once dispatched a reporter to Chinatown with no clear assignment. The fellow wandered around aimlessly—until a tong-war battle erupted around him. Chapin was the only editor with a man on the scene.

He plotted the city's neighborhoods on a grid and assigned a reporter to each box. When news broke, the man was already in place. He got the story and, instead of rushing back to write it, called in the facts to one of the *World's* three or four telephones manned by star writers who could quickly pound out the copy. Chapin invented rewrite.

Chapin was in the newsroom the June day in 1904 when one of the top rewrite men received a call and shouted out to Chapin: "There's a boat burning in the East River, at about a Hundred Twenty-fifth Street." It was the *General Slocum.* Over the next few hours the mangled, blackened bodies of 1,021 excursioners, almost all women and children, floated in on the tides and were stacked up in high piles on North Brother Island.

Veteran reporters taking down the details turned away to vomit, but Chapin cruised the newsroom ecstatically shouting out the bulletins: "Women and children jumping overboard with clothing afire! Water full of charred bodies!"

At times like these his gaze, which usually seemed strangely blank and dead, appeared to flicker with unearthly fire. Some thought him serpentine. "His eyes were curious," wrote Irvin S. Cobb, the staff humorist who was as droll as he was homely. "The light which lit them seemed not to come from within his skull but from without. Ophidians have such eyes, but they are rare in human heads." Chapin was flattered.

He had no patience for ineptitude. When a starting reporter asked how to cover a fire, Chapin barked, "Find the hottest place and jump in."

He pushed his men hard, but he pushed himself harder. No one quit Chapin's *Evening World.* He had a rare eye for talent, letting other editors train promising reporters and then hiring them away. He was tolerant of professional hazards like alcoholism and womanizing. When a snitch tipped Chapin that one of his star reporters was keeping two households, one with his wife and one for his blonde, Chapin was impressed. "The son of a gun," he said. "I'll double his salary."

He disdained the practice of "journalism," preferring to be known as a plain newspaperman. He treasured terseness, and he posted the word as a commandment over each reporter's desk. He even spoke in headline words like "probe," "rift," "fray," and "slay," although when an inspired reporter one day invoked the "melancholy waters" of the East River, Chapin offered him a rare bouquet: "Pretty good phrase, that." Soon "melancholy waters" was finding its way into every story, until Chapin ordered that the next man to parrot the tired formulation would be fired.

Dwight Perrin, a young reporter who hadn't got the word, began his story of a suicide, "The melancholy waters of the Hudson . . ." Incensed, Chapin called him over. "You're fired! Melancholy waters!" How, he demanded, could waters be melancholy? "Perhaps," ventured the panicked Perrin, "because they had just gone past Yonkers?"

"Not bad," Chapin relented. "You're hired."

There was pathos in the volume of sweets he consumed, ice-cream cones and jam from the jar and canned peaches, a desperate substitute for a not-quite-conquered craving for alcohol that continued to haunt him.

When he moved to the *World*, Chapin installed himself and Nellie at the châteauesque Hotel Plaza on Central Park, the most palatial of the city's hostelries, and then so new it was still under construction. The Chapins and their maid, Katie, and another guest were the first residents. The hotel matched his debonair lifestyle: the daily barbering, hair brilliantined and perfumed with bay rum, the sartorial splendor of his tweeds and herringbones, his gilded watch fobs and boutonniere, and ogling smirks at pretty girls. He had fancy friends like sporting goods king Al Spalding, the Ringling Brothers, and Jack London.

Nellie, his onetime Juliet, wilted in his frequent absences. She had no home of her own, no possessions. They had no children. She was showing her age.

Chapin had a yacht, a touring car, horses, and European vacations, extravagances far above the means of even a well-paid editor earning twenty thousand a year. Newspapermen were notorious spenders, but his improvidence was deliberate. He fully intended to inherit the eighty million of his great-uncle, Russell Sage.

Chapin cultivated the quirky financier, getting him seats to the opera and prize fights and rallies at Madison Square Garden and taking him on his first automobile ride. Sage could well afford a fleet of limousines, but he was notoriously cheap, wearing suits until they were threadbare and refusing to waste money on underwear. He was one of the largest stockholders of the elevated lines, but when they rode together, he made Chapin buy a ticket while he used his pass. "You'll be a very rich man someday," he promised Chapin. But Sage died leaving Chapin a mere fifty thousand dollars, hardly enough to pay back the loans Chapin had taken out in anticipation of the fortune to come. Furious, Chapin assigned one of his reporters to write articles challenging the will, to no avail.

More reverses followed. Chapin's stocks plummeted, wiping him out. He skipped out on a three-thousand-dollar bill at the Plaza and moved with Nellie into the modest Cumberland on the fringe of the Broadway theater district. He sold his yacht, car, and horses, emptied Nellie's savings accounts, and, still deep in debt, misappropriated the bonds of a young relative whose guardianship he held. There was only one way out, he resolved. Suicide. But what would happen to his wife? His shameful death would shatter Nellie. She would have to die too.

Chapin borrowed a revolver from Police Commissioner Rhinelander Waldo and laid his plans. He would shoot Nellie and then himself. But first, with creditors hounding him, he told her everything—everything, that is, except his planned murder-suicide.

She was forgiving, telling him, "My dear husband, I know better than you can tell me that there was nothing intentionally dishonest in what you have done." He had lot of friends, she soothed; they would help him.

Sure enough, understanding bankers replaced the lost securities, gaining him a reprieve. But like a gambler unable to leave the table, Chapin was no sooner whole than he plunged in again, borrowing heavily and betting on tips from friends. He kept on winning until Germany declared war in 1914, crashing the stock market and ruining him. For the next four years, Chapin struggled to fend off creditors, eventually having his pay garnisheed. He borrowed from the few friends he had left, but he was cracking under the strain.

The time had come. In September 1918, he took Nellie on a trip to Washington, D.C., to celebrate their thirty-ninth anniversary. He made a quick, surreptitious detour to nearby Glenwood Cemetery to reserve two plots. That night, he waited until she fell asleep and pointed the gun at the back of her head.

Suddenly, he saw a wraithlike form materialize in the room, the ghost of his beloved dead mother. "She stood in the room but a few feet from the bed, not the white-haired old woman, wasted with disease, that I had come to see a few days before she died, but the beautiful mother I had idolized when I was a child. She looked at me with the same sweet smile and gently shook her head, just as she had done in childhood days when reproving me for something I shouldn't have done. Then she faded away."

Whether it was indeed his mother's spirit or his fevered brain, Chapin didn't know, but he put away the gun, took the sleeping Nellie in his arms, and breathed a silent prayer that she was still alive.

They returned to New York and Chapin went back to the paper, terrorizing reporters as usual. But he had not abandoned his murderous scheme. At the cigar stand in the lobby, he cashed a check for a hundred dollars, knowing there were no funds to cover it. He spent the weekend with Nellie in the hotel and mailed a farewell letter to the *World*. "When you get this I will be dead. My wife has been such a good pal. I cannot leave her alone in the world."

That Sunday night he lay in bed, waiting for Nellie to turn away from him and fall asleep. When she finally did, he pointed the revolver at a spot slightly above her right ear and pulled the trigger.

Nellie didn't die instantly. She lingered, writhing unconscious as Chapin comforted her, amazed that no one had reacted to the shot. It took two hours for her life to ebb away. Now was the moment for Chapin to turn the gun on himself, but he changed his plan. He donned a gray summer suit and bright orange tie, hung his pince-nez on its silken cord, and adorned his buttonhole with a bright calendula.

There was a knock on the door. He answered tremblingly, but it was only the bellboy with the newspapers. Chapin accepted them casually and called down the hall to the maid, "Mrs. Chapin was up late last night, I want her to sleep late this morning." He posted a DO NOT DISTURB sign on the door, pocketed his revolver and a backup pistol, adjusted his black derby, selected a cigar, and left the room.

Meeting the advertising manager of the *World* in the lobby, he said he would be late for work. He stopped for a shave in the hotel barbershop, then hailed a series of taxicabs, leaving one to jump into another in case he was being followed, and rode to Central Park, which he thought a good place to shoot himself. Again he hesitated.

Then he migrated to Brooklyn, by which time his letter had reached the *World* and an extra had hit the streets.

"CHARLES CHAPIN WANTED FOR MURDER!"

In Prospect Park, he lifted a gun to his head, but a passing policeman sent him fleeing. He rode to the Bronx and then back to Manhattan, where he bought a newspaper and read that the police, taking him at his word, believed he was dead. The story sobered him enough to call the police and surrender.

At police headquarters he told his story to astonished commanders and the district attorney. He was overcome with relief. "Today is the first happy day I have known since falling into financial difficulties."

He signed a confession and was marched off to the Tombs, where he immersed himself in news accounts of his crime and picked apart the stories with a practiced eye. "As well as I know newspapermen," he said, "I cannot understand how the reporters managed to distort my story as much as they did."

Meanwhile, the twelfth-floor city room of the *Evening World* was in an uproar, staff members dancing and clapping one another on the back and passing around celebratory bottles. The more cynical among them were dubious of Chapin's explanations. Had he really killed Nellie out of kindness, twisted as it was? Or had he simply grown tired of her dowdy looks? Had he really lost all that money gambling on the market? Or was he being blackmailed over an old scandal, perhaps a liaison with some demimondaine? No one knew. But in the absence of proof to the contrary, Chapin's account stood.

A sanity commission was appointed to see whether he should go to a lunatic asylum. To Chapin's indignation, a parade of reporters testified that his actions in the city room proved he was deranged. But when the four-month inquiry closed with Chapin's own narrative, he was judged completely sane.

Although he insisted that he had no desire to present a defense, behind the scenes he was calling in some of the chits he had collected in his years as a news titan. As a confessed killer in a capital case, he could not legally plead guilty—that is, sentence himself to death. But in a maneuver remarkable for its audacity, when asked in court to enter a plea, Chapin made his play: "Guilty of murder in the *second* degree."

The judge on the bench was no stranger to Chapin. He quickly assented to the scaled-down admission, sentencing the sixty-year-old editor in January 1919 to twenty years to life in Sing Sing but sparing him the chair.

6

Three weeks after Esposito's rapturous date with death, Lawes was steeled for his second execution, this one likely to draw far more attention than his first.

Prisoner no. 70292, Gordon Fawcett Hamby, alias Jay B. Allen, more widely known as the Brooklyn Bank Bandit, was devilishly handsome, with blond hair and fine aristocratic features. Hamby could also have been, Lawes thought, the most intelligent man ever to find himself in the death cells, but in his delusions about his shooting escapades, he may well have been insane.

In their brief time together, Lawes had come to know him well. Hamby came from a good family and had been to college, where he was expelled for gambling. Expecting no sympathy from his severe father, he took to robbing banks, rationalizing his outlaw trade with the insight "They rob the people, anyhow, and I was sort of righting the wrong." He struck boldly, staging his robberies in the middle of the business day, often with crooked cops as accomplices. But one Brooklyn robbery in 1918 went awry and two men were killed. Hamby and his partner made their gateway with ten thousand dollars. Hamby was later arrested out west for killing a pal he mistakenly thought was drawing on him. In remorse, Hamby confessed to the Brooklyn murders as well, welcoming death. He put up no defense and was quickly convicted. He ruled out any appeal, but one of his many women admirers made one anyway, begging the governor for a commutation. To Hamby's relief it was turned down. In Sing Sing, he refused to answer to the name of Hamby and painted himself as a desperado of exquisite humanity who gave his victims every chance.

For the press jackals of Park Row, Hamby was red meat, and they descended on Sing Sing with pencils poised. One of the first to arrive was a striking, bubbly woman with a sweet smile who had made his travails her own.

Ushered through the gates by awed guards, she made a point of asking to see Charles Chapin. He was editing the *Bulletin*, she was told. She could find him down by the print shop.

"Well, well, well, if it isn't my old beloved editor!" she cried as he jumped, startled by her piercing laugh. Energized by his obvious discomfort, she rattled on, "How are you, old dear? I've often thought you ought to be in a cage but this is the first time I've ever seen you in one!" She laughed again, drawing the attention of all inmates within earshot.

Chapin leaped up, face flushing scarlet. "Get out of here!" he roared. "Get out of here you dirty ragamuffin, before I break your goddamn neck!"

The woman backed off and walked away, smiling. She winked at the audience of puzzled convicts. "Now I can understand why he killed his wife," she said. "Thank God, I'm through with him."

One of the men asked the sergeant at arms who the lady was.

"She was one of his old reporters. Her name is Nellie Bly."

That name spoke for itself. For more than three decades, going back to the 1880s, her exploits as the nation's first celebrity newswoman and stunt reporter, and her gamine zest and lithesome figure, had won hearts around the world, catapulting her to the forefront of the young science of investigative reporting.

Born Elizabeth Jane Cochran in Pennsylvania in 1864, she grew up with an abusive stepfather who left her with a burning intolerance for injustice. As a freelance writer for the *Pittsburg Dispatch*, she signed her pieces "Orphan Girl." But with her promotion to the staff, she needed a real byline. It was risqué in those days for a woman to write under her own name. Her editor solicited suggestions from the newsroom, eliciting a chorus of "Nelly Bly!," the name of a pretty black servant girl in a popular song by a great son of Pittsburgh, Stephen Foster. The editor was not a fastidious speller and no matter that Cochran was white, "Nell*ie* Bly" she became.

By 1887, on the strength of her shrewd intellect, fetching smile, and radiant sex appeal, she joined Pulitzer's *World*, where she applied her maxim: "Energy rightly applied and directed will accomplish anything." In her first big scoop, she feigned insanity and had herself committed to the women's asylum on Blackwell's Island in the East River. Her harrowing two-part undercover series, "Inside the Madhouse," recounted the wretched treatment of the unfortunates there.

Her greatest feat began on November 14, 1889, when, on four days' notice from her editors, she set off alone with just an overnight satchel to challenge Jules Verne's fictive voyage around the world in eighty days. She did it in seventy-two days, six hours, eleven minutes, and fourteen seconds, assuring the *World* a publicity bonanza and herself journalistic immortality.

Nothing, of course, could top that exploit, and in the years since, Nellie Bly's fortunes had waned, through a stormy marriage to an elderly millionaire and exposés, however inventive, that paled in comparison to her global adventure. By 1920, she was fifty-five, no longer girlish but statuesque, with silvered locks and a smooth-faced beauty that transcended time.

Having broken with the *World,* she had moved to William Randolph Hearst's *New York Evening Journal* and was making headlines with grievous stories of abused and abandoned children when editor Arthur Brisbane, with whom she had been romantically linked, offered a new challenge. Did Nellie Bly want to be the first woman in years to witness an execution? Making it even more irresistible was the chance to trump the exalted Brisbane, long the highest-paid editor in the business. After witnessing the first electrocution at Sing Sing in 1891 while in his last months at the *New York Sun*, he turned green and fled the autopsy. Surely, she thought, she could do better. She readily volunteered to go up the river to cover Hamby's execution.

Having tweaked her old nemesis Chapin, whom she was comforted to see behind bars, Nellie Bly joined Lawes and his wife, Kathryn, in the death vigil.

She threw herself into the story, interviewing Hamby in his cell a week before the execution. She found his blond boyish good looks mesmerizing. Like many women before her, she was captivated by his élan and repulsed by the idea that he was about to be destroyed before her eyes.

She fixated on the commandment "Thou shalt not kill." If it applied to Hamby, she thought, why not to the state?

As the hour approached, Lawes excused himself to look in on Hamby in his death cell, and when he returned, Nellie Bly thought she could see tears in his eyes.

Hamby had made some final requests. He asked to wear his own white shirt and collar instead of the prison's customary black one, and Lawes readily assented. He wanted to wear a tie, and Lawes agreed to a little bow tie that didn't carry the risk of a length of silk that Hamby might use to hang himself. After all, Lawes reflected, Hamby shouldn't do to himself what the state had to do to him. Hamby asked to walk to the chair unhandcuffed, and again Lawes agreed. What risk was there that anyone so determined to die would try to escape? Hamby also asked that an escort who looked particularly glum be replaced by one with a smile, and that was granted too. But when he asked Lawes himself to walk him to the chair, the request so anguished the warden that Hamby hurriedly withdrew it.

Hamby, a jailhouse convert to Spiritualism, also confided to Lawes that he would try to return from the dead the following night and visit the warden.

Lawes told him he needn't go to the trouble—and sincerely hoped he would not.

Earlier, Hamby had dined extravagantly on delicacies of his most fanciful imaginings, as the custom dictated: lobster Newburg and strawberries, mushrooms and more strawberries. Kathryn Lawes had dutifully hunted them down in Ossining.

Shortly before eleven, Lawes called the other reporters and invited witnesses and officials into his office, motioning Nellie Bly to a seat by his side. The warden took out his pocket watch and stared at the sweeping second hand. No one spoke.

The room was heated, but Nellie Bly began shivering. Where was Hamby? she wondered. What was going through his mind?

At the stroke of eleven, Lawes stood and walked out, gathering Nellie Bly and the others. Outside in the bitter cold, the group trudged down a dark and icy road. Lawes was coatless. Gates were swung open by unseen hands.

They filed into a small chamber blindingly lit from above. Nellie Bly had to shield her eyes from the piercing glare. Four oak benches like church pews awaited them, and then suddenly she saw the chair. Above it dangled a thick black electrical wire coiled like a viper.

Along one wall behind the chair stood twelve men, the witnesses. Opposite them stood Lawes, Squire, and the executioner, John P. Hulbert, a pudgy man with a few strands of gray hair tangled atop his balding pate. He was being paid $150 for the night.

Behind Hulbert, Nellie Bly could see a set of hideously large electric switches with handles of burnished copper. She had promised Hamby to gaze into his eyes at the fateful moment, but courage failed her, and she asked Lawes if she could move back to the seat farthest from the chair. He nodded. Minutes ticked by.

The brown door swung open, and all heads swiveled toward it. For a long moment there was silence. Then, a distant voice down the corridor: "Goodbye, boys."

There was a muffled chorus of responses and Hamby appeared. Nellie Bly was amazed to see him smiling. He looked different now, his long hair cropped close.

He stood in the doorway and shouted back, "I will try anything once, boys."

He walked in and seated himself in the chair, flung aside a last cigarette he was smoking, and looked inquiringly at Lawes. "May I speak?"

"Yes," Lawes said.

"Why, I would just like to say that I thank you for all that you have done for me. You have treated me with the greatest kindness in misfortune and I would like to express my appreciation. I also want to say that no matter how badly I needed money, no man ever faced Jay B. Allen's gun without a chance."

Attendants in blue quickly strapped him in. He winced and asked, "Is it necessary to make them so tight?"

In response, the strap dangling over his head was pulled down and a black leather mask like a football helmet was buckled over his face. A face, Nellie Bly thought, that would never again be seen in this world. Grotesquely, though, his mouth was uncovered. His teeth were bared and he was still smiling grimly.

The executioner stood by the switch. Squire looked at the executioner. He looked at Hamby and waited for him to exhale. Squire raised his right hand. In his left hand he clasped a gold watch. His right hand dropped.

The executioner stepped forward, grasped the handle of the switch, bent his knees, and, straightening up, threw the switch home. There was a droning hum. No sound came from Hamby, but at once his body surged up as if it would rise out of the chair. Nellie Bly shut her eyes.

When she opened them, someone was tearing open Hamby's shirt and Squire was presenting his stethoscope, listening. She could not take her eyes off the white throat and neck, bones now vivid under the collapsed flesh. So this, she thought, was death. No, it wasn't. This was murder.

Headline from Hamby execution. (NEW YORK EVENING JOURNAL)

She saw Hamby being carried out. She took Lawes's arm and filed out with the others. She saw the warden shivering, perhaps not from cold, and his eyes glistening with unmistakable tears.

The next day's *Evening Journal* blared her account in huge headlines, giving her, typically, top billing.

"Horrible! Horrible! Horrible!" the story began. It ran for nine columns.

That night, twenty-four hours after the execution, Lawes was mounting the stairs to the bedroom when he heard some faint musical notes. He froze, listening, but they had stopped. He took a few steps and heard them again, mystic chords that seemed to reverberate in his suddenly pounding heart. Hamby had said he would return.

He tried to shrug it off and continued upstairs. Then, telling himself it was not possible, he crept back downstairs. The parlor was in shadow. Small dark forms flitted about. On the couch he saw a round white shape, a banjo. Kittens had been scampering over the strings.

7

While Hamby was waiting to die, Chapin had accepted Lawes's offer to edit the *Bulletin* and moved into the newspaper office next door to the book-bindery, with ten prisoners groaning under the weight of his belongings. Though making a pretense of his great sacrifice, Chapin was buoyed beyond measure to inhale once again the elixir of printer's ink and bend to the roar of the rotary presses.

Fellow inmates looked on agog as Chapin unloaded crates of fruit, jams, jellies, boxes of crackers, sugar, tea, and coffee, gifts from solicitous friends. The place soon looked like a grocery store.

Under Chapin's command, the prisoners moved the delicacies into the closets and cupboards, leaving the overflow, for which there was no room, on the floor. They eyed the extra cans and jars hungrily.

One of the men spoke up. "Don't we get anything for helping you?"

Chapin regarded him icily. "Why should you?"

Under the ministerings of Lawes and Kathryn, Chapin had emerged from his cocoon of depression. He was no longer the gaunt, 133-pound specter of his arrival. He had put on nearly 20 pounds. Some saw his gray eyes flash bright blue. He walked about in a white silk shirt and tie, shielded from the sun by a newsman's green eyeshade. And when visitors asked if he was happy, he replied, "Well, no, not happy, but this is better than the *World*."

Inmates nudged one another knowingly as he passed, exchanging tidbits of his notorious history. Lawes had spared him the coal pile of other newcomers and put him to work as the chaplain's assistant in the library, at Sing Sing's standard wages of a cent and a half a day. Chapin was the only prisoner whose letters bypassed the censor in the Correspondence Department, to be reviewed, instead, by Lawes's accommodating secretary. Clearly he was the warden's pet.

Chapin's professional hand was quickly evident. With his name on the masthead as editor, his maiden issue of February 1920, double the size of its predecessor and dressed in a handsome new typeface, examined the business activities of the Mutual Welfare League. It carried articles from inmates on the hardships of prison life and news of prison band concerts, vocational courses in the shops, new books in the library, and ball scores of the prison teams. With Chapin ghosting articles under a host of pseudonyms, the paper began to take on the authoritative tone of its new master.

Chapin's view of Lawes was evident enough in a fawning piece he head-lined "RIGHT MAN IN A BIG JOB IS THE NEW WARDEN OF SING SING."

"There is not a man in Sing Sing whose heart is not filled with gratitude to Superintendent Rattigan for having chosen a man like Major Lawes for the big job of Warden," Chapin wrote.

From the tone of the article, Lawes was clearly using Chapin to send messages to his fellow prisoners. Chapin got his exclusive interview; Lawes got his word out.

Brutality was no longer the order of the day at Sing Sing, the article made clear, but Lawes was no sentimentalist. Every man would be accepted on trust, until he violated it, and then retribution would be harsh. Under Lawes, Sing Sing would be "an honor prison." Only those proved worthy would be allowed to remain; the others would find themselves shipped out to Auburn or Dannemora. Lawes was a reformer. Every man would have an op-portunity to help himself. He believed in the prisoners' Mutual Welfare League, as long as it remained a democratic and positive force. Staff courtesy would be the watchword. But woe to the inmate who confused it with weak-ness. Lawes favored liberal letter-writing and visiting privileges, but privi-leges given could be revoked. He believed in fresh air and recreation, baseball, handball, and tennis.

Chapin even loosened up enough to poke fun at himself in the paper. "Think of the advantage of always knowing where your reporters are and of being able to place your hands on them when their services are needed. Re-porters of our prison paper don't come down at irregular hours and sing the editor a song about a blockade in the subway. They are never called away by sickness in the family or to attend the funeral of a mythical grandmother. There are no besetting temptations to lure them from duty, no racetracks, no poker games, no cabarets, no wild women."

Chapin also filled his pages with an extraordinary confessional. He called it "Autobiography of My Forty Years as a Newspaper Man."

Since his arrest, he had been writing his memoirs as a distraction. He printed excerpts in his *Bulletin* and they were seen by the publisher George Palmer Putnam, who asked Chapin if he would consider a book. He offered Chapin a thousand-dollar advance plus fifty-cents royalty per copy sold and 75 percent of newspaper reprint sales.

Chapin hardly needed convincing.

The March 1920 issue of the *Bulletin* carried the second installment of Chapin's memoirs, and movie reviews of films to be shown at Sing Sing— *The Feud* with Tom Mix, *The Hayseed* with Fatty Arbuckle, and *The Mother and the Law* by D. W. Griffith. He campaigned for a new death house. "Make it light and airy and cheerful," Chapin wrote.

He also ghosted items, including a gossip column bylined "Bill the Burglar," a behind-the-walls roundup signed "The Observer," and a piece on community singing at the nightly movie show, credited to "The Old Lifer." The issue also contained an erudite legal column interpreting an appellate division decision that dashed the hopes of many prisoners eager for earlier release. Two years earlier Governor Smith had signed a law allowing convicts to deduct from their sentence the time spent in jail before their conviction. Now the court ruled that the law was not retroactive. Prisoners sentenced before May 1919 got no credit for their pretrial time behind bars. The legal pundit explaining the decision—he signed his column "The Counselor"—was also none other than Chapin.

With a newspaper under him again, overstocked food shelves, and other privileges, Chapin was as happy as a man could be behind bars. But a bout of illness reminded him of his ultimate prospects, so with the April issue put to bed, he sat down at his typewriter and, with the two-fingered method that had served him throughout his newspaper career, hammered out a document addressed to Lawes.

"The day I complete my term of imprisonment will you kindly arrange to have my body buried by the side of my wife in Glenwood Cemetery, Washington, D.C., the expense to be paid from my personal funds." The deed to the plot was held by his only close kin, his unmarried sister, Marion, in Washington, whom he had forbidden from ever visiting him in prison.

He wanted, he specified, to be laid to rest in the least expensive black-cloth-covered casket, the casket to be placed in a hardwood zinc-lined box and sealed, never to be opened. There was to be no autopsy. He did not want his body disfigured. His last belongings were to go to old, friendless prisoners of the warden's choosing, "irrespective of color or race."

8

The hot July sun of Lawes's first Sing Sing summer was baking the cellblocks, sending whiffs of sewage blowing east from the Hudson, where the men emptied their slop buckets. Lawes lit up a fresh Robert Burns panatela, flinging away his old chewed one.

For more than two years now, long predating his arrival, prison crews had been grading the land for a new Sing Sing, a six-million-dollar reconstruction that, he thought, should go a long way toward curing that stench. It would be up the hill, open to the breezes and high above the present plant that hugged the fetid river, where, the original builders must have believed, it would be invisible, sunken from the sight of the world. The new cells would have plumbing, and each would have a window to the outside world. There would be a new hospital and a new mess hall laid out like a Maltese cross. There would be a new administration center, and the old buildings down below would become the workshops.

The original cellblock would be erased as surely as the original Bastille. Demolition had already begun. In November 1917, as the prison's white-uniformed Aurora Band wheezed "The Star-Spangled Banner," a first ceremonial slab had been pried loose and lowered to the ground. Governor Charles S. Whitman watched it descend and quipped, "It took a long time to come down." Indeed, replacing the cellblock had been a goal of reformers since the early years of the century.

By 1905 conditions at Sing Sing were seen as so abysmal that a legislative commission came up with a plan for building a replacement that could engage inmates in healthful and productive labor. A site was soon found at

Bear Mountain some fifteen miles north across the Hudson, and within a few years 150 convicts were at work clearing the land and installing power lines and a water supply. It was to be a model institution, with sanitizable enamel cells with toilets and sinks, and advanced public address and telephone systems. But it all evaporated in 1910, when the Prison Department lost the land to the Parks Department.

The project was shifted to a new site at Wingdale in the Harlem Valley some forty miles north of Sing Sing, and again crews began building. This time it was almost completed before partisan bickering doomed it. The governor halted construction, and after years of lying empty, the would-be model prison opened as a state psychiatric facility.

Scandal followed scandal, as grand juries and special commissions investigated prison conditions and reform became a battleground between the Tammany Democratic machine and its foes.

In 1913 Governor William Sulzer, styling himself an independent Democrat and populist progressive, announced an attack on Tammany-led prison corruption. But the holdover Republican superintendent of prisons refused to appoint Sulzer's choice, Charles Rattigan, as warden of Auburn. Sulzer then dismissed the superintendent; appointed his own candidate, John B. Riley; installed Rattigan at Auburn; and commissioned a newspaper court reporter and crony, George Blake, to conduct an investigation of the prisons as a playground of graft. Blake dutifully found rampant brutality, mismanagement, and theft.

Citing Blake's findings, Sulzer kept up a barrage of charges against prison officials of prior administrations. He singled out Warden John S. Kennedy of Sing Sing as especially callous and lax, even accusing him of condoning perversity among the prisoners.

Kennedy, outraged, beat his tormenters to the Westchester County district attorney, demanding a grand jury investigation that he insisted would clear him.

Sulzer, meanwhile, removed Kennedy as warden and named an anti-Tammany prison reform commission under a former Auburn mayor, Thomas Mott Osborne, a staunch ally of Rattigan's.

Tammany, in turn, struck back from Albany and cut off funding to the prisons, raising the threat of violent insurrections.

To Kennedy's consternation, the Westchester grand jury issued a present-ment confirming many of the worst charges. "The cells are unfit for the housing of animals, much less human beings." They were so cramped they had less than half the space required by law per person in a lodging house and were so damp you could wet your hand by running it over the stone walls. Inmates bunked two to a cell, ensuring rampant sexual relations and an epidemic of syphilis and gonorrhea. In short, conditions were barbaric and scandalous. The jurors were aghast not only that elderly degenerates were sharing cells with young men but also that Negroes and whites were doubled up together. Sing Sing's problems were so extensive, the panel found, that there was little remedy but to abandon the prison altogether in favor of a new facility where inmates could farm outlying acres, growing their own provisions.

Warden Kennedy and four of his staff were indicted for misdemeanors. The governor, triumph at hand, readied a major shake-up.

Tammany counterattacked. Legislators appointed their own committee to investigate Sulzer's and Blake's finances. Under oath, Blake could not ex-plain how he had spent his money, and several of his key witnesses and in-vestigators were exposed as frauds. The evidence against Kennedy looked increasingly flimsy. And now Sulzer looked like a dupe.

He seized the initiative once more, naming a loyal Democratic supporter and real estate assessor from the Bronx, James M. Clancy, as Kennedy's suc-cessor. Clancy arrived at a Sing Sing about to explode.

The state's withholding of funds had starved the prison. Stirred up by the embittered Kennedy, the men were seething over rumors of impending mass transfers upstate. Soon enough the mattress factory was aflame, with the blaze spreading to other shops and burning down Sing Sing's north gate. As hundreds fought the fire, townspeople and news reporters gathered on the hill overlooking the prison, within earshot of inmates shouting their griev-ances. Over the next few days, there were more fires, work stoppages, and window smashing. One black prisoner, fingered as an informer, was fatally slashed in the head.

Now the Ossining townsfolk—the village had changed its name from Sing Sing in 1901 to distance itself from the prison—were growing alarmed, calling for the state naval militia and National Guard. But after ten ringleaders were sent to the dungeon and 170 prisoners were transferred to other institutions, the revolt petered out.

Warden Clancy and Superintendent Riley, shaken by the uprising, soon instituted reforms. They renovated much of the prison and established an honor group of prisoners privileged to pick apples outside the walls. They closed the dungeon, fixed up the death cells, and let the prisoners out for longer periods.

But the hapless Sulzer suffered the fate of many would-be reformers. The hostile legislature, concluding that he had stolen party funds, impeached him. Tammany exulted.

Osborne, the chairman of Sulzer's reform commission, had emerged un-tainted. Born in the city of Auburn in 1859 to a wealthy manufacturing family, he attended Harvard and took over his father's farm machinery busi-ness making mowers and reapers until it was sold to J. P. Morgan's Interna-tional Harvester Company, leaving Osborne a rich man. A widower—his wife had died after bearing him four sons—Osborne joined with the econo-mist Henry George Jr. and publisher William Randolph Hearst in backing the George Junior Republic, an upstate enclave teaching self-government to street boys. He soon broke with Hearst, charging that the publisher was us-ing philanthropy to promote his newspapers.

A renegade Democrat in a family of Republicans, gifted in art and music and strikingly tall and handsome, Osborne entered public life, serving on the school board, founding a newspaper, the *Auburn Citizen*, running for lieutenant governor, challenging Hearst for the gubernatorial nomination, and eventually winning office as Auburn's "millionaire mayor." Later, inves-tigating rail service for the state's Public Service Commission, he went undercover, dressing as a hobo to spy on crews of the New York Central Railroad. It was a favorite ploy. From his days in amateur theatricals, Osborne had liked to dress up, sometimes donning disguises to infiltrate Auburn's dives and taverns to see what people were saying about him.

A terrifying childhood visit to Auburn prison attuned him to the suffer-ings of men behind bars. That experience and a recently published memoir, *My Life in Prison*, by Donald Lowrie, serving fifteen years in San Quentin for a single burglary, helped Osborne, as a member of Sulzer's prison reform commission, decide on a bold caper in 1913. He would put himself in Auburn for a week and see firsthand what it was like.

He thought at first he would enter incognito but soon realized he would be quickly unmasked by fellow prisoners and undoubtedly labeled a snitch, with potentially dire consequences. So with the agreement of his friend Warden Rattigan and Superintendent Riley, he addressed the fourteen hundred men in stripes, explaining his wish to be treated as just another convict, "Tom Brown," no. 33333X, the only man in Auburn with a Harvard education. "I suppose," Osborne noted, "the others come from Yale."

"I have put myself on trial in the court of conscience and a verdict has been rendered of 'guilty'—guilty of having lived for many years of my life indifferent to and ignorant of what was going on behind these walls," he told the inmates who gaped in silence (talking not being allowed at Auburn), not knowing what to make it of all.

"Brown" said he knew many would regard his mission as a "fool's errand." Yet he was determined to carry it through. "For somehow, deep down, I have the feeling that after I have really lived among you, marched in your lines, shared your food, gone to the same cells at night, and in the morning looked out at the piece of God's sunlight through the same iron bars—that then, and not until then, can I feel the knowledge which will break down the barriers between my soul and the souls of my brothers."

With that, mustache shorn, he reported to the warden's office and entered the world of the convict, confined to cell 15, second tier north, a cubicle four feet wide by seven and a half feet long. The floor was concrete; an iron bed and table hung from the wall; and a stool, locker, water basin, and toilet bucket completed the furnishings. He was on his own, although allowed writing materials to keep the journal that would become his 1914 book, *Within Prison Walls*. The guards were under orders to treat him like any other inmate. But even that smacked too much of privilege. Osborne was determined to experience the punishment cells. Deliberately, he provoked a guard in the basket shop, defying orders, and was consigned to the dungeon.

He was strip-searched and given a dirty shirt and trousers. His handkerchief was taken away as a precaution, for a prisoner had once strangled himself with one. The jail, as the punishment unit was called, sat in a vaulted stone cavern between the death house and the powerhouse with its ceaselessly grinding dynamo. His cell was solid sheet iron studded with projecting rivets, except where Warden Rattigan had magnanimously installed a smooth floor. A small hole in the roof provided the sole ventilation. Almost no light leaked in.

Through a slot in the door he was handed a slice of bread, and shreds of newspaper for toilet paper. The spout of a tin funnel poured him his gill of water, an inch and a half in his tin cup for the night. There was no bed—but still there were bedbugs. Osborne picked one off his neck in the dark.

From the next cell came an anguished wail. "Oh my God, I've tipped over my water!" He listened helplessly as a thirst-tormented prisoner gibbered insanely in the pitch-dark solitude. Even knowing his prospects for release, Osborne nearly went mad himself, overcome with hatred for the guards and "this hideous, imbecile, soul-destroying system."

He already thought capital punishment insane, "as if one crime of such nature, done by a single man, acting individually, can be expiated by a similar crime done by all men, acting collectively." Now he felt the whole system was demented.

At the end of his week Osborne was reprieved. He left Auburn a changed man. In an impromptu farewell to his fellow prisoners, he vowed: "Believe me, I shall never forget you. In my sleep at night as well as in my waking hours, I shall hear in my imagination the tramp of your feet in the yard, and see the lines of gray marching up and down." The men roared their approval, and Osborne was overcome. "Probably I am the only man, in all the years since this prison was built, to leave these walls with regret."

Public reaction was mixed. Rattigan and Riley seemed to regard the experiment as a success. The *New York Tribune* applauded Osborne for his courage. "Intelligence and sympathy may go a long way toward lighting up the dark places in our system of criminal administration and putting to a test the growing conviction that a prisoner need not be consigned, from the time he enters prison, to the social scrap heap."

But other editorial writers heaped ridicule on Osborne. The great reformer, one said, might have achieved similar insights in an equal amount of time spent in a Turkish bath. Cartoonists drew him in his cell supping on wine and caviar. The *New York Times* called him an "amateur prisoner." If Osborne wanted to know how it felt to be very ill, commented the *Kingston (N. Y.) Freeman*, he could check into a hospital and have a pretty nurse take his temperature every half hour. The *Bridgeport Standard* asked if it was "necessary to wallow in a mud hole to know how a pig feels."

Undeterred, Osborne persuaded Rattigan and Riley to let him set up a system of prisoner self-government at Auburn. He called it the Mutual Welfare League, a way of giving the inmates themselves through their elected delegates responsibility for their actions and preparing them for eventual freedom. Minor infractions of the rules would be dealt with by the men themselves, while the warden would remain in ultimate charge of discipline. "The state will patrol the walls, that is their business, but inside the walls it is up to you," Osborne declared. The league put on musicals and minstrel shows, sports contests and baseball games, and kept in touch with its members through its own newspaper, the *Bulletin*.

Downstate at Sing Sing, conditions were deteriorating once again. Warden Clancy, who had calmed the prison after its outbreak of rioting, had been caught trying to help his disgraced mentor, Governor Sulzer, by clumsily wiretapping a Tammany state senator doing time for bribery. Clancy had also been interfering in the tangled death row case of New York City police lieutenant Charles Becker, who had probably been framed for the killing of the gambler Herman Rosenthal. Four other men, "Gyp the Blood," "Dago Frank," "Lefty Louie," and "Whitey Lewis," had already been electrocuted for the crime.

Clancy's successor, Warden Thomas J. McCormick, a Tammany ally and plumber from Yonkers, imported some of Osborne's ideas from Auburn, starting a Golden Rule Brotherhood patterned after the Mutual Welfare League. But then an influential prisoner, convicted Brooklyn banker Daniel A. Sullivan, was caught living it up outside the walls. Furthermore, Sullivan had "loaned" money to McCormick to buy a fancy new car and was driving the warden around as his chauffeur. McCormick was out.

In November 1914, little more than a year after his self-exile in Auburn, Osborne heard that he was a candidate to succeed McCormick at Sing Sing. He was dubious. He had been mayor, state fish and game commissioner, and a member of a prison reform commission, but never a warden. Sulzer's downfall, moreover, had doomed the reform panel and dimmed Osborne's prospects. Osborne also felt that Clinton, New York's "Siberia" in the wilds of the Adirondacks, required attention even more than Sing Sing. He cabled Superintendent Riley to take his name off the list.

Riley would not take no for an answer. The newly elected Republican governor, Charles S. Whitman, the former Manhattan district attorney who had railroaded Becker for the Rosenthal murder, also urged Osborne to take the job and pledged his support.

Rattigan at Auburn understood Osborne's reluctance. "I cannot understand for the life of me why you want to consider that Sing Sing proposition," he said. "It is perfectly 'impossible.'" But Osborne said he would take it, provided the men of Sing Sing wanted him. Two hundred fifty of them promptly petitioned for his appointment.

He took over in December 1914, and immediately installed the Mutual Welfare League, supplanting McCormick's Golden Rule Brotherhood. As at Auburn, the league administered discipline and organized entertainment and sporting events, going so far as to convert part of the Hudson River into a pool where hundreds of inmates swam daily. It also improved vocational training in the prison shops. Henry Ford and John D. Rockefeller were among the benefactors donating money and equipment for prisoner rehabilitation. Ford in particular supported Osborne, vowing to employ released prisoners in his Detroit auto plants, although many ended up in a strong-arm force.

To further prepare inmates for life on the outside, Osborne created a prisoner economy backed by the league's own scrip, aluminum coins and notes. Everyone earned a basic wage of six dollars a week and more for extra work. Out of this, inmates paid for meals (10¢ for breakfast, 25¢ for dinner) and rent ($1 to $1.60 a week, depending on the desirability of the cell). There was a bank for savings and an insurance plan.

Superintendent Riley, stricken with cancer, viewed Osborne's growing popularity with dismay. Was Sing Sing a prison or a country club? Particularly rankling were Osborne's freewheeling comments to the press.

The two were soon at odds over a more volatile issue—sex.

Perversion in prison, especially with two convicts in a cell, was widely recognized, as evidenced by the routine hospital examinations for anal penetration. But officially the problem was denied, with complainants often suffering punitive transfers to Clinton.

Osborne, who spoke out against sexual relations in prison, drew distinctions among degenerates or effeminates who welcomed advances, wolves who preyed on them, and ordinary men driven to homosexuality by loss of their normal sexual outlets. The solution, he said, was physical activities and entertainment. He also tried to limit double-bunking to blood relatives and in-laws, and sought a new housing unit to disperse the population.

Superintendent Riley opposed new space at Sing Sing and preferred to transfer the overflow upstate. But Osborne argued that transfers were punitive and that the Mutual Welfare League put discipline largely in the hands of the prisoners themselves.

They had other differences. Osborne imperiously fired guards he didn't like. He subscribed to a clipping service that tracked his growing renown and went on the stump to address influential audiences. He opened Sing Sing to celebrity tours, some 250 visitors a day, from evangelist Billy Sunday to bare-knuckle fighter John L. Sullivan and presidential candidate William Jennings Bryan.

Riley was now bent on Osborne's ouster. The night of Lieutenant Becker's electrocution, Riley dispatched an agent to seize Osborne's files while Osborne was away, for he always left the prison during executions to protest capital punishment. But tipped off to Riley's raid, Osborne rushed back, intercepting Riley's agent at the Ossining station and snatching back his documents.

Plots swirled. Loyalists tipped Osborne to schemes by guards to foment a riot or to sneak prostitutes to the road gangs working outside the prison, and to frame Osborne himself in sexual liaisons with prisoners' wives. The battle for control of Sing Sing was on. Who was in charge—Riley or Osborne? Governor Whitman assured Osborne of support, but did nothing to call Riley off.

What occurred next was indisputably sordid. An inmate told the league's court that he had had sex with twenty-one fellow prisoners. Osborne quietly suspended the men's privileges without reporting the case to Riley, as regulations required.

Riley learned of it anyway and went to the Westchester district attorney. In November 1915, the zealous prosecuting attorney, William Fallon—later to become known as "the Great Mouthpiece," a legendary defense lawyer who never lost a homicide case—secured a grand jury indictment of the twenty-one for sodomy. Fallon's crusade continued. The following month, a year after taking over Sing Sing, Osborne himself was indicted on seven counts of perjury, neglect of duty, and "various unlawful and unnatural acts"—sodomy. Although none would testify against the warden, Fallon quoted a convict as reporting that Osborne had told him: "You are a good-looking boy; if I were a girl I would fall in love with you."

As word of his indictment spread through the prison, Osborne assembled the men in the mess hall and climbed atop a table to face them. "I have just heard that I have been indicted by the Westchester grand jury," he said. "I presume that you will congratulate me."

When the laughter died down, one of the men shouted: "Now, Warden, you know how it is yourself."

He went on leave while his friend, George W. Kirchwey, former dean of Columbia University Law School, temporarily took over Sing Sing. Months later, 3,500 people, from ex-convicts to Harvard president Charles W. Eliot, antivice crusader Charles Parkhurst, philanthropist Adolph Lewisohn, psychiatrist Dr. Felix Adler, social reformer Lillian Wald, and general sessions judge William H. Wadhams, filled Carnegie Hall to show their support for Osborne.

He went on trial in March 1916 with the evidence against him rapidly evaporating. A perjury charge that he had falsely denied the existence of sodomy cases was thrown out. He had never denied there was sodomy in prison. Sodomy charges against the prisoners were also withdrawn on the grounds of double jeopardy—they had already been disciplined in the prison. Without evidence, the rest of the case against Osborne collapsed. But though he was cleared, he was irredeemably tainted, and in October 1916, Osborne resigned.

Over the next three years, five wardens would waltz in and out of Sing Sing's gates.

9

Back on his feet after his disturbing brush with mortality, Chapin was once again basking in his exalted status as editor of the *Sing Sing Bulletin*. With the blessing of Lawes, he and his paper were doing splendidly, perhaps a little too splendidly.

The April 1920 issue carried Chapin's third installment of his memoirs and lively ghosted columns on inmate doings and homespun wisdom. "Science is said to be developing a way to prolong human life to 190 years. Pleasant outlook for us 'Lifers.'" As usual, there were bouquets aplenty for Lawes, including praise for his morning calisthenics, compulsory for men forty and under, and optional for those older. Chapin's investigative instincts were in play too, the paper pressing state officials on a food-poisoning outbreak at Clinton, traced to tainted salmon, that had felled thirty-four prisoners, killing two of them. And there was an editorial against capital punishment, again clearly by Chapin. "We have studied it at close range, some of us in the solitude of the condemned cells, in the gloomy shadows of the execution chamber and its hideous electric chair." But killing a man didn't punish him, the editorial went on. Better "to send the culprit to prison and keep him there until he has worked out his redemption." Let him labor in prison and divide his pay between those who were dependent on him and on his victim.

The front page, however, carried the most compelling—and ominous—item of all.

In Albany, Superintendent Rattigan had been taking a dim view of the goings-on at Sing Sing and the avalanche of publicity Lawes was reaping.

AN ANNOUNCEMENT

An order in the interest of economy has come from the Superintendent of Prisons to restrict the output of the Sing Sing Bulletin to 1,500 copies for each issue. As it takes almost this number to supply the officers and inmates of the Institution, it will not be possible hereafter to mail copies to the many persons on the outside who have requested that our paper be sent to them. After this issue the mailing list will be practically eliminated. The law forbids us to accept subscriptions.

Although well disposed toward Lawes and his camaraderie with the prisoners, Rattigan shared little of the warden's affection for Chapin and his *Bulletin*. To have a paper so popular run by a wife killer smacked of trouble. There were only eleven hundred men in Sing Sing, but five thousand copies of the *Bulletin* were being printed every month, going out free to prisoners throughout the state and a long mailing list of penologists, law enforcement officers, philanthropists, women's clubs, even subscribers abroad. The law forbade the sale of subscriptions, but that hadn't curtailed the paper's reach—the reach of a murderer regaling readers month after month with his self-aggrandizing memoirs. The Republicans could make a lot of hay with that.

Rattigan sent a message with his order curtailing the print run, a message Lawes and Chapin could not mistake. Lawes seethed and considered a response. Did they think he was another Tom Osborne they could push around?

The paper's May issue stopped Rattigan cold. Chapin had added another autobiographer to the *Bulletin*'s contributors. Charlie Wilson, a convicted polygamist with seven wives on the outside, was now telling his story. "They say a good wife is a rare jewel. I have been a collector of jewels."

Prisoners got a laugh, but Rattigan was not amused. Seizing on a minor lapse—another prisoner's complaint that he was named in the paper in violation of a privacy policy—Rattigan decided to act. The *Bulletin* had to go altogether.

Lawes, meanwhile, was puzzling over a letter that had come to him in the institutional mail, an eight-page, single-spaced, typed manifesto so engaging and literate it could scarcely have come from a prisoner. But he saw, flipping quickly to the end, that it did.

It may be said that I had you under "observation"—to decide to my own satisfaction whether you were the man that I have been convinced you are, or—just a mere "flash-in-the-pan" like so many others that I have seen come here and elsewhere, with honeyed phrases and multitude of promises and then, have seen make their exits as dismal failures.

Lawes had to grin, crinkling his blue eyes. The man had *him* under observation! He read on avidly.

The writer hardly bothered to introduce himself—if Lawes was that good, his spies already knew who he was—but noted that he had been there for almost two years and had managed, in his fifty-eight years, "to crowd the experience, compared to the average human being, of a thousand years." He readily admitted having "prostituted talent, ability, etc." He was working in the industrial superintendent's office, having come from the Shipping Department, and he proceeded, with clinical detachment, to critique shipping's shortcomings and rate its staff, along with those of the key industrial shops—knitting, brushes, shoes, sheet and metal, and cart and wagon.

The Mutual Welfare League was a joke. "The moment that it was put into the exclusive control of 'cliques,' 'gangs,' &c., it per force lost its mutual features." He had high hopes for the progressive prison movement but thought Osborne, who predated him at Sing Sing, had squandered his capital by the appearance, if nothing else, of personal indiscretions. While Osborne may have been vindicated in court, he "left impressions behind which to this day prevail in the mind of quite a few," the writer noted pointedly. "It is a matter of history that in those days 'roof-sleeping-gardens' were maintained atop that part of the building where your residence is, for the special delectation of the favored few, etc." It all ended, as it had to, in scandal. Of course, he conceded, a reformer was bound to excite jealousies, "but, a man occupying the high and important position of Warden of this institution, particularly during that period of transition when he was the focus of the eyes of public opinion—should at least, like Caesar's wife, have endeavored to 'be above suspicion' and it was a mighty poor way to avoid that suspicion or reasons for

it, by fraternizing so promiscuously with a certain set whom he had placed in
full control of league affairs."

The writer closed with an apology for having monopolized Lawes's valuable time and a pledge to do all he could to support efforts to clean "the pu-
trid accumulations of years."

Lawes, unable to suppress a chuckle at the man's audacity, studied the cal-
ligraphic signature: Ernest Sawyer # 69280. Per force, indeed. He would
have to keep an eye out for that one.

Rattigan was also getting mail, and he didn't have to wait long to see his
worst political fears materialize.

A letter arrived at the end of June 1920. He didn't recognize the sender—
a John G. Purdie of 129 East Fifty-eighth Street—but the threat was unmistakable, though Purdie was too apoplectic to get the name right: could
Rattigan explain "why it is that Major Ernest Lawes, warden of Sing Sing
prison," is permitted to behave as though his position were that of press
agent for a burlesque show instead of prison warden?

"There is hardly a day passes but one notices some idiotic item in the papers to the effect that 'Major Lawes says the "boys" in the death house prefer
Caruso to McCormick and he has ordered Caruso phonograph records' or
'Major Lawes has ordered an easy chair for Hattie Dixon the woman murderer because the prison stool hurt her back' or 'Major Lawes says one of the
men in the death house snores and keeps the others awake' or 'Major Lawes
with tears of gladness in his eyes brought the reprieve to the condemned
man himself.' And so on, ad nauseam."

What was Sing Sing anyway, Purdie demanded, a place of punishment for
those who break the law or "a house of amusement for cranks, perverts and
nuts"? He lumped Lawes with Osborne "and all the crowd of maudlin 'reformers'" and demanded that Sing Sing be put back in the hands of "stern
men of discipline" who would abolish welfare leagues and baseball games
and make the streets safe again.

The last paragraph went straight to Rattigan's concerns. "Please give me
your opinion of this prostitution of the prisons to the personal ambitions of
the wardens and the cranks who control them. I am making this a very defi-
nite issue in the forthcoming campaigns."

Lawes learned of the matter several days later when Rattigan sent him a copy of Purdie's letter, "parts of which I entirely agree with."

Lawes was staggered. The superintendent was siding with this nobody against him! The rest of Rattigan's letter was unmistakably hostile to Lawes. "Please send me your views of the subject before I fully answer Mr. Purdie. And do you know who he is? I agree with some of his criticism, and will discuss this with him and you later."

Lawes would not give Rattigan the satisfaction of an angry reply. More than fifteen years in the state penal bureaucracy had taught him the virtues of stoicism. Yes, he wrote back, he had received Rattigan's letter, and Purdie's, "and I wish to advise you that I do not know Mr. Purdie and, furthermore, I do not care to discuss his views."

Rattigan had not been entirely candid with Lawes. He had already replied cordially to Purdie, who now corresponded with the superintendent as if he were an ally. Purdie was also emboldened enough to show more of his hand. He knew many important people, Democrats and Republicans, and was working to line them up against any reelection bid by Rattigan's boss, Governor Smith, "because of the leniency he has extended to murderers and criminals." It was people like Smith and Lawes, he railed, who were responsible for the crime wave. He wasn't out to get Smith, Purdie insisted. "I am doing it because I know criminals for what they are and alone and unaided I intend to stir up popular sentiment against this coddling."

He enclosed some newspaper clippings "as an example of the press agent stuff which Warden Lawes is continually getting out." The "idiocy" of the items, he said, "indicates a bad attack of that disease known as 'craving for the limelight' and should be severely repressed." Purdie voiced hope that he and Rattigan could meet when the superintendent was next in New York. He would prove to Rattigan that he wasn't a crank.

Rattigan, in turn, sent Purdie's latest letter to Lawes, demanding "that you write me your views on the subject."

Lawes's patience was dwindling. "I wish to advise you that Mr. Purdie, or any other of ten million people, is entitled to his views, but I did not come here to be dominated by any nonentity who does not realize that the world is progressing, and I am very much surprised that you should correspond with any individual who criticizes Governor Smith, as well as a warden of one of the institutions over which you have jurisdiction, on matters which plainly show his lack of knowledge." It was a bold rebuff of his boss, but Lawes well knew that as warden of Sing Sing he was lord of his fief and powerfully independent.

Less than a week later, Purdie wrote Rattigan again, this time enclosing newspaper clippings reporting that Lawes had refused to permit an artist access to the death chamber to paint a picture of the electric chair. But by ostentatiously rejecting publicity, was not Lawes really courting it? Purdie sensed another publicity stunt. "I ask you as an officer of this State and as his superior officer if a man who deliberately seeks public attention by means of such imbecilities in the public press is fitted for the responsible position of warden of Sing Sing prison."

Rattigan made sure Lawes saw this, too.

Lawes had had enough. He was not to blame for the press's obsession with Sing Sing, he insisted. His predecessors Kennedy, Clancy, McCormick, Osborne, Kirchwey, Moyer, Brophy, and Grant had all encountered the same. He couldn't control news coverage any more than they could. Was it his fault Sing Sing was less than an hour's train ride from the city rooms of New York's sensation-starved press? All he could do was try to manage the prison in a modern and efficient way and steer it clear of scandal. And no editorial page had taken issue with his administration. He was not surprised at the sniping from the occasional John Purdies, Lawes told Rattigan, "but what surprises and disappoints me is your attitude in reference to the matter."

That ended his exchanges with Rattigan, but Lawes would not let it rest. Who was this Purdie anyway?

Two weeks later, he had a confidential investigator's report in hand. "P." was employed by the Astor estate to look after its real estate interests. The investigator had called on P., who was about thirty, and learned that he had studied law at Fordham but had never taken the bar exam, and had served as a U.S. intelligence officer in Europe during the world war. Earlier, he had investigated prison conditions for Governor Whitman and been convinced of the need for strict punishment and the death penalty. His opposition to Governor Smith arose from the murder of an elevated-train operator by two men who years later were still in the death cells, boasting that their Bronx political connections would win them a commutation from Smith. P. believed that the crime wave engulfing New York was attributable to prison leniency and that prisons were there not to reform but to punish.

Lawes tucked away the report, scratching out the investigator's name.

He didn't have to wait long for Rattigan's next move. But this time Lawes was ready.

In August 1920, B. Ogden Chisolm, a prison reformer from one of New York's oldest families, asked at Sing Sing for his usual copy of the *Bulletin*. He was told the paper was not available, but had been suspended. Chisolm was stunned. He notified reporters, always hungry for any stories about strife at the prison, and they thronged Lawes.

"The *Sing Sing Bulletin* has suspended publication" was all Lawes would say, knowing the answer would be unsatisfactory.

But, they persisted, had the order come from the state prison officials?

"I have nothing to say," Lawes insisted.

Whispering in reporters' ears, however, he clearly implicated Rattigan, and the ensuing stories quickly put Lawes's spin on the affair.

SING SING'S NEWSPAPER
KILLED BY POLITICIANS

Order from Superintendent of Prisons
Stops Publication of the *Bulletin* Which Was
Widely Read and Quoted.

The *Morning Telegraph*'s special dispatch from Ossining said the suspension of the "most talked-about prison paper in the world" came "like a thunderbolt." The warden refused comment, the *Tribune* solemnly affirmed. "It is regarded as certain, however, that the order suppressing its publication was not of his giving." The *Brooklyn Standard Union* went further: "It is rumored that politicians in the State service at Albany have shown jealousy of the prison management under the administration of Warden Lawes." Lawes's hometown paper, the *Elmira Gazette*, also leaped to his defense, laying the paper's suspension to "a clique of politicians" in Albany who had been trying to stymie Lawes "in every way possible."

The press frenzy was now engulfing Governor Smith himself. Chisolm wrote Smith to protest the "outrage" and told reporters, "I believe politics is behind the suspension of the paper and I don't believe that Governor Smith will stand for it."

Rattigan, thrown on the defensive, denied giving the order to suppress the *Bulletin* and insisted he would open an immediate investigation into the paper's suspension.

Lawes, meanwhile, was rallying support. Warden Brophy, whom Lawes had relieved half a year before, spoke out on Lawes's behalf. "Discontinuing the prison newspaper is pretty dangerous stuff. They tried to stop it when I was in charge. Rattigan put obstacles in the way. The latest deed was only to try to embarrass Major Lawes. It is a great help to the prison officials, I found, as well as to the inmates. Warden Lawes ought to be let alone and allowed to turn it out again."

Another predecessor, Warden Kennedy, who had overcome the vilification of the Sulzer years to become president of the State Prison Commission and had extolled the *Bulletin* under Chapin, lent his support. "I think all the commissioners favored the prison newspaper and we'll take the matter up."

A hero army officer and prison crusader, Captain T. A. Brady, who had been instrumental in ousting Warden McCormick over his improprieties with his chauffeur-inmate, lent his powerful voice to the paper's cause. "Major Lawes made the *Sing Sing Bulletin* a great force for good and it's a pity the interlopers cannot be made to leave them alone."

Amid the finger-pointing, Lawes recalled Smith's assurances of a free hand and asked to see him. The governor was at the Biltmore and invited Lawes down.

Lawes found Smith in his suite in shirtsleeves and red-and-green suspenders, hunched over a plate of corn on the cob dripping with butter. As Lawes tried not to stare, Smith mowed off row after row of kernels, discarded the cob, wiped his chin, and went on to the next glistening ear.

The corn had been flown up fresh from the South, Smith said by way of conversation, motioning Lawes into a chair at the table. The development boys were trying to show what the airlines could do for interstate commerce. Smith was supposed to pose for photographers, but by the time they showed up there'd be nothing left but husks.

Then he turned his big-domed face to Lawes. "What's up, Warden? Trouble already?" His eyes twinkled mischievously. "You told me you could run that place. The boys too much for you?" Lawes explained about Rattigan and the *Bulletin*, although Smith surely knew all that.

"Pretty good sheet," Smith conceded. "But hell, is that all the trouble there is?"

It was enough, Lawes said. The story was already making headlines. He was trying to close the floodgates. But the pressure was building. He wanted the free hand Smith had promised him, Lawes said. Otherwise he might as well resign.

Smith picked up another ear of corn and salted and peppered it. Lawes was right, he said. He could go back to Sing Sing and tell everyone he had the governor's approval to run the place as he saw fit.

Lawes shook his head. No, he repeated, he was prepared to resign unless the governor himself put out the word.

Smith looked up, annoyed. "All right, all right," he muttered. He'd never known a paper yet that didn't start trouble. Now, was there anything else on Lawes's mind?

As a matter of fact, there was, the warden said. He described the death house and mortuary and the whine of the autopsy saw.

Smith set down his corn distastefully. That was enough, he said. "We'll give 'em a new death house."

Back in Sing Sing, Lawes found Chapin anxiously standing by his silent presses. Lawes gave him the thumbs-up. The presses could roll.

Rattigan, meanwhile, had journeyed to Dannemora—about as far from Sing Sing as he could get without falling into Canada—and had his Albany office issue a statement that he was demanding to know who had suspended the *Bulletin* and insisting that publication be resumed at once.

After returning from upstate, Rattigan went straight to Sing Sing with Deputy Superintendent James Long to meet with Lawes. They emerged from behind closed doors to find a crush of newsmen and photographers.

Rattigan was tight-lipped. "I'm not here to give out news," he said. "I'm here on official business. The warden may make a statement."

Lawes stepped forward. "The *Sing Sing Bulletin* will be continued," he said evenly. "The suspension has been lifted."

Long tried to save face. "It will be run as it always has been. It will be carefully edited and censored."

"Here or at Albany?" someone shouted out.

"Here," Long conceded.

Lawes had won.

Chapin had even more reason to be happy. He had found an amorous pen pal, a young Minneapolis woman named Viola Irene Cooper whom he had met years earlier; he wrote to her in an infatuated correspondence, "Won't you please not be shy, but hold out your arms and your lips to me, as you did when you were a very little girl?" He begged, "Greet me as though we had parted only yesterday and not a thousand years ago." Soon the two were exchanging steamy letters of a fantasy idyll away together. As a special favor, Lawes did not run the correspondence through prison censorship.

With the *Bulletin* back in circulation, Sir Thomas Lipton, the bachelor tea magnate and yachtsman, seventy and walrus-mustached, paid a visit as the guest of the State Prison Commission. The son of grocers in Glasgow, Scotland, young Thomas had stowed away on a ship to America during the Civil War, earning a living as a farm laborer in the South and then migrating to New York. In 1870, he returned to Scotland, where he founded a chain of groceries keyed to direct purchasing of bacon and cheese from Ireland and aggressive advertising. During the 1880s he began selling tea, purchasing his own plantations in Ceylon and developing a revolutionary new technology—tea bags. He moved his headquarters to London, reaping a colossal fortune and entering the lists for the America's Cup. But despite his wealth, he never could wrest the coveted sailing trophy from the Americans.

At Sing Sing, the prisoners presented him with a joshing award. "To a good loser, Sir Thomas Lipton, from some good losers of the Mutual Welfare League of Sing Sing."

In return, Sir Thomas endowed a sports trophy, the "Lipton Baseball Perpetual Challenge Cup," inscribed "There Never Was a Man Who Did Not Make a Mistake." He acknowledged his own share of mistakes. The trick, he said, was not to make the same ones twice.

By December, five who had made fatal mistakes—or had failed to persuade a jury that they hadn't—were living their last days on death row, set to be executed the same night, the first time since 1915 that so many were to go to the chair at once. One of the men, Howard Baker, who had been convicted of killing a night watchman near Rochester, was only twenty. His wife, sickly and destitute, with three babies, visited to say good-bye. Kathryn

Lawes drove her around and Lawes got Maud Ballington Booth of the Volunteers of America to provide clothes for the children.

Lawes's first year as warden ended with an unexpected drama. A few weeks before Christmas, 1920, Fred Rothermel, a bank robber barely into a ten-to-twenty-year sentence for holding up the First National Bank of Freeport, Long Island, was on a work crew repairing the roof over the cellblock when he declared he was missing a tool. Allowed to retrieve it, he walked to the roof of the warden's residence and made his way inside and down four flights of stairs to the ground, where he passed himself off as a trusty and walked through the gate to freedom.

When Rothermel was discovered missing, Lawes rounded up a posse of sixty guards and twenty state troopers to chase him down. Seven hours after the escape, the motorcade was speeding down the road when a lone figure stepped out of the brush. Lawes, recognizing Rothermel, screeched to a stop. "Hop in," he said.

Rothermel gratefully accepted the ride, then did a double take when he saw who was at the wheel. "Well, I'll be damned. . . ."

"You can count on that," Lawes said.

Lawes's triumph with the *Bulletin* turned out to be short-lived. By the spring of 1921, budget cuts ordered by Rattigan doomed the paper. Chapin's influential friends came forward with offers to privately underwrite it, but that smacked of charity, which Chapin could not abide; he wrote to his beloved Viola Irene, "More than a dozen similar offers have come to me but, of course, none of them will be accepted. I would prefer to shovel coal rather than edit a prison paper that existed solely by generosity of men who take a kindly interest in it. If the State cannot supply the funds to buy the necessary material, I would have no heart in trying to carry on."

10

Kathryn Lawes, her svelte figure enveloped in the generous curves of coming motherhood, negotiated the steep hills of Sing Sing with weakening stamina. As the damp Hudson Valley spring yielded to sticky summer, she was suffering through a fourth difficult pregnancy, though she tried not to dwell on her personal discomfort. She had become a patron saint of the prisoners, particularly Chapin, who had hailed her in a handwritten note not long before his presses were forever stilled: "To the dear lady who gave me my first ray of hope and perhaps saved me from the worst fate that could have befallen me." The other men, too, were touched by her tender generosities, her willingness to keep their secrets, and her regular visits to the potter's field on Sing Sing's hill, where she laid flowers on the unmarked graves of unclaimed victims of the chair.

Her beloved first babies—twins, a boy and a girl—had died at birth. Then by the grace of God came Kathleen and, eleven months later, Crystal. Now, in mid-1921, Kathryn—thirty-six, the mother of two girls, thirteen and twelve, and a devout Roman Catholic—was, to her own guarded delight and that of her surprised husband, expecting again.

Her history left her anxious. Then, too, the embattled Lawes was preoccupied with prison problems and often off traveling. Typically, he had been away at a convention in Ohio the spring night two prisoners sandbagged a guard and fled to the warden's residence, trying to force open the door to the upstairs private quarters, where Kathryn was dining with Kathleen and Crystal. Terrified, she cowered with the girls until the inmate chef, hearing the commotion, hurled his body against the door, bracing it

against the intruders. They threatened to shoot but he held firm.
Finally they retreated, fleeing
through the laundry and smashing
though a screen door to freedom.

The baby came not long afterward, a third daughter, born in June
1921. Kathryn, whether out of su-
perstition or exhaustion, hadn't prepared a name, so Lawes improvised,
calling the baby Joan Marie after a
horse that had showed some promise at the track. Kathryn didn't care
much for the name or its derivation.
She called her Cherie—darling—
and the nickname stuck.

Kathryn Stanley had met Lawes
in Elmira in 1904 when she was
nineteen, he not yet twenty-one.
One of three sisters in a family
that had fled Ireland during the

Kathryn about the time she met Lawes in Elmira.
(JOAN L. JACOBSEN)

potato famine, she had taken a business course and landed a rather risqué
position as an office worker at a wholesale paper company. Lewis, a seven-
dollar-a-week office boy in an insurance brokerage, soon contrived to be
standing outside the Stanley home as Katy left for work in the morning.
They made a handsome couple, he blond, tall, and rugged, she slender and
fine-figured with a delicate pink complexion and warm blond hair piled high
in the fashion of the day.

Lawes's family roots in the area went deep. The Abbotts on his mother's
father's side had settled Massachusetts and later migrated to upstate New
York's Iroquois territories during the American Revolution. His mother's
forebears, Sullivans, had migrated from Ireland during the potato famine as
well. Lewis was born on September 13, 1883, the second child of Sarah Abbott and Harry Lewis Lawes, an English Protestant who acceded to his wife's
insistence that their sons be baptized and raised Roman Catholic. Lewis's
elder brother died in childhood. Lewis's uncle, his father's brother John, was

a blacksmith reputed to weigh six hundred pounds and sought by a traveling circus as its giant and strongman. When he died, his coffin could not fit through the door but had to be taken out through a window, hefted by ten pallbearers.

Young Lewis grew up delivering the *Elmira Telegram*, accompanying his grandfather Charles Abbott through Woodlawn Cemetery, where the old man worked as sexton, and getting into mischief. His were all the usual petty larcenies of youth. His father, Harry Lawes, was foreman of an iron yard—a junkman, to put it plainly—an avid violinist and backyard gardener who assigned his son to weekend duty hoeing the vegetables. One morning, tending the tomatoes and seeing his father emerge in his Sunday best, Lewis was overcome by an irresistible impulse. He plucked a ripe tomato and let fly, with perfect aim. The tomato splattered deliciously on the boiled white shirt.

Lewis took his licking, mystified by the origins of his errant criminal impulse and, when he took some time to think about it, relieved that his victim was only his father and not some stranger who might have hounded him into prison.

And in Elmira, prison was hardly an abstraction. Looming over the city—where a local son, Samuel Langhorne Clemens, could be seen clattering through the streets in his horse-drawn victoria—was the towered fortress of the Elmira Reformatory, opened in 1876, seven years before Lewis's birth. Rising just half a mile from the Laweses' simple clapboard house, it was the world's first institution for reforming youthful offenders. But behind its bright promise and the progressive image of its autocratic superintendent, Zebulon Reed Brockway, lurked terrible secrets, some of which were revealed by the *Buffalo News* and then the *New York World* in a sensational exposé in the early 1890s. An ensuing investigation by the State Board of Charities confirmed the horrors. To prevent masturbation, doctors chloroformed inmates and inserted a metal ring through the skin of the penis. Offenders accused of infractions were taken to an isolated bathroom where they were stripped and flogged bloody by Brockway himself. He used not only a water-soaked leather strap—nearly two feet long, three inches wide, and a quarter inch thick—but also his fists and feet, often kicking and stomping his victims in the head and kidneys in what some later described as psychopathic rages. When questioned, Brockway called the punishments "harmless parental discipline" and defended his measures as necessary to correct the moral deficiencies of the inmates. He was never out of control, he insisted. It was all an act. The scandal soon blew over. Brockway remained in charge.

The brassy blare and drumrolls of the reformatory band were siren songs for the youth of Elmira, but Harry Lawes cautioned his son to keep his distance, even when the boys paraded in their martial finery outside the walls. But Lewis was intrigued and stayed close, looking at them hard to discern any difference between them and himself; he found none, except that he envied their fierce discipline, contrasting it with his own dreary existence. As a twelve-year-old, he dreamed of glory, posing with Harry and Sarah

Lawes in his Spanish-American War army uniform. (JOAN L. JACOBSEN)

and the family dog outside their simple wood frame home for a photograph he entitled "Future Pres. of U.S. and Parents."

Calls to action abounded. Gold was discovered in the Yukon. American troops were ousting the Spanish from their last colonial outposts in the New World. Lewis and a school chum decided they were needed in Cuba. Skipping school, they caught a train to Binghamton and tried to enlist in the army. The recruiter eyed the callow pair and sent them home. The army was looking for men, not children.

Harry thought that Lewis should get a job on the trolley, but instead he entered a business college in Elmira, where he learned that a figure six without a long upstroke was in grave peril of being taken for a zero. A graduate at almost eighteen, he disdained the office life, yearning for glory. There was war in South Africa and China. He was determined to enlist. He returned to Binghamton, this time with another buddy, and they were accepted—in the Coast Artillery.

Harry Lawes was resigned. If their son was determined to scale Fool's Hill, all they could do was watch him climb up and hope he'd make it down the other side.

Lewis never did go overseas. The closest he got to Manila or Shanghai was Portland Harbor in Maine and Fort Hamilton in Brooklyn, and his only injuries were a fractured collarbone and dislocated shoulder from an army football game in Madison Square Garden. One day on the artillery range the captain ordered him to open fire. Lewis saw that the coordinates were dangerously off, so he recalculated, made the adjustment, and fired. The officer chewed him out. Who was he to make his own decisions? Lewis decided that perhaps after all the army was not for him.

The Fort Hamilton Post Office posted civil service openings. Lawes noticed an opening for prison guard and took the exam.

Mustering out, he staked his army savings on a crap game. In an hour, he had cleaned out the outfit. He had no doubt what to do with his winnings. He headed for Brooks Brothers and emerged in a blue serge suit, starched shirt and collar, silk tie, black derby, and buff suede gloves, glorying in the nap of the woven wool and the bouquet of supple leather. His parents were

Lawes, age twelve, with parents, Harry and Sarah, in Elmira. (JOAN L. JACOBSEN)

ready to throw out their pretentious fop of a son. But the neighbors noticed, particularly Kathryn Stanley.

She herself was a virtual outcast, an office girl who consorted with men in a commercial setting. She loved music and yearned to buy a piano with her first earnings, but her mother wouldn't hear of it, fearing her daughter would become something even worse than an office girl—an *entertainer*.

They were soon courting, dancing to "Bedelia" and downing bottles of Moxie. On Valentine's Day, he saluted her as "The Typewriter Girl":

> *Oh the belle of the office is she,*
> *Office boy, clerks and boss all agree*
> *That her manners are grand,*
> *They are "hers to command"*
> *Oh, who'd not a typewriter be?*

They went through the pas de deux of the age, "going together" but not engaged, free to meet others yet committed to each other. Still, Sarah Abbott thought that at twenty-one her son Lewis was too young to marry.

He searched for work, his hopes pinned on a testimonial on the letterhead of the mayor's office in Elmira:

> *To whomever it may concern:*
> *I have known Mr. Lewis E. Lawes, the bearer of this letter, for many years and know him to be honest, industrious and gentlemanly. He comes of a highly respected family in this city and I can recommend him as capable and deserving.*

Lawes was selling insurance when the civil service results came in. He had won appointment as a prison guard. He had assumed he would be assigned to the Elmira Reformatory, where Brockway had finally retired five years earlier, in 1900, to win election as the city's reform mayor. But it wasn't to his hometown that Lawes was posted, as he struggled to explain to an uncomprehending Kathryn. It was to Clinton Prison, the state's harshest lockup, at Dannemora, high up north in the Adirondacks twenty miles from the Canadian border.

She was devastated. What kind of a life would they have up there?

None, Lawes agreed.

Then he wasn't going?

Oh yes, he said. He was. Alone. Maybe after a while he could transfer to Elmira. Then they could get engaged. Maybe.

Fine, Kathryn sniffed. Maybe she didn't know him that well after all. Why, she wanted to know, would anyone want to spend his time locked up with a bunch of criminals?

Snow blanketed the upstate landscape. As the train chugged north to Clinton that March, carrying prisoners up and passing lumber coming down, Lawes tried to imagine the bleak journey through the eyes of an arriving convict. No wonder they called it Siberia. The stationmaster in Plattsburgh told him not to take it so hard. He was lucky; the others came for a ten-year stretch.

His first view of Dannemora and the grim prison only reinforced his gloom. The caged inmates, sentenced to perpetual silence and bristling with menace, were a sea of gray. Second offenders bore two stripes, third offenders three, and the incorrigibles—the zebras—four. They shuffled through the yard, disdaining to meet his glance.

But then, he thought, brightening, from here there was nowhere to go but up. He might actually be able to do some good for his fifty-five dollars a month. (He was supposed to kick in twenty-five dollars a year to the party in power in Albany, but there he drew the line. His pay was meager enough.)

He drew the rookie's standard night shift of twelve hours, seven days a week, patrolling the gallery in prison-made sneakers with a pistol and a leather-wrapped club. His partner's advice was succinct: "Watch out for these fuckers—they're bad." Most of the time, though, his biggest challenge was simply staying awake. The night captain sympathized and made sure to kick the spittoons loudly as he made his rounds so as never to catch his men napping.

There was one sure way to day duty, he learned. The assistant principal keeper, who made the schedule, had two daughters he was eager to marry off, and Lawes was invited to draw his own conclusions. He looked the girls over and decided that the night shift wasn't so bad.

Still, homesick and missing Kathryn, he pulled whatever strings he could for a job closer to home. In October 1905 he received encouraging word

The Lawes family at dinner in the Sing Sing warden's mansion. Cherie is a blur at left, then daughter Kathleen, Lawes, his wife, Kathryn, Crystal, and Kathryn's mother. (JOAN L. JACOBSEN)

from the warden of Auburn. He could use a new guard and would write his counterpart at Clinton, but Lawes would have to be patient.

Now he got to know the prisoners as more than snoring hulks. One of the stranger ones was Frenchy Menet, a demented hunchback serving twenty years for murder, who, on his arrival from Sing Sing, was found to be concealing no fewer than six small saws. One day, clad in a red blanket fashioned into a makeshift dress and wearing an orange peel on his head monkey-style, he stood at his cell bars bellowing the "Marseillaise." After subduing him, Lawes and his partner searched his cell, where they found carved wooden keys that fit locks on some of the gates and a makeshift blackjack, a sock filled with sand that he had collected under his long fingernails, grain by grain. He had been laying for a rookie like Lawes.

See, Lawes's partner warned, they couldn't be trusted. He had to be ready all the time. And when he brought down his club, he had to bring it down hard.

Lawes was torn. Clearly Frenchy was dangerous, but he also seemed insane. Did he belong in Clinton?

There were many like Frenchy too, "bugs" with the mental capacities of six- and seven-year-olds, who were all concentrated in the stone shed, where they worked crushing rocks. By way of a long-standing joke, each new guard was rotated through the stone shed, where he was invariably welcomed with a shower of rocks. When it happened to Lawes, he stood rooted to the spot, too terrified to move. It was taken as courage, and he passed the test.

The next time trouble erupted he was ready. During a fight in the yard, he muscled his way into the melee and saw an upraised hand clutching a knife. He brought his club down, hard. Unfortunately, he brought it down on the head of the prisoner about to be stabbed.

In the prison hospital, Lawes apologized to the innocent victim and came to know the assistant physician, Walter N. Thayer Jr. An avid penologist, Thayer had a fine library and opened it to Lawes.

He had ample time to read, even with his mile-long runs or walks each day from his boardinghouse outside the prison. He was particularly drawn to the books of Cesare Lombroso, an Italian criminologist whose works, beginning with *L'uomo delinquente* in 1876, propounded a biological theory of criminality. Incorrigible offenders were born criminals, Lombroso contended, throwbacks to an early evolutionary stage and thus clearly identifiable by physical and mental abnormalities.

Lawes was intrigued. If criminals could really be picked out by type, his work would be a lot easier.

But his doubts grew after he met the bookkeeper at the prison clothing shop, Joseph Chappleau, a fifty-five-year-old college-educated intellectual with prematurely snow-white hair and the saddest eyes Lawes had ever seen. Old Chappleau, which is how everyone knew him, had been at Clinton for sixteen years and would never leave. He had argued with a neighbor near Plattsburgh over the poisoning of some cows and his accusations that the man and Mrs. Chappleau had become unduly close. Chappleau had settled the matter by killing his neighbor. Chappleau, like Frenchy, was a murderer, but Lawes found him one of the gentlest and wisest men he had ever met. Chappleau was in for life. Frenchy was doing twenty years and would surely one day be out. Lawes found the anomaly crazier than Frenchy. Shouldn't the sentence fit the criminal, he wondered, and not just the crime?

Visiting Chappleau at the clothing shop one day, Lawes hefted his club and remarked how reluctant he was to use it. Old Chappleau was sympathetic. "Carry it as a badge of authority," he advised, "but never use it." Better yet, he said, leave it on the rack. If trouble came, it would be useless. Hung there, it became "the emblem of authority, not the symbol of punishment."

. . .

After six months in Dannemora with no days off, Lawes took two weeks' leave to visit home. He and his parents had exchanged only a few letters, and Kathryn's were stilted, as if she dared not really write her mind.

Their reunion was passionate. Swept away, Lawes presented Kathryn with an engagement ring. But he told her he was leaving again to return to Clinton. She rebelled and they quarreled. She took off the ring and threw it at him. It rolled away and vanished. He didn't care. "I'll be damned if I'll hunt for that ring," he told her.

On the day before he was to return to Dannemora, they met again, and Lawes brought a small diamond ring "for the one you threw away." They hurried to Elmira's St. Patrick's Rectory and were wed, after which they informed both sets of scandalized parents.

The newlyweds kissed good-bye at the train station. The assistant keeper and his daughters would not take the news well, Lawes joked. He could look forward to going back on nights.

Six months later, in March 1906, after just a year at Clinton, he was transferred to Auburn Prison, as he had sought, with a raise of six dollars a month. Now he was within fifty miles of Elmira. Kathryn quit her office job and joined him in a rented room.

If his first view of Clinton had dispirited him, Auburn, with its pretensions of progressivism, only disillusioned him further. Here prisoners condemned to silence communicated in sign language, one finger for a second helping of bread, two fingers for more soup, three fingers for extra potatoes. Discipline was harsh, dungeons with bread-and-water diets, and no outdoor exercise except for the time it took prisoners to walk from their grim cells to work in the shops and back again. Not much, he thought, had changed in the eighty years since Lynds press-ganged his army of forced laborers from Auburn down the river to build Sing Sing.

Some things were beyond him, Lawes thought, and making a dent in Auburn was probably one of them. He was wasting his time there. In May 1906, two months after arriving, he took an exam for reformatory guard. Elmira would be closer still to home, and Kathryn was homesick—and pregnant.

At twenty-two, he was grappling with his own ideas of crime and punishment. When a man entered prison, hadn't all other institutions failed him—his family, his school, his church? Was crime just the criminal's responsibility, or was it in some measure society's? When exactly did criminality begin?

In September 1906, six months after he moved to Auburn, the exam results came in. With a score above 96 percent, Lawes emerged at the top of the eligible list, but his preeminence also reflected the level of the competition. One of his fellow civil service applicants was a candidate for a Health Department position. He was asked, "What are rabies and what is to be done for them?" His reply: "Rabies are Jewish priests and there's nothing you can do for them."

The next month Lawes was transferred again, this time to Elmira. Finally, he was home.

In Elmira, there were no striped uniforms, no shaved heads or lockstep. The repressive spirit of Zebulon Brockway still held sway, but Brockway's ideals of the reformatory had taken root as well—indeterminate sentences, a grading system, schooling, vocational training, physical education, and military discipline.

Lawes had turned twenty-three, the average age of the 340 inmates of the reformatory. He scrutinized them for the telltale signs of criminality that Lombroso had warned of. He found none, just boys and young men aged sixteen to thirty who seemed discomfortingly similar to himself. Each morning after he hung up his suit and donned his uniform, he found that his pockets overnight had been picked clean of stray shreds of tobacco, a contraband treasure denied the inmates. He wished the prisoners had a worthier outlet for their talents. He tolerated some infractions but meted out his share of punishment. When a problem prisoner struck at his squad leader during drilling one day, Lawes landed him one on the chin that knocked him cold. He was soon revived and, Lawes was relieved to see, bore him no grudge. He guessed that prisoners were used to it. He didn't like using his fists but wasn't afraid to. Still, he had seen enough whippings to feel it brutalized not only the whipped but the whipper, and everyone else from the warden down. He had a favorite saying: "Treat a man like a dog, and you will make a dog of him."

He and Kathryn had rented a house close to the reformatory, across a field from his parents and close, too, to hers. It was a tight-knit community. The buddy with whom he had enlisted in the Coast Artillery five years before had married one of Kathryn's sisters and was also a guard at the reformatory.

Kathryn had given birth to a daughter they christened Kathleen. Then, eleven months later, came Crystal. The girls were practically twins. Nights, Lawes dandled them on his knees, telling stories of the reformatory as Kathryn sewed in the electric light. Her one eccentricity, if it was that, was an aversion to the kitchen. She did not like to cook, choosing soups and the simplest of meals to feed her family. "Stay out of the kitchen," she advised her girls at an early age, "and you'll never have to cook." Yet theirs was a sweet domesticity, devoid of the distractions and excitement of big-city life.

Mornings, Lawes dog-trotted to work, convinced the exercise would do him good. At the end of the day, he took his time returning home, mulling over the events of the day. What exactly had made the inmates criminals? Their biology, as Lombroso said? Or other factors more amenable to correction? People loved to read about lurid crimes, every sordid detail. But where was the information about the criminal's early life, and the causes of his downfall? Where had Brockway gone wrong?

Again and again, Lawes tried to put his finger on what was wrong at the reformatory. He and the institution's doctor and assistant superintendent, Frank Christian, had become close. The physician, seven years senior to Lawes and destined to take over Elmira, was mentor to the young guard. Together they tried to puzzle it out. Brockway's rule had been hostile, they agreed. What was lacking was . . . wholesomeness.

Lawes and Dr. Christian were tossing a baseball back and forth one day, drawing envious glances from some of the inmates. Impulsively, Lawes tossed them the ball. Soon an impromptu ball game was under way, overturning the ban on fraternization of staff and inmates. Before long, organized sports were introduced to the curriculum and the reformatory had its first ball team, the Mustered-Outs.

Lawes's teachers of penology were a mixed lot. Old Chappleau and Frenchy Menet, Dr. Christian, Walter Thayer, Cesare Lombroso, and Cesare Bonesana, marchese di Beccaria, the eighteenth-century aristocratic Milanese economist and father of modern penology, whose writings Lawes was now taking home to study. Never having finished high school, Lawes had always been drawn to reading as a way of filling gaps in his education. His favorite book was *Les Misérables*. Beccaria, he was intrigued to see, seemed to have been preoccupied by the same inconsistencies of criminal justice a century and a half earlier: "We see the same crimes punished in a different manner at different times by the same tribunals." The aim of punishment, Beccaria further asserted, was not to torment a criminal or undo his crime but to prevent him from doing further injury to society and keep others from committing similar crimes. With a humanitarianism far ahead of his time, a generation before the French Revolution, he urged an end to torture and secret trials, legal rights for defendants, and sentences just severe enough to serve as a deterrent. At the same time, he favored imprisonment as a penalty in itself—not just a prelude to trial or execution. Interestingly, Lawes thought, Beccaria sanctioned the death penalty for violent robbery and other serious crimes but felt there was a worse punishment—perpetual slavery.

Lawes also marveled over the exploits of another model reformer, John Howard, a wealthy and high-minded British Puritan who sailed to Lisbon to aid survivors of the devastating earthquake of 1755. He was captured at sea by a French privateer and thrown into a military jail in Brest. Freed and back in England, he became high sheriff of Bedford and grew interested in the ordeals of prisoners. All sheriffs were supposed to inspect their prisons, but he took the task to heart, probing their cells and dungeons. Soon he was visiting other jails, shocked by what he found—starving men and women, racked by disease and dying amid their fellow prisoners. Jailers earned small stipends supplemented by fees from the prisoners they supervised, and to save the tax levied on each window, they barred light and air. After his visits, Howard stank so much that stagecoaches would not have him, so he had to travel alone by horseback. Even his notebook and pencil reeked—he had to air them out over the fire at night before he could even enter his information. He carried around vials of vinegar to repel the vile odors, but even these had to be periodically discarded as tainted.

Prisoners, he found, slept on cold stone or straw that was never changed and were fastened with irons so heavy that jailers could charge fees for lesser weights. Vices of every conceivable variety flourished. And except for debtors, who were permanently confined, this was not even punishment: this was detention before trial. If acquitted, prisoners emerged as living skeletons. If found guilty, they were exiled or hanged. And this was progress. Prior to reforms ordered by a House of Commons committee in 1728, prisoners were routinely tortured. Some in the bishop of Ely's prison were found chained to the floor for months with spiked collars to prevent them from lying flat.

Howard's revelations spurred further reforms. Jailers were put on fixed salaries, and prison sanitation measures were ordered to stem disease. He then turned his attention to prison conditions on the Continent. He found prisons in Holland, Belgium, and Switzerland relatively humane. But in Vienna, he found men chained to the walls of dungeons. In Munich, he uncovered a black-clad torture room with bloodstained machines whose workings, he said, were too terrible to relate. "Even women are not spared."

Howard proceeded to St. Petersburg, then Moscow, then Kherson on the Dneiper, eighty miles east of Odessa, which he reached in November 1789. With soldiers and refugees from the Russian-Turkish War flooding the town, plague was rife. His work in the prisons had made him a deity of sorts, and sufferers begged for his intervention. But his ministrations were cut short by his own infection. He died in January 1790. Grieving supporters erected a block of marble at his grave.

JOHN HOWARD
Whoever thou art, thou standest
at the tomb of thy friend.

Howard, Lawes thought, was his kind of hero.

11

In March 1912, after five and a half years at the Elmira Reformatory and study at home, Lawes took an exam for chief guard. He came in first of forty applicants. The *Elmira Telegram* headlined his triumph.

LOUIS LAWES WINS PROMOTION AT THE ELMIRA REFORMATORY ON HIS WAY TO PRISON FAME

Even his hometown paper couldn't get his name right.

When a notice for a six-week summer course in penology and sociology at Columbia University's New York School of Philanthropy caught his eye, he thought his new stature as chief guard warranted his application.

The young science of sociology had its roots in the founding of the University of Chicago in 1892 and the staging of the Columbian Exposition, which drew millions of fairgoers to a city struggling to apply scientific remedies to the social ills of poverty, vice, and crime. In New York, Columbia University had moved from Madison Avenue and Forty-ninth Street way uptown to Morningside Heights in 1897, and the following summer the *New York Times*, under its visionary new publisher Adolph Ochs, announced a class in "practical philanthropic work" sponsored by the Charity Organization Society, one of the many good-works groups that had sprung up after the Civil War. The class had begun as a summer offering and by 1904 had expanded to a year-round program of Columbia's School of Philanthropy.

But the summer fee was a stiff $350, almost half Lawes's annual salary at

Auburn a mere six years before, and he didn't have it. He confided his disappointment to Kathryn. He could go, she said. Lawes looked at her strangely. "I have the money," she said. "I've saved it up."

The class, at the imposing limestone-and-brick Charities Building on East Twenty-second Street at Park Avenue, featured lectures by public officials, university professors, and philanthropists, including social scientists financed by the Russell Sage Foundation, endowed by the Wall Street tycoon and great-uncle of Charles Chapin, then still the tyrannical city editor of Pulitzer's *Evening World* with dreams of inheriting Sage's millions.

Lawes felt intimidated by academe. Who was he? Just a prison guard, twenty-eight years old. But unlike many of his intellectual fellow students, eager do-gooders, the strapping blond upstater had a grip on real life. If nothing else, he knew how to size men up and how to ask questions. He was also burning with ambition and he couldn't wait to turn thirty. Nobody was taken seriously under thirty.

His lecturers came to appreciate his sharp edge, his way of getting to the heart of an issue. Among his admirers was Burdette G. Lewis, state inspector of penal institutions, and George W. Kirchwey, about to be named the state's commissioner for penal reform.

In particular, Lawes asked what society was doing for young people to keep them out of places like Elmira. From his posting there he knew that a large proportion of inmates at state prisons were under twenty. How did the city propose to deal with them?

Lawes answered his own questions. Police stations weren't enough. There should also be boys' clubs and settlement houses. Youngsters had to be kept off the streets. The boys he saw at Elmira were living proof of that. He warmed to his topic. "Sometimes the schools are to blame. Sometimes the homes. Usually both. Almost always the environment has been unhealthy. There has been no training for the proper use of leisure and these lads have made heroes out of the neighborhood bad boys. Because of the dullness of their lives they have felt an incitement to crime for the excitement and danger connected with it."

Delinquency, he contended, was neither destined nor hereditary, feeble-mindedness excepted.

"The delinquent boy is the potential adult criminal. It is therefore essential that we do everything in our power to redirect socially maladjusted boys before it is too late. . . . In the end, what sends an offender to prison is failure in character. Whatever helps build and strengthen character—whether it's religion, or athletics, or the discovery of an ability in some craft and the development of that ability—cuts down the number of crimes and the number of potential offenders."

That, Lawes said, was the task of the state and every city and town. There should be less talk about reforming criminals and more about eliminating the causes of crime. And crime, that summer of 1912, was dominating the New York headlines, particularly after Herman Rosenthal was gunned down, setting off an explosive corruption scandal and the swift arrest of Lieutenant Becker.

His professors were impressed. Young Lawes showed promise. Burdette Lewis praised him to Katharine Bement Davis, a social work pioneer and the founding superintendent of the Reformatory for Women at Bedford Hills. Born in Buffalo before the Civil War, Davis, large and plain-faced at fifty-two, traced her American roots to the 1630s and counted Ethan Allen among her ancestors. Her grandmother was an abolitionist and attended the women's rights convention led by Elizabeth Cady Stanton in Seneca Falls, New York, in 1848.

Davis studied sanitary science at Vassar College, taught school in Brooklyn, and, after taking graduate courses in food chemistry at Columbia, was appointed to supervise a model workingman's home at the 1893 Chicago Columbian Exposition, where the world's attention was riveted on the new social sciences and their promise for the betterment of society's outcasts. After applying her reformist theories at a settlement project in Philadelphia, Davis continued her studies at the University of Chicago under the charismatic economist Thorstein Veblen. With a growing interest in sociology, she set sail for Europe in 1898 to study the oppressive living conditions of farmworkers in Bohemia, coming away with special sympathy for exploited women and intrepid emigrants to America. By 1901 she was in charge of the new women's reformatory at Bedford Hills in Westchester County, not far from Sing Sing.

Determined to turn it into a model facility for rehabilitating women convicted of prostitution, vagrancy, theft, and drunkenness, and believing, too, that crime had its roots in the social environment, Davis opened a range of prison shops for teaching trades. She learned how to mix concrete and trained the inmates in construction skills. She started literacy and math classes and lectured on democracy and law.

Now, as she was hearing about this promising young progressive Lewis Lawes in the School of Philanthropy, she had just won a pledge of two hundred thousand dollars from John D. Rockefeller Jr. to establish the Laboratory of Social Hygiene at Bedford Hills. Rockefeller had recently led a special grand jury to investigate prostitution and had decided that Bedford Hills could be the best institution of its kind in the country to study its pathologies. He called Davis a woman of surpassing intellect, sympathy, and common sense. With his father's money, he bought seventy-one acres adjoining the reformatory and ordered buildings and roads, the property to be leased to the state. The laboratory's first project was a landmark study of prostitution that examined the business in exhaustive detail, with particular emphasis on its victims, some 650 prostitutes who had landed in the reformatory. It was underemployment, not simply poverty, that drove women to selling their bodies, the study found. Heredity was a factor too. About one in five of the women showed a history of family alcoholism, insanity, venereal disease, or criminality. These women were poor candidates for reformation.

After Columbia, Lawes returned to Elmira with more than a modish New York haircut. He was authoritative and self-assured. Dr. Christian, his baseball partner and confidant, sensed that Lawes had gotten a lot out of his courses. But, he asked, how did he plan to put it to use?

"The opportunity will come," Lawes said. He knew that promotions usually went to those with political connections in Albany, but he had a stubborn confidence in his destiny. He had come to memorize the poem on a Christmas card that someone had sent Kathryn and that she had framed and hung in their bedroom. It was by the naturalist John Burroughs and it was called "Waiting."

> *Serene, I fold my hands and wait,*
> *Nor care for wind, or tide or sea,*
> *I rave no more 'gainst time or fate,*
> *For lo! my own shall come to me. . . .*

He didn't have to wait long. A year after his summer course—and still not yet thirty—he was put on the list for warden of the Massachusetts State Prison at Charlestown, opened in 1806. It seemed too good to be true. It was. He was dropped as too young and offered instead the post of deputy warden.

Lawes turned it down. As deputy, he said, he wouldn't be free to try out his ideas. And as a New York carpetbagger, he'd be blamed for whatever went wrong. He'd continue waiting.

Then, almost two years later, in March 1915, his moment came.

CAN YOU COME TO NEW YORK IMMEDIATELY
TO DISCUSS POSSIBILITY OF ACCEPTING POSITION
OF OVERSEER NY CITY REFY FOR MALE MISDEMEANANTS?
TELEGRAPH EARLIEST POSSIBLE DATE.

It was signed Katharine B. Davis.

A year and a half before, as Lawes was rejecting the Charlestown offer, Davis too had come to a momentous decision. She had decided to leave Bedford Hills to accept a historic appointment as Mayor John Purroy Mitchel's commissioner of correction, the first woman to hold a cabinet-level office at city hall. The reformist Mitchel (who was to die falling out of an airplane over Lake Charles, Louisiana) had asked John D. Rockefeller Jr. about her, and the philanthropist was unstinting in his praise. "Dr. Davis is the cleverest woman I have ever met." Not everyone had applauded the appointment. The *Times* denounced it as "appalling," arguing that handling criminals was "a man's job."

As commissioner, Davis oversaw some 125,000 prisoners who passed through the city's fifteen prisons every year. Among her first steps was to infiltrate two of her researchers into the Tombs, the ominous lockup near the lower Manhattan courts. They witnessed drug dealing, alcohol smuggling, and bribery. Davis banned outside food and tobacco deliveries and ended the special comforts afforded moneyed prisoners. She also abolished the dreaded zebra stripes that branded prisoners as human animals. The psychology of clothes was important, she said. Every woman knew that. To feel your best, you had to look your best. The press cackled—but knew she was right. And now she was reaching out to Lawes.

Eight days later, Lawes was moving Kathryn and their girls, Kathleen and Crystal, into the overseer's cottage on Hart Island, a mile-long sliver of 101 acres off the Bronx in Long Island Sound. Kathryn was instantly repulsed. During the Civil War it had been commandeered to confine Confederate prisoners. After the war, the city bought the island from the Hunter family for a public burial ground for the poor and unclaimed. Nearly two thousand bodies went into the earth the first year alone. When a yellow fever epidemic erupted in 1869, a section was set aside to quarantine the stricken. The island also came to house a women's charity hospital, an insane asylum, a jail for prisoners working the burial detail, an old men's home, a tuberculosis hospital for women, and, starting in 1904, a reformatory for young men. Later, overflow prisoners from the city's penitentiary were also moved in. It was the poorest, meanest, worst-provisioned reformatory in the state, perhaps in any state.

This was the Laweses' new home, their cottage tucked picturesquely between the workhouse for hoboes, drunkards, and drug addicts and the graveyard, where boatloads of bodies were deposited daily.

Hart Island Reformatory was scandal-plagued as well. The *New York Evening Mail* had exposed brutality, depravity, and corruption on the island, where five hundred inmates lived without heat because guards were stealing the coal to sell. The superintendent had been fired, ushering in a period of general anarchy that erupted one Friday afternoon shortly before Lawes arrived. The boys had been out at exercise and returned to the mess hall well armed with rocks. At a signal, the fusillade began, raining down on a stunned guard. This was followed by a barrage of dishes and yells of triumph that brought reinforcements scurrying from the penitentiary. The insurrection was quickly put down with flailing clubs. Such was Lawes's welcome.

Looking on the bright side, as he liked to do, Lawes realized it was hardly a riot in the usual sense, nothing like what he'd seen upstate. There had been no gunfire, knifings, or breakouts. Some rocks and dishes were thrown. But retribution was harsh. Touring the jail, Lawes found twenty-seven of the supposed ringleaders locked into seventeen cells. Buckets served for their natural functions. And, Lawes wondered, seeing all the doubling up, what about their *unnatural functions*? The other inmates weren't treated much better. After daily work assignments, they were marched into their dormitories to sit on their beds until nine. The only activity they were permitted was hymn singing. Those who violated rules were forced to kneel on the cold concrete floor for two hours.

The worst of the lot, Lawes was assured, was Mike the Rat Catcher.

Mike was a pale, skinny youth with a piercing gaze who owed his notoriety to a penchant for catching rats with his bare hands to tame as pets. At his call, they came running, burrowing into his pockets. When he commanded "Scram!" they fled. Hart Island's resident celebrity, Mike had been orphaned at five, eked out an existence stealing from pushcarts, and grew up in various institutions, where he became known as an incorrigible. Lawes had him examined and concluded he was mentally defective. Still, he had a rough charisma that in another life might have propelled him, Lawes thought, to a political career, perhaps even landed him in Congress. Lawes saw from Mike's record that he had once stolen a dog. "Sure I took him," Mike admitted. "I wanted a dog, that's why."

Lawes took it as a hopeful sign. At least Mike cared for something. On a hunch, he sprang Mike and the other instigators from the cooler on their promise of no more trouble. In return, Lawes improved the food and loosened the regimen, allowing games and sports.

Now his troubles began with the staff, a surly bunch of rejects from other penal institutions who had reached rock bottom at Hart Island, where they waited for their pensions, secure in a tenure that good political connections afforded.

One June Sunday, during a baseball game, players started collapsing as if felled by lightning. Then others began dropping until close to ninety boys lay writhing on the ground. They overflowed the hospital beds and were laid out on the floor on mattresses. The doctor suspected poison. The Bronx district attorney sent investigators. How bad were conditions on the island that inmates would attempt mass suicide?

Lawes was called before the grand jury. As he stepped off the elevator in the Bronx County Courthouse, a man called him aside. "Major?"

He hadn't been called that for some time, not since his days at Elmira. He thought the face looked familiar. One of the boys?

The man nodded. Years ago, he said, Lawes had been sent to escort him from Sing Sing to the reformatory. On the train, Lawes had asked if he wanted a meal and offered to remove his handcuffs if he gave his word not to escape. He agreed and they ate together in the diner, facing each other across a white tablecloth, conversing man to man like any two traveling companions. Lawes didn't reapply the cuffs until they were entering Elmira. The man never forgot that. Now he was a court stenographer. A court stenographer heard lots of things. He heard the prison staff was trying to frame Lawes and Commissioner Davis with a phony scandal.

Lawes understood. On his second day on the island, he had found the drug supplies scandalously unsecured. He removed the medicinal morphine, cocaine, and heroin to his office safe but left non-narcotics behind. Now, he told the grand jury, some of these must have been stolen to poison the prisoners and taint his rule.

The panel believed him, exonerating him and urging that he be given a free hand to replace the staff. The *Evening Mail*, skeptical, sent a reporter in search of a new scandal. He returned disappointed. Lawes had Hart Island in hand. There was, however, a scoop that eluded the paper. Mike the Rat Catcher had a new pet, a mutt, rescued from the city pound. Mike finally had his dog.

The winter of 1915–16 was brutally cold. The boys shivered in the icy winds, envying the bodies dumped into the frozen trenches. At least they were beyond feeling. Lawes decided something had to be done. He knew that several years before, the city had purchased six hundred acres of farmland for a new reformatory upstate across the Hudson in Orange County. His mentor, Katharine Davis, had left the corrections post to become chairman of the Parole Commission, but her successor was another admirer, Burdette Lewis, the former state penal inspector under whom Lawes had studied at the New York School of Philanthropy nearly four years before. Lawes wrote Lewis urging a move to the country.

The commissioner was dubious. The property was undeveloped.

He and the boys would develop it, Lawes said.

There were no walls or fences, Lewis argued.

There wouldn't have to be, Lawes promised. He'd guarantee no escapes.

Lewis was unyielding. The boys would have to travel through New Jersey. There was no extradition agreement for misdemeanants between the two states. And even when they reached the New Hampton rail station, they'd have to march a mile to the farm.

There wouldn't be any escapes, Lawes repeated. "I'll put the boys in charge."

The commissioner threw up his hands. Lawes had worn him down.

Kathryn and the girls were long gone, Lawes having sent them home to Elmira to wait out the migration. They would have been happy enough to join the trek—anything to get away from Hart Island.

On moving day—April Fool's Day—reveille sounded at 4:15, but many of the boys were already up, excitedly readying their packs and ridiculing the ungainly rubber boots that Lawes, anticipating the upstate spring mud, had gotten an extra appropriation to provide.

Piped out by their own reformatory band, 547 youths provisioned with meat sandwiches and shouldering heavy wooden parade muskets marched down to the dock and the department's steamer *Correction*. Bringing up the rear was Mike the Rat Catcher, his mutt roped to his belt. As the ship cast off, the band broke into "Auld Lang Syne."

When the ship docked in Jersey City, Commissioner Lewis and Katharine Davis of the Parole Commission were there to escort Lawes and the boys off to a waiting train. Davis watched as Lawes waved from the last car. She shook her head in disbelief. "I believe he has actually done it," she said. Commissioner Lewis was fumbling in his pocket for change. He had to telephone Mayor Mitchel, who was nervously awaiting word of a safe transit.

At the New Hampton station, Lawes and the boys disembarked to trudge through the mud to the new camp, where an advance guard had been putting up temporary quarters and a field kitchen. Mike the Rat Catcher's dog had trouble keeping up, so Mike finally scooped him up and carried him the last stretch. Behind Lawes, the bedraggled and famished army followed the aroma of beef stew to their new home.

Except for the welcome victuals, there was little to it. Water had to be carried in from a spring. There was no electric power or gas. Light came from kerosene lamps.

The local populace was hostile. Why was "the scum of the earth" being deposited on their doorstep? But they soon saw they were just boys, and even offered to hire some of them after they served their time. That delighted Lawes. Nothing, he thought, could be more rehabilitative than a waiting job.

Most of the boys pitched in eagerly with picks and shovels to build the prison farm, but one young delinquent, a onetime Wall Street runner, rebelled. Digging from sunup to sundown wasn't his idea of a reformatory. Besides, he knew he couldn't be sent to the cooler, since no detention cells had been built yet. He refused to work.

Lawes contemplated his first crisis. He could send the rebel back to Hart Island, but then others might also opt for a return to avoid the hard labor. Nor did he want to make a martyr out of him. For want of a better idea, Lawes sent him to the gate and told him to stand there.

"Can I walk up and down?" he asked.

Of course, said Lawes. He had legs; he could walk up and down.

"Can I sing?"

"If you have a voice, sure."

The boy pranced back and forth singing and smirking at his passing buddies.

At chow time he took his place in line. Lawes yanked him out. "Nothing doing," he said. "No work, no eat."

The rebel resumed his place at the gate, walking around and singing. But he walked a little slower and his tune was off.

The boys stopped envying him. "What a boob," one said.

Lawes made sure the name stuck. "Good idea, boys," he called out. "That's the Boob Squad from now on." From then on, shirkers were assigned to the Boob Squad. They didn't have to work but got no privileges either, and it became a dread punishment.

Yet a few tested their luck, making a break for freedom. Three boys escaped into what they thought was the Promised Land of New Jersey. Lawes would have none of that. He tracked them down and hustled them back to New Hampton for a lesson in pragmatic justice, to the gratification of Commissioner Lewis, who happened to be visiting New Hampton at the time. "As fine a thing as I have ever seen," he told Lawes.

"It is possible we were guilty of kidnapping," Lawes conceded. But he did what had to be done. Some had dismissed him as soft, but this changed their minds. He could be tough when he wanted to be. "Not when he wants to be," a Lawes deputy corrected them. "When he has to be."

Mike the Rat Catcher, who had also groused about the harsh labor, asked to work with the horses at the barn a mile from the camp. Lawes wondered if he was also planning to escape but found it hard to refuse him. If anyone was to get away it might as well be Mike. So Lawes showed him how to care for the horses, and Mike became a devoted groom, if occasionally stealing the oats from other steeds for his favorites.

Lawes was away on business in the commissioner's office in New York one day when an urgent message came from New Hampton. The boys were in an uproar over the stew. It was inedible, and revolt was in the air.

Lawes demanded to speak to Mike the Rat Catcher. He was summoned and put on the line.

The boys were taking advantage of his absence, Lawes began, and he didn't like it. "Now, Mike," he commanded, "I want you to round up the gang, whoever they are, and tell them to stop it." If they had a complaint, they should wait until he returned and discuss it like men. If they wanted to be on the level with him, they had to deal with him directly, not wait until his back was turned.

Lawes rushed back, armed with an appropriation from the Board of Estimate for a new herd of cows. The farm was quiet. Lawes didn't know what Mike the Rat Catcher had done, but the peace spoke volumes. There was good in everyone, Lawes decided. He would never give up on any man.

Word of the farm's success spread. While Lawes was visiting home in Elmira, Zebulon Brockway, nearing ninety and long retired from his tarnished superintendency of the reformatory, asked to see him.

"I hear you have a reformatory without walls," Brockway said. "If you haven't any walls you must have something else."

"We have morale, Mr. Brockway," Lawes said. "It is more effective than your strongest walls."

He was soon to put that theory to the test. Riding his horse along the Walkill River one morning in October 1916, he came across two men who seemed to be inspecting the landscape. They said they were agents for a moving-picture company scouting a location for a picture, *The Brand of Cowardice*, about the U.S. Cavalry and Mexican troops along the Rio Grande. The Walkill looked more like the Rio Grande than the Rio Grande did, they said.

Lawes thought fast. He could arrange for permission. But what about the soldiers? Where would they come from?

The two moving-picture men pondered that. From the neighboring towns and villages? Could they find 150 men there? A hundred infantrymen and 50 horsemen?

Lawes had a better answer. He could provide the land *and* the manpower, robust youths with good physiques.

The scouts were intrigued but asked what he wanted in return.

Not much, Lawes said, just a moving-picture projector for his boys. They liked to watch pictures too. He had wanted an outfit for the farm but had been afraid to put it in the budget.

The deal was struck. One morning soon after, a large crate arrived at the farm. Inside were more than a hundred Krag Jorgenson rifles and fifty .45-caliber Colt revolvers, with a large quantity of blank cartridges. Sound couldn't be heard on the silent screen, but there would be convincing puffs of gunsmoke.

The stars soon arrived: Lionel Barrymore, Louis Wolheim, Grace Darling. Uniforms were handed out to the boys, and then the guns, too.

Lawes put on a brave front, but he was nervous. There were now hundreds of armed boys charging around on horseback and in foot formations, and although their guns were loaded with blanks, who knew how they might react?

And then Commissioner Lewis showed up. He took a look around and turned on his heels, aghast. He was heading back to New York. He wouldn't be caught dead there, not in the middle of a shooting war starring his reformatory inmates. If anything bad happened, he warned Lawes, there wasn't a place in the world far enough away for Lawes to hide.

Fortunately for Lawes, the skirmish ended peaceably. All guns were returned, and no one escaped. Even the final sequence—the burning of enemy headquarters—proceeded without incident, and soon after, the farm had its own moving-picture apparatus.

Within a year the boys were marching to a different tune, a patriotic parade celebrating draft registration day in Orange County. America was at war and nearly half the boys were in the army. "I don't think the Germans will last very long when we get over there," one of them wrote Lawes. Even Mike the Rat Catcher served, going overseas with the Twenty-seventh Division and coming back a proud corporal.

The Great War was over but peace not yet a signed formality when Lawes received his cable from Rattigan.

He knew it was about Sing Sing long before Al Smith said the words "It's yours, son."

12

Into his third year at Sing Sing, Lawes never knew quite what to expect. The men were still glumly mourning the death, or murder, of the *Bulletin*, and tensions were running high. He generally retired by eleven after an hour or two of reading to ease the strains of the day. He may have seemed easygoing, but inside—as few but Kathryn knew—he was a bundle of nerves, with high blood pressure and an anxious stomach. He liked to sleep in the nude, with his pajamas and robe folded over the foot of the bed for emergencies. He often had trouble falling asleep. One night he was up late reading the latest Edgar Wallace thriller, in which the hero, imprisoned on a frame-up, tries a daring escape. Lawes was rooting for him to make it out when he heard a shuffling noise outside. He switched off the light and saw a dark figure crawling around the top of the wall. There was a thump as the man jumped twenty feet to the ground, followed by a second shadowy figure and another thump. Lawes snatched up the phone to sound the alarm and threw on his pajamas, rushing down to join the hunt. The two would-be escapees were quickly seized. Lawes went back upstairs and returned to his novel.

Mornings he liked to come downstairs early, collarless and coatless, and stand at his desk leafing through the morning mail, selecting the letters and newspapers to take back to the breakfast table. On this winter morning in early 1922, he was stopped cold by a headline in The *New York Herald:*

PRISONS TOO GENTLE, ENRIGHT'S COMPLAINT

He read the story through several times. Speaking at a church in uptown Manhattan, Police Commissioner Richard Enright, a career officer plucked from the lower ranks by Mayor Mitchel's successor, John F. "Red Mike" Hylan, was ridiculing talk of a crime wave. Enright was insisting that serious crimes were down 35 percent since 1916, but arguing nevertheless—as nearly as Lawes could follow it—that any increase was the fault of leniency in prison.

Enright denounced "too much prison reform, too easy bail, too much parole and too much ease and comfort in the penal institutions," and the paper went on to detail his complaints. "There are no longer shaved heads; prisoners no longer wear prison garments and perform hard labor. Instead they have the best food, the best treatment, medical attention of the highest order, baseball, lawn tennis, motion pictures every day, drama often and sometimes grand opera. Convicts are treated better than 90 percent of the people who have homes in this city." Criminals had to be scared into going straight, Enright insisted. They had to fear prison.

Lawes stewed for a while and then called the newspapers. Criticism of the penal system was not new, he began. But what did Commissioner Enright know of conditions in prison? He had never visited Sing Sing, nor had any of his deputies. His mention of "the best food" was just one example of how little he knew. The papers were full of articles telling housewives how to prepare a meal for as little as twenty-five cents, but the state spent only six cents a meal for each man at Sing Sing, eighteen cents *a day*. And who were the prisoners Enright pretended to know so much about? They ranged from sixteen to seventy, some with a mental age of six. Most were unskilled; 12 percent were drug addicts; more than a third were foreign-born; and most of the others were of foreign parentage. Their sentences ranged from a single year to life, with thirty-three the year before bound for the chair.

Yes, Lawes agreed, there were diversions. To keep the men confined in their cells would only mean more tuberculosis, pneumonia, insanity, and suicide. The prison authorities used the yards and auditorium to keep the despair and desperation at bay, and to prove it, he said, assaults were down by a fifth over the last decade. Most of all, the men were industrious, producing nearly six hundred thousand dollars' worth of manufactured products the year before, at pay of a cent and half a day.

"To my mind," Lawes said, "there is no such thing as a single prison problem to be settled by one general prescription for all who come to us. There is

Picnic of inmates at old warden's mansion before 1930. (OSSINING HISTORICAL SOCIETY MUSEUM)

a separate problem in each one of these men. We have, if you please, about a thousand different kinds of prison problems at Sing Sing." He summed it up for Enright: "Six-cent meals, a three-and-one-half-foot unventilated stone hole to sleep in, and one and a half cents a day to save up for the future—these are the fundamental facts about the coddling of our prisoners at Sing Sing."

The papers backed Lawes, giving him this round. He was buoyed, too, when the legislature passed Republican governor Nathan L. Miller's bill to give prisoners a share of the profits they generated for the state with their products from prison industries.

But the debate about coddling soon erupted anew over another bill, introduced by Westchester assemblyman Walter W. Westall, to allow the state parole board to grant supervised release to any first-term felon, no matter how long his sentence, who had served at least one year in prison. So far, prisoners had to serve their minimum sentence, up to half the imprisonment term, before becoming eligible for release.

Judges and prosecutors rose up in fury, arguing that the measure could free as many as twelve hundred criminals, from pickpockets to murderers. Prominent among the opponents was none other than Lawes's boss and recent nemesis, Superintendent Rattigan, executioner of the *Bulletin*, who had stayed on under Governor Smith's successor Miller, and who now urged the bill's rejection. Lawes, who believed that the sentence should fit the criminal, not the crime, endorsed the Westall bill. So did Sing Sing's Catholic chaplain, Father Cashin.

Then intriguing new information began circulating. One prominent beneficiary of the Westall bill, the papers reported, would be Robert P. Brindell, former czar of the New York City building trades, who had arrived in Sing Sing in April 1921 to serve a five-year stretch for wholesale extortion and graft. As a first-timer already behind bars for almost a year, Brindell, probably the richest man in Sing Sing, would be eligible for release under the bill, within days, in fact. The news outraged Samuel Untermyer, one of the nation's leading investigative lawyers, who, as counsel to the Lockwood legislative committee that had exposed corruption in the construction industry, was most responsible for Brindell's conviction. Questioning why the bill materialized without notice in the stealthy final days of the legislative session, Untermyer called it a "thoroughly vicious measure" intended solely to spring Brindell.

Westall insisted that the bill had been suggested by the Prison Association, not Brindell or his lawyer, and had occasioned so little debate in committee that no hearings were thought necessary. But the press, stirring the pot, quoted unnamed friends of Brindell boasting that pressure from President Harding and Attorney General Harry Daugherty would sway their fellow Republican in Albany, Governor Miller, in favor of the bill.

Thrown on the defensive and insisting they held no brief for Brindell, Lawes and Father Cashin could only repeat what they had said before. "For every Brindell," the priest said, "I could point out a hundred deserving cases." He then confounded everyone by revealing that he himself was the author of the measure.

Lawes ridiculed the idea that Brindell was behind the bill. "There is not a warden in the state who would have the nerve to grant special privileges to such a prisoner."

But soon a second bill turned up, this one also potentially helpful to Brindell. It provided that whenever two or more sentences had been imposed on the same person, the court could revoke or suspend the additional sentences. And this bill was sponsored by an assemblyman who had been one of Brindell's lawyers. Once that nasty bit of business was exposed, the measure's prospects were nil, and it threw a new cloud over the parole bill.

In an effort to seize the initiative, Lawes offered a fervent defense of probation and parole, time-tested ways used by some forty states and the federal government to supervise lawbreakers in place of incarceration or before prison terms were fully up. With typical thoroughness, he attached a summary of parole laws around the country, showing the many states more progressive than New York. Even in New York, he wrote, parole was clearly successful 80 percent of the time. There were more convicts out of prison than in it, he noted, with close to twenty thousand given noncustodial sentences the year before. Only 8 percent had been rearrested for violations, and another 6 percent had escaped supervision. Let anyone, he challenged, "show better results under the older methods of brutal punishment for long and inflexible terms."

It made perfect sense, Lawes reasoned. A prisoner coming up before the parole board bared his entire history, his crime and his progress in confinement. No one, and certainly not the judge who had sentenced him in the first place, would know so much about the prisoner and his rehabilitative prospects. The Westall bill was, moreover, a logical stepping-stone to a system of completely indeterminate sentencing, the goal of progressive penology. "Just as a person declared insane is committed to an institution until cured or until death," Lawes declared, "so a person sent to prison ought to be committed until reformed or until death." Under truly indeterminate sentences, he went on, the prisoner had a strong incentive to improve himself, to advance his prospects for release by learning a trade and taking educational courses. Besides, parole didn't mean an end to the sentence, just a change of supervision from the prison to the community. The board could step in anytime and send the prisoner back to his cell, another powerful incentive to remain straight. Only 18 percent of Sing Sing prisoners over the previous year were repeat offenders, he said. And hadn't Attorney General Daugherty recently declared that nine out of ten federal prisoners could be trusted on parole?

"Parole and probation," Lawes concluded, "have saved many thousands of men and women from the crushing effects of a rigid form of imprisonment which holds out no hope of redemption on merit." It was too late in penal history to let reform be held hostage to "a few glaringly bad cases."

The public was cynical. Crooked union bosses, businessmen, politicians, and prison wardens knew how to take care of one another. And prisoners did seem to have it soft. Movies for inmates seemed a particularly striking luxury to a public smitten with the silver screen. Just weeks before, the papers reported, twenty-three prisoners in the death house had been treated to two comedies, including an unreleased Buster Keaton feature. The projector, donated by one of Lawes's Hollywood friends, the actor Thomas Meighan, had been set up at the end of the row of condemned cells, and first one line of prisoners leaned into the bars to view it aslant, and then the screen was shifted for the other line of men to do the same. It was arranged, said Lawes, to take their minds off a pending execution.

The governor ordered a hearing. Father Cashin, appearing as the Westall bill's now acknowledged author, testified that the prisons were full of men who ought to be returned to their families and that "sixty percent of the prisoners have been admitted to jail on their own pleas of guilty."

The governor was dubious. "Innocent men do not often plead guilty," he said. And a year was a rather short minimum sentence. That, the priest countered, was precisely what the parole board would determine.

The parole board itself dramatically announced that it did not want the new broader power. Its president, George W. Benham, formerly warden of Auburn, testified that many first felony offenders were not really first-time criminals but had previously committed offenses not covered by the bill. Then, too, he said, "owing to the unsettled state of the country and the atrocious increase in crime, this is an inopportune time to open prison doors for any first offenders."

The hostility of Rattigan and the parole board was impossible to overcome. Governor Miller, calling the bill far too radical, vetoed it.

As the Westall bill was still gasping for life, Lawes took comfort in some perversely good news. Sing Sing had gotten a new death house. True to the pledge he had extracted from Governor Smith during the fracas over the *Bulletin* less than two years before, Sing Sing's twenty-seven death row inmates were now, in the spring of 1922, about to move into a modern new home where they would not have to hear mortuary saws autopsying their freshly executed predecessors.

The new building, in a remote southwestern corner of the prison facing

the steely Hudson, was squarish and stark—the only public structure in New
York, explained state architect Lewis F. Pilcher, to have been designed to-
tally devoid of ornamentation. Considering its purpose, Pilcher said, embell-
ishments were rather beside the point, and their absence was perhaps one
reason the building had come in under budget, about fifteen thousand dollars below the three-hundred-thousand-dollar appropriation.

It was liver-colored, one story high, with two stubby two-story wings
flanking the entrance. The interior, behind gates of sawproof steel, was
labyrinthine. An inmate who might manage to slip out of his cell would not
have an easy time finding his way out.

The cells boasted the latest in death house technology. Each had a toilet
and sink, but with the plumbing and faucets out of reach to thwart mischief.
Drinking water came at the push of a button. Prisoners used their hands to
slurp it up—there were no cups to be fashioned into weapons. The light-
bulbs were set high in the ceiling, unreachable to prisoners looking for a way
to slash their wrists. The keyholes were protected so prisoners could not
stuff them with paper, delaying guards while they attempted suicide. And
every ten feet along the corridors were alarm buttons for the guards to summon urgent help.

Upstairs were six isolation cells for the mentally disturbed, one padded for
the particularly violent. There was a kitchen so food would no longer have
to be prepared in another building and carried in to be eaten cold.

Beyond the entrance were three visiting cages with screens to separate
the condemned from their visitors. Next came three separate cells set aside for
women given priorities awaiting death—ladies before gentlemen, as the state's
grim joke went. Two other long corridors were lined, on one side only, with
twelve cells each. In the old death house, the cells faced each other, so inmates were forced to witness the excruciating moments when their fellows
were summoned for their last walk. No longer. The cells of the new death
house all faced out, to an exercise yard, and sunlight marched through each
cell part of every day.

At the end of another corridor radiated six other cells—the preexecution cells, where those who had lost their final appeals spent their last
hours. One guard stationed in a central gallery could see what was happen-
ing in each. The vigilance was intense. Some years before, a prisoner with

an eye infection used bits of cotton given him by the doctor to weave a rope, which was discovered just before he was able to hang himself.

From the preexecution cells, the condemned were led across the corridor to a holding cell, connecting, through yet another corridor and three brown doors, to the death chamber.

Here too there were innovations. In the old death house, the executioner was gruesomely visible to the witnesses as he got the signal and threw the switch home. Now he would sit in a small shielded booth. When the doctor gave the signal, no one would see the executioner's fatal response. And witnesses who fainted could now be expeditiously removed to an anteroom expressly built for their recuperation, no longer disrupting the killing process.

There was a slight delay in inaugurating the new facility as Lawes waited for new guards, who would not be available until July. Meanwhile, the chair continued to take its toll in the old death house. In a desperate effort to save their client, lawyers for one convicted murderer, Julius Rosenwasser, won a court order to have him examined by alienists seeking evidence of excess "gland juices" that could prove that insanity ran in his family. When the results failed to win him a new trial, Sing Sing's Jewish chaplain, Rabbi Jacob Katz, approached Governor Miller at a funeral the day before the scheduled execution and whispered a plea that Rosenwasser be granted a reprieve, or at least a postponement, since the next day, the rabbi said, was a Jewish holiday. Offended, Miller shooed him away, scolding, "This is not the time or place to bring up such a matter."

Rosenwasser and a fellow death house inmate then complained that turning the clocks ahead for daylight saving time would shorten their lives and hasten their deaths by an hour. They had lived their misbegotten lives by standard time—shouldn't they at least have the right to die by it? And wasn't it particularly sneaky that the precious hour would be stolen from them while they slept?

That drew little reaction except for some chuckles from newspaper readers, amused by doomed men fighting for an extra hour of life.

Killing days at Sing Sing were eerie. The scheduled execution of Rosenwasser and four others drew forty-eight witnesses, including a Binghamton couple, Patrolman James Donnelly and his wife. They toured the old and new death houses and experienced the thrill of giddily sitting, if only for a moment, in the well-used electric chair. Mrs. Donnelly begged to be allowed to view the executions, but Lawes had to tell her that aside from Nellie Bly, women had never been permitted to do so. He assured her, however, that someday they would, and he would be pleased to re-invite her then.

As the preparations proceeded, a harrowing scene erupted. The mother and sister of an eighteen-year-old sentenced to die collapsed in hysterics. Moments later, word came that he had been reprieved.

Lawes paled, his relief edged with anger. What if the reprieve had come too late?

Then Rosenwasser was led in, accompanied by Rabbi Katz reading prayers. He was strapped in and three minutes later was a corpse. Two other men followed, the last cheerfully waving down the corridor to his fellows. "Good-bye, boys, see you tomorrow." Minutes later he too was dead.

Patrolman Donnelly left exhilarated. Everyone should see an execution, he declared. In fact, he said, executions should be filmed. Then, instead of going to the movies to cheer gangsters, bank robberies, and shoot-outs, people could see the wages of crime.

Lawes was less certain that putting people to death deterred killing, and the more he saw, the more confused he became. Shortly before Rosenwasser's execution, another death row inmate, condemned for killing the husband of a woman he loved, had been stricken with appendicitis. He was rushed from his death cell to the hospital, where Squire arranged for emergency surgery, the first death house prisoner of record upon whom a lifesaving operation was performed. Save the life of a man condemned to death? Why? Squire asked. So the state, not nature, could kill him? Lawes also found it bizarre, and the fact that the condemned was later spared on appeal made the episode even more tormenting.

Coddling, meanwhile, remained a volatile public issue, fed by perceptions of a postwar crime wave that cropped up in the press, it seemed, whenever there was a news lull. One newspaper symposium juxtaposed Lawes with several prosecutors and a judge in an impromptu debate on dealing with criminals. "Brutalizing men and boys, giving them hell, will not solve the problem," Lawes declared. "There is no coddling at Sing Sing."

At any rate, he was tempted to add, it wasn't prisoners who were getting coddled. For years the Victorian warden's residence had been a convenient hostelry for state officials with business at or near the prison. Sometimes they made a point of stopping there to overnight or dine while passing through Westchester to and from Albany, and at times they brought along family members and other guests. In his brief tenure, Lawes's predecessor Brophy had been commanded by Rattigan to put up the state's chief prison engineer, who ended up Brophy's houseguest for six of his eight months at Sing Sing, with the man's wife joining him for three weeks. At the same time, Brophy was having to feed as many as ninety-four other official visitors a month, going broke doing it. Under Lawes the open door continued, with one prison commissioner sometimes arriving with a horde of friends in a convoy of automobiles for lunch. Lawes left orders that the next time the freeloader returned he was to be escorted into the mess hall to dine with the prisoners. He did return with another large party several weeks later but Lawes was away, and the group was entertained again in the house, after which they treated themselves to a sight-seeing tour of the prison. When Lawes learned of it, he was apoplectic. He was getting a two-thousand-dollar-a-year entertainment stipend, but he found himself digging into his pocket to put up all his unwanted guests.

Now, in November 1922, the household was hosting a state efficiency expert who was investigating prison industries and had already spent some six weeks in the Laweses' home. Then, the day before Thanksgiving, yet another state official telephoned from New York to invite himself and his wife up for the holiday. Kathryn had had enough. She summoned the efficiency expert, invited him to the front hall, where his coat and hat were hanging, and bade him retrieve them and depart. Hotel Sing Sing was closed.

Lawes was in a strong enough position to weather any repercussions. That October in Detroit, his national colleagues had handed him a singular honor. Though only thirty-nine, he was elected president of the American Prison Association, the leading penology organization, founded in 1870 under Ohio governor Rutherford B. Hayes. Lawes had been a familiar figure at the congresses going back to 1916, when he was at New Hampton and Mayor Mitchel had sent him to Buffalo to represent New York.

Among the laudatory telegrams arriving in Detroit was one that drew a particular smile from Lawes.

THE AMERICAN PRISON ASSOCIATION IS TO BE
CONGRATULATED ON HAVING CHOSEN THE
FINEST MAN I HAVE EVER KNOWN FOR ITS PRESIDENT
BUY THEM A DRINK ALL AROUND AND COME HOME
I AM GROWING SOME LOVELY FLOWERS FOR YOUR WELCOME

A drink? That was a good one. The country was winding up its third officially dry year under Prohibition.

The telegram had no name at the bottom, just a familiar number: 69690.

13

Charles Chapin, Sing Sing's celebrity wife-murderer and unabashed favorite of Lawes and Kathryn, had rebounded yet again. His newspaper quashed, his autobiography written and published, his amorous correspondence with Viola Irene dashed by a reimposition of prison censorship, he had, in the summer of 1922, plunged into one of his familiar depressions, when Lawes once more came to the rescue. The Sing Sing yard under the cellblock was a mess of cinders and rubble, the warden said. It could use some flowers. Was Chapin interested?

The old editor barely lifted his grizzled head, muttering, "What's the use?"

Father Cashin tried next. He had previously attempted to interest Chapin in redemption through the grace of the Holy Spirit, but Chapin had turned him away. Then, scolding Chapin for staying cooped up in his cell without exercise or fresh air, he dropped off a seed catalog and a set of garden tools like one he had gotten his mother.

"Maybe if you could dig a little garden, Charlie . . ."

"The hell I would," Chapin growled.

But that night, as it happened, the *Evening World* that Chapin never missed reprinted a poem by Thomas Edward Brown that seemed to speak directly to him.

> *A garden is a lovesome thing, God wot!*
> *Rose plot,*
> *Fringed pool,*
> *Ferned grot—*

The veriest school of peace; and yet the fool
Contends that God is not—
Not God! in gardens? when the even is cool?
Nay, but I have a sign,
'Tis very sure God walks in mine.

Chapin clipped it and slipped it into the seed catalog. The next morning he asked Lawes if he might take care of the lawn. "It's pretty desolate," he ventured. "Do you suppose I could plant some seeds in the bare spots?"

Lawes was happy to oblige. "I can furnish you with all the rough labor you need, but no money."

Chapin, doing what he did best, fired off letters to garden magazines appealing for bone meal for fertilizer. Manufacturers, touched by the letters postmarked Sing Sing, sent it by the ton. Having polled the inmates to ask their favorite flower—the rose was the sentimental choice, naturally—he wrote the American Rose Society, which dispatched hundreds of rose-bushes. Nurseries sent irises, peonies, hyacinths, daffodils, crocuses, and petunias. Abjectly, he wrote Adolph Lewisohn, the millionaire prison reformer who had rallied for Osborne and had since become a friend of Lawes's. "I hope to have some very beautiful flowers if only I can procure what I need in the way of bulbs, shrubs or plants. Seeds I am able to buy out of my own slender funds. Do you know that I actually get a heartache every time I look through the catalogues and read of the many fine plants in greenhouses and nurseries that I covet?"

Lewisohn sent two trucks with plants, including a crate of rare orchids that Chapin installed in the old morgue to exorcise the tormented spirits of those autopsied on its concrete slabs.

There were no tulips, so Chapin asked Father Cashin to pray for tulips. Within a day a bulb importer on Long Island wrote that he was sending five hundred. Thousands more quickly followed. "For the love of heaven, Father," Chapin begged, "will you stop praying for tulips?" Instead he asked for Madonna lilies. They began arriving in short order, and he stacked them on the Virgin's altar in the chapel.

Chapin had his garden, rose plot and ferned grot, but he was still short his fringed pool. The priest suggested he settle for a fountain—there were cement workers at Sing Sing. Soon the grounds held a fountain, fringed by rosebushes. Around the new death house, Chapin planted lilacs to perfume the last mortal days of the condemned. He lined the walkways with splashy tropical cannas, favoring blossoms of deep hemoglobin red, the color of life.

Throwing himself into gardening with the same fervor he had once reserved for newspaper work, Chapin drove his Garden Squad hard. Lawes finally had to intervene. "Look, Charlie," he said, "these men working for you are wards of the state. You can't treat them like men on the *Evening World*."

The Associated Press had been working on Chapin's advance obituary. Now it decided he was very much alive and instead ordered up a piece on the old editor's fabulous prison garden.

As he delighted in Chapin's latest redemption and its beauteous effect on Sing Sing, Lawes was grappling with an agonizing decision, no less momentous than life and death.

The grim distinction of christening the new death house had fallen to Henry Brown of the Bronx, a twenty-three-year-old black man convicted of killing a white woman. Weeks into the new year of 1923, he walked stoically to his fate as the 201st victim of Sing Sing's electric chair. It was not the most dramatic of executions, meriting only a short news item. There was no last-minute claim of innocence or any clamor over a reprieve. After all, as the *Ossining Democratic Register* said, he was a Negro. But for Lawes the time had come to speak out.

He had entered Sing Sing an instinctive supporter of the death penalty—who wasn't? How else to enforce the Fifth Commandment? But, he began to wonder, didn't state killing itself transgress the commandment? And the more he saw of the official mechanism of death and its political implications, the more his qualms grew.

The previous Thanksgiving, Governor Miller had asked him for a list of death row inmates worthy of clemency. "It is more than likely that nothing will come of it," Miller confided, but he wanted to consider the cases "without regard to efforts from the outside often put forward for the sake of financial reward." In other words, he was making a brave effort to exclude bribery. But, he cautioned Lawes, "let no one know that I have asked for such a list."

It made Lawes wonder. Was the process so corrupt?

In a talk before the Government Club, a women's civic group that met at the Hotel Astor in Times Square, Lawes finally gave voice to what he and

Squire and Father Cashin had debated in the private recesses of Sing Sing. The death penalty was useless, a colossal failure that needed to be abolished. The ultimate deterrent to crime was no deterrent at all. This argument was a heresy, to be sure, and all the more shocking in the mouth of one who, after all, was no sob sister or tweedy academic preaching from some ivory tower but a prison boss who walked daily among killers, child molesters, corrupters, and thieves.

As the audience listened raptly, not sure what it was hearing, Lawes asked, "If it is a fact that it is a deterrent, why not have these executions in public and make persons who might commit murder fear execution?" Why, indeed, was the electric chair hidden away in a chamber at Sing Sing? Why not set it up, say, right in Times Square?

Enjoying the looks of consternation, Lawes plowed on. Slayers who escaped the chair or the noose made the finest prisoners, as he could testify. "The point I am making is that men who took human life and served time are the best behaved and the best trusted in Sing Sing and the very few returned shows that this class of inmates are more readily reformed than other offenders." In the last five years, he said, 180 men in Sing Sing for murder or manslaughter had been paroled and only 3 had been recommitted. If society really wanted to fight crime, he said, it had to wipe out the scourge of illegal narcotics.

The newspapers were slow to catch on. The *Times* gave the item three paragraphs and stuck it under an equally obscure brief about rubber growing in the Philippines.

ASSAILS DEATH PENALTY

Sing Sing Warden Says It Is Not
A Deterrent of Murder

Others gave it similar prominence or ignored it entirely.

Lawes realized he had to do a better job of getting out the word. A few weeks later, in mid-March 1923, he called in a reporter from the *Ossining Democratic Register* and laid out his arguments. The theory of punishment, Lawes began, rested on deterrence, retribution, and reformation. Clearly, the death penalty ruled out reformation. Retribution was just another word for revenge, a barbarism discredited by modern penology. That left deterrence.

If executions served to deter, Lawes continued, "why weaken this deterring or terrifying effect by making it the most humane affair possible under the circumstances by selecting the quickest and most painless method?" Why, he asked, use the electric chair with its nearly instantaneous lethal jolt or the merciful sleep of gas? "Why not give this benefit of this deterring influence to as wide a number of people as possible? Why not give to the execution of the condemned the character of a public function, by holding them in the public square with the greatest attendance possible, even forcing or coaxing people to witness these executions that may save them from a crime which otherwise they may commit?"

No, he said, capital punishment did not deter, because death was not a deterrent. Many, plainly, did not fear death—or else why did prisoners have to be so closely watched lest they commit suicide? Then too, he said, people about to commit murder did not stop to consider the consequences. They killed in a frenzy trying to escape capture or abscond with bootleg whiskey or drugs or burgled booty. And simple poor marksmanship or blind luck kept more criminals off death row than the electric chair.

Twelve states had already abolished the death penalty, Lawes noted. Was murder on the rampage there? And if so, wouldn't those states reinstate capital punishment in a hurry?

Henry VIII punished no fewer than 263 crimes by death, executing seventy-two thousand people, Lawes told the reporter. But had that cured crime?

Capital punishment was inequitable, he continued. "Who of wealth and influence ever suffered the extreme penalty of death?"

Were mistakes made? Of course. It came with being human. But with the chair, the mistakes were irrevocable.

"There is nothing softly sentimental about me," Lawes said. "Let me confess however that my worst duties are those which are in connection with executions. I dread the thought that someday a reprieve or a commutation may come too late. Last month one came within a few hours before an execution. It has been closer than that. A condemned man who is free today— it having been proved that he was convicted on perjured testimony—was commuted within an hour of the time set for the execution. He had already gone through all the preparations—his hair appropriately trimmed, his black suit donned, his trouser legs slit open—still hoping against tremendous odds that his life might be spared. He never fully recovered from that shock. As a result of that nervous strain, although a big and robust man otherwise, his voice cracked—that is, a partial paralysis of the vocal cords look place, giving him a thin piping voice which persists until today."

When the interview was published, other papers ridiculed his arguments. Regardless of the penalties, every possible crime was being committed somewhere by someone. Should the laws against them be repealed too? Laws didn't deter everyone from wife beating, counterfeiting, or white slavery either, but they deterred some. And without those laws, surely those offenses would soar. So it was with the electric chair and murderers.

But Lawes stirred enough interest with his stance to generate a Democratic bill in the state legislature to outlaw capital punishment. It quickly became a matter of merriment.

Yes, a supporter of the death penalty said, he knew that Lawes had argued that prisoners preferred to die than spend their lives behind bars. So why not give them what they want?

It was fine to feel compassion for "these poor downtrodden murderers," said another, but "what might become of them if they were permitted to escape the chair?" Wouldn't they degenerate into burglars, pickpockets, or even "corner loafers"?

The bill to kill the death penalty died.

14

As Lawes was beginning to speak out against capital punishment he was also discovering a way to magnify his voice beyond all bounds of public imagination. A miracle called radio was captivating the nation, spiriting sound by no visible means over hundreds of miles into living rooms and hobbyists' garages. An age of invention unparalleled in human history had upended the lives of Americans in a few short decades with fast-multiplying new technologies—electric light, the telephone, sound recording, movies, the automobile, airplanes. But nothing seemed so extraordinary, so utterly unexplainable, as the wireless radio telephone, which spoke from the void like a phantom link to the hereafter. Indeed, there was something deeply spiritual about a medium that leaped space to enter through the ear and go straight to the heart in a listening ritual both intensely private and comfortingly communal.

Lawes quickly saw the possibilities. The previous July, shortly before the lightweight champ Benny Leonard was to meet Lew Tendler of Philadelphia in a title bout, Lawes installed a splendid radio set with a Western Electric loudspeaker in the chapel. It was, he explained, an experiment. "What the future will hold is difficult to predict. The radio telephone cannot be an instrument for anything but good and for that reason, if no other, every effort will be made to find its permanent place in prison life."

He was utopian enough to see its greatest value in educational terms. Prisoners hearing instructional talks could not help but be uplifted. Music "of the better type" would also elevate. If a man lacked knowledge of the better things of life, then it was society's duty to educate him to know and desire them.

Whether or not a prizefight was one of those better things, it was Sing Sing's introduction to radio. It was, Lawes maintained, a singular opportunity to introduce the men to the mysterious new medium and lure them in a way that might draw them later to sermons, lectures, and classical music. At the same time, Lawes could follow the bout.

With both men just under the prescribed weight of 135 pounds, and forty-three thousand fans packing Boyle's Thirty Acres in Jersey City, Tendler owned the first six rounds, marauding toward an upset. But Leonard rallied in the sixth, survived a crushing left to the jaw in the eighth, and then, in one of boxing's great comebacks, savaged Tendler to retain the title and the prize of $120,000, with Tendler pocketing the loser's share of $62,000.

Every man at Sing Sing not in a hospital bed or a death row cell had crammed into the chapel to hear it.

Not long afterward, Lawes traveled to the studios of WEAF, the station of the American Telephone and Telegraph Company on lower Broadway, to make his radio debut and early broadcast history with a talk called "Prisons and Prisoners."

His voice steady and his enunciation precise, and cribbing freely from his recent comments to the newspaper, he argued that those locked up would someday be set free again, so what happened to them behind bars was of very real concern to everyone. There was a moral dimension as well, Lawes continued, laying out a vision of progressivism. People had a responsibility to society, but society had a responsibility to its members. "In numerous instances, the crime committed by the member of society is but the natural result of the environment in which the offender was brought up. It may be a case of total illiteracy and ignorance, of a childhood spent in the slums, reared in crowded filthy tenements which make modesty, physical and moral cleanliness, unknown. Should the product of an environment like that be held solely responsible?"

Crime *was* preventable, Lawes insisted, calling for a ban on gun sales. "I would have the slums razed to the ground and in their places model tenements erected at reasonable prices." He called for more schools, compulsory classroom attendance, and a ban on the employment of school-age minors. Prohibition was clearly a disaster. The universal availability of alcohol bred only contempt for the law. Criminal procedure had to be simplified, with fewer adjournments, speedier and more certain convictions in cases of guilt, and indeterminate sentences and parole geared to a prisoner's rehabilitation. As for capital punishment, there was no measurable correlation between the use or nonuse of the death penalty and the homicide rate.

Lawes's hometown of Elmira was agog. His parents did not have a radio set but had been invited by neighbors to listen in. "Isn't it wonderful to hear Lewi's voice so plainly?" asked his mother, Sarah, to everyone in the house. There were times, she admitted, that she became so eager to hear him that she willingly spent as much as a dollar to call him on the telephone. But this—hearing his voice come out of a box—this was *miraculous*.

Lawes received seventy-five letters from listeners as distant as Boston, Washington, Detroit, and New Brunswick, Canada. A Brooklyn lawyer so carried away by the intimacy of the experience that he presumed to address Lawes as "Dear Louis" wrote to say, "Your diction was perfect and the way the waves carried your enunciation was astounding." As for Lawes's remarks on the humanitarian care of inmates, he said, "to use the vernacular of the stage, you went over big."

Stimulated by his reception, Lawes spoke out more widely. Condemning the inequities of sentencing, he revealed that first offenders at Sing Sing served longer terms on average than convicts with prison records—three years and six months versus three years and three months. Drug addicts released from prison went right back to their habits, he complained. He knew a hundred different cases of prisoners who used drugs before being committed, and all went back to their addiction upon being freed. "If the rest of the cases of rehabilitation were like this one of drugs, the prison problem would be absolutely hopeless."

He knew how to grab a headline too. The death rate in prison was five per thousand. Outside the walls it was eight per thousand. (That Sing Sing housed largely robust young men and the general population factored in the high infant mortality rate of eighty-five per thousand and the death rate of the elderly went unmentioned.) The *Buffalo News* and other papers loved it.

SING SING FOLKS
HEALTHIER THAN
FREE PEOPLE

Lawes received support from other penologists, notably B. Ogden Chisolm of the American Prison Association, the reformer whose dismay at not receiving his copy of Chapin's *Bulletin* three years before had helped spark the uproar over censorship. He joined Lawes in condemning Prohibition as a sadly misguided cause of American womanhood that doubled the daily number of murders across the nation to one each half hour.

Lawes was savoring his good publicity at the end of May 1923, when he got some bad news, a whispered tip from one of his many friends among the prisoners. The next morning, Lawes rounded up his head keeper, his secretary, and the superintendent of the Ossining waterworks and sped through the gates so fast that rumors spread of an escape.

The car screeched to a stop at a wooden reservoir house east of the prison, outside the walls but still on Sing Sing grounds. Lawes leaped out. He ran into a guard and asked what he was doing there. Repair work, came the answer. Lawes knew better.

"Where's Brindell?" he demanded.

The guard looked stricken. In the reservoir house, he said.

Lawes ran to the rear and threw open the door. Inside indeed was Robert Brindell, the imprisoned building trades czar thought to have masterminded the doomed Westall parole bill more than a year before. With him were his wife, son, and daughter.

"Come out of there!" Lawes ordered. "Lock them up."

Betrayed yet again by a privileged inmate, he was incensed. With the earlier suspicions of Brindell's influence, this painted Lawes as a crooked crony of the influential racketeer. Brindell had been allowed off the grounds to supervise a construction job at the chlorinating plant, not to hold family reunions. As stories circulated in Ossining that Brindell had a regular connubial love nest in the reservoir shack and received packages through drop-offs in town, Lawes fired the guard-lookout and sent Brindell into solitary confinement, eventually packing him off in chains to Dannemora. Let his family drive all day into the Adirondacks to see him.

This time Governor Smith demanded answers from Lawes. Was Brindell still running his rackets from Sing Sing? Had he banqueted with state officials outside the walls? And how many other influential prisoners had also wormed their way outside the prison?

The papers were merciless. One cartoonist drew a convict in striped suit strolling out of his cell with his golf caddy. "If anyone wants me, Warden, I'll be over at the country club."

Lawes insisted it was an aberration and fought back, challenging his critics: "If anyone has evidence to the effect that I extended courtesies to Brindell or any other prisoner, I would be gratified if he would present it. If I had granted these courtesies, it would be time for me to quit."

He needed the distraction of some good publicity, and mysteriously, it arrived in the form of a last-minute death reprieve. Teddy, Sing Sing's Great Dane, had been suffering what the prison veterinarian called an incurable case of eczema, and had been ordered executed. Sensing his doom, he escaped. He was recaptured, but somehow word of his plight reached the press. Children by the hundreds wrote in begging for Teddy's life and deluging the prison with home remedies for skin disorders. Lawes magnanimously commuted Teddy's sentence, prescribing diet therapy and rehabilitation. Teddy was cured and saved, and Brindell's name faded from view.

15

Sunshine, open air, sports, and music were the civilizing influences that Lawes prized. "Men have been taken out of isolation and put into the sunshine and they have done splendidly," he told a visiting reporter. "We don't take them away from their sunshine except for a serious offense against discipline. If they're in good standing, they're out in it every day." A third of the twelve hundred inmates worked outdoors and stayed out until just before dark. The rest had three daily outdoor recreation periods. It was simple common sense, but it also had a scientific basis. Lawes had seen studies showing sunlight to be a powerful prophylaxis against rickets, but only if it was direct, not filtered through glass. Sunlamps had their value, but nothing equaled nature's pure golden light. Color, too, improved the men's mood, and Lawes repainted Sing Sing's grim dun buildings orange, the same bright hue as New York City's elevated lines.

The new Sing Sing, too, continued to rise on the hill, four brick buildings including a new cellblock, long in the making but finally nearing completion in 1923. Soon the men would trade their dank stone cubicles and slop buckets for the airy new cells with plumbing and plenty of sunshine. Another of the new buildings was the hospital, including a floor for psychiatric studies. The mentally disabled and retarded were usually easy to spot; it was the borderline cases that proved troublesome, Lawes found. The hospital had floors for surgery, dental and optical treatment, and X rays.

Construction had been delayed. From his earliest days at Sing Sing, Lawes had asked the state for money for a prison hospital. He had found the

Lawes (second from left) with Sing Sing baseball team. (OSSINING HISTORICAL SOCIETY MUSEUM)

perfect site, an open area stretching back from the river, and he was pacing it one day when an inmate said, "Gee, boss, wouldn't that make a great base-ball field?" Lawes mulled it over. Would he have the nerve to go back to the state and say that instead of the hospital, he wanted a ball field? Asking himself the question, he knew he had already answered it. Now he had Lawes Field *and* the hospital.

Squire was still the physician in charge, contributing his own supplies of radium to treat inmates with cancer. In a bizarre series of experiments on electrocuted corpses, he sought chemical factors that might influence crimi-nality. He also tested the efficacy of the chair by trying to revive the dead with a solution of adrenaline chlorate injected into the heart wall. Ever since the contraption had been invented, doctors had been yearning to make medical history by bringing back the dead, to no avail. Now Squire was trying too. He was able to produce some fibrillar contraction over an hour after death but no real contraction of the heart muscle.

The pharmacy, still housed in old quarters, looked like an ancient apothe-cary, with bottles of pills and unguents and syrups in bulbous jars of indigo and periodontal pink and bile green, medicaments made largely in the pharmacy

View of Sing Sing and ball field. (OSSINING HISTORICAL SOCIETY MUSEUM)

itself and no longer purchased expensively from outside contractors. The clinic next door was where incoming prisoners still presented themselves for mental and physical examination upon arrival. Those found addicted to drugs or ill with tuberculosis were packed off to Clinton at Dannemora. The mentally ill were sent closer, to Napanoch. The illiterate were kept at Sing Sing, where they attended compulsory classes, an hour and a quarter a day, taught by six inmates under a principal brought in from the outside. The youngest in school was eighteen, the oldest fifty-nine. One class counted no fewer than twenty-three nationalities. For those who could read and write, at least a little, there was night school. Some men went because it swayed the parole board. Those with loftier aspirations competed for the thirty-five scholarships for home study through Columbia University. And almost everyone who could read used the fifty-thousand-volume library.

Sing Sing baseball game, probably in 1920s. (© NEW YORK DAILY NEWS, L.P. REPRINTED WITH PERMISSION)

Outside on the grounds, thanks to Chapin, there were pansies and roses, a hothouse where the old morgue once stood, and emerald patches of lawn with no need for any Keep Off signs. Any inmate who trampled the plantings faced a hanging jury of his peers. The illicit shacks that had outraged Lawes on his first visit had been razed to expand the ball field and allow for two grandstands. The baseball team practiced an hour a day, and on weekends played visiting teams from local civic clubs. The men could watch from their assigned and numbered seats or toss a ball around themselves, or they could play handball or boccie, read, or practice music for the twenty-four-piece band. But most watched the ball games. There was even an annual field day with events like a high jump and a fifty-yard dash for fat men. The record was seven seconds. Pole vaults, however, were banned.

The shops thrummed with activity: the shoe factory, the sheet metal plant turning out street sweepers' carts, the barbershop, the tailor shop, the automobile school. Entrepreneurs prospered. Sam the Bootblack walked out of Sing Sing after fifteen years with a conditional pardon and a fortune of $890—one of the few inmates to leave with more money than he came in with.

As Lawes walked the grounds, sometimes with visitors, he was freely ac-
costed by petitioners with a grievance to air or a favor to ask. Once he stood
coatless in the rain, wet and dripping, patiently listening to a prisoner explain his wish to be deported to Russia. The man walked away amazed at
Lawes's compassion, as he wrote afterward to tell him. Another time a prisoner asked Lawes for permission to write a letter to a nonrelative.

"Who visits you?" Lawes asked.

"Nobody."

"You've never had a visitor?"

"No sir."

"How long have you been here?"

"Nine years."

Lawes scrawled his approval.

Penology professionals from around the country, hearing about Lawes's
successes at Sing Sing, came to see for themselves. Envoys from Panama,
Germany, China, and Imperial Japan also scheduled tours.

But progress, Lawes thought, was relative. Awaiting a date with the chair
was a woman, Anna Buzzi, a voluptuous, round-faced thirty-year-old divorcée
convicted of shooting to death her ex-boss and lover, Fred Schneider, a
wealthy Bronx contractor long separated from his wife. Buzzi, an expert shot
and veteran of the Women's Motor Corps in the world war, had begun as
Schneider's bookkeeper and later became something more, supporting him
when he was broke. They had been living together on the Grand Concourse
and were planning a home in Riverdale overlooking the Hudson when she
became aware of his unseemly closeness to an office stenographer. His body
was found slumped at the wheel of his heavy-curtained touring car near a
snowbank in a deserted part of the Bronx, a bullet in his right ear and another in the back of his head. There was a .38 Colt revolver on the seat beside him. A woman was seen fleeing the car. The trail led quickly to Buzzi,
and despite her tearful denials, she was convicted.

Sent first to Auburn and then to Sing Sing, she took one look at her
cell and declared she would go completely insane. Lawes and Kathryn
contributed a rug and curtains from their home. Fellow prisoners who regarded the execution of a woman as the ultimate atrocity built her painted
furniture.

None of the inmates, of course, was allowed to see her, but accounts of her movements and utterances were breathlessly passed on, told and retold among the prison population. She had her own clothes sent to her and insisted on dressing in black "in mourning for Fred." But sometimes her mood shifted and she donned a sleeveless pink silk negligee, reports of which drove the men to heights of sexual ecstasy. The wife of a prison staff member complained about her risqué attire, but Buzzi laughed in derision. She was, after all, in solitary confinement. Lawes found it all silly. Who cared if Buzzi wanted to flash her bare fleshy arms to the unseeing walls?

She spent her time crocheting, embroidering, and making bead bags. "Anna's Boudoir," it came to be called, and her creations soon threatened to overwhelm her narrow cell. Lawes would happily have let her listen to the radio, but the equipment was installed in the chapel. The Salvation Army had offered to purchase a set for the prisoners on death row, which Lawes thought a fine idea, but state officials rejected the gift. The condemned were to be held in an isolation not to be breached by entertaining voices from outside. Instead, Lawes commandeered the prison phonograph for Buzzi's exclusive use.

She listened to music as she did her handiwork and her morning calisthenics. Allowed into the yard to exercise, she played furious games of solitary handball against the towering brick death house wall.

Then her mother died and Buzzi seemed close to a breakdown again. One night she awoke in excruciating pain. Squire diagnosed acute appendicitis. He asked her permission to operate. She refused.

Squire sent for Father Cashin, who tried to persuade her, but she was adamant.

Lawes offered her an entire ward to herself if she would relent, but still Buzzi refused.

Father Cashin returned with his kit and prepared the oils for extreme unction.

Finally Buzzi understood. "Am I that ill?" she asked.

Yes, Father Cashin said. Now would she consent to the operation?

"No," she said. She was going to die either way. She had rather it be like this.

Father Cashin reminded her that she still had hope; her sentence could be commuted.

"Live the rest of my life behind bars?" She shook her head and lay back to let the priest administer last rites.

But she didn't die that night. Or the next day. Or the day after. Her execution was scheduled for August 1923, but delayed when her lawyers won a stay.

Who could have any confidence in this system? Lawes wondered. There was no end to the tormenting cases. Hours before their appointment with the chair, two other condemned men, convicted of killing a store clerk in Albany, scrawled impassioned pleas of innocence; the ink was still wet on the paper when it was placed in Lawes's hands. "I am going to die," wrote twenty-one-year-old Thomas Kindlon. "I know it. I can tell my God that I don't know anything about this case at all. I am innocent." He named two others he said had confessed to him in jail. Desperate to buy time, he even admitted to a train robbery for which another prisoner was serving time in Dannemora. Lawes tried urgently to reach Governor Smith at a party and failed. Kindlon marched to the chair with a blank smile. In seven minutes he was dead.

To forcefully make his case against capital punishment, Lawes put his arguments between hard covers, in a book for G. P. Putnam's Sons that he called, grandly, *Man's Judgment of Death: An Analysis of the Operation and Effect of Capital Punishment Based on Facts, not on Sentiment*. For inspiration, he chose a quotation from Lafayette: "I shall ask for the abolition of the Penalty of Death until I have the infallibility of human judgment demonstrated to me."

He began with a strange tale of two Eskimo judges in the Canadian Arctic who executed a tribesman and were then themselves hanged by the government for murder. Their judgment was deemed killing, and the government's, simple justice. "Thus," Lawes wrote, "do we again see the illogical futility of a method of punishment which is older than civilization itself."

England had had its hundreds of capital offenses—and still crime was rampant. George Kirchwey, the Columbia University dean who had replaced the embattled Osbsorne at Sing Sing in 1915, had said it well before him, Lawes wrote: "It is not the murderer but the murder that is the enemy. The primitive method of striking blindly in impotent rage at the life of the offender has had its day, but still it obscures our vision as to the real nature of the problem."

Lawes was a great believer in facts and statistics. In the previous thirty-four years, he wrote, nearly 60 percent of all murderers sent to Sing Sing were below the age of thirty. Were they likely to have had the maturity to evaluate the consequences beforehand? Did people realize how rarely the death penalty was imposed, and that in 80 percent of the forty states with capital punishment, the judge or jury had the right to impose life imprisonment rather than execution? Who should get life and who death? And who was qualified to render such fine distinctions?

Death was hardly a certain punishment for murder. Barely one out of eighty killers actually paid with his life. And who was the one? Rarely the guiltiest. Often the poorest, stupidest, or unluckiest.

But wouldn't spared murderers serving life soon be paroled or commuted back onto the streets? Not at all, Lawes found. In the bulk of the states, nearly 80 percent of the lifers remained behind bars after eight years—in New York it was nearly 70 percent. More lifers went insane behind bars than gained release.

In short, he said, the death sentence was wildly uncertain in its application. Juries and judges given a choice usually shunned it. Life imprisonment remained a good alternative, certain enough as a punishment when warranted, flexible when justified, and in cases of miscarriage of justice, reversible. Finally, convictions were more readily obtainable in states that did not mandate death.

He was hardly alone in his views. Seventeen wardens around the country agreed with him. Twenty-three others favored capital punishment, and seven voiced mixed opinions. With such confusion among the professionals, how could the public put any faith in the death penalty?

The trend was clear, he concluded: the severity of punishment was on the decline. The death penalty was an anachronism. It failed every test. And could anyone ever explain why homicides were rising faster in states with the death penalty than those without it? He appended sixty pages of state-by-state statistics and expert testimony.

Lawes gave an extensive preview of his case to *Outlook* magazine, which ran a long interview with him headed "Why I Have Lost Faith in Capital Punishment." Finding him a big man with slow movements, deliberate speech, and "a jaw that can stay put," the magazine summed up his beliefs with a simple formulation: "Crime is a social disease with roots deeper than such as could be cured or prevented by punishment."

Asked by a Civil War veteran why the United States had so many more homicides proportionally than England, Lawes scribbled his answer in the margin of the man's letter: "Newspapers give crime too much glamour."

As departing president of the American Prison Association, he presented his brief in person to the three hundred delegates at the September 1923 congress in Boston, calling the death penalty barbaric and, worse, ineffective. "Capital punishment should be done away with," he concluded, startling the delegates with the severity of his attack.

Lawes's adversarial position, well known enough in New York, astounded the *Boston Globe*. *The Nation* took notice too. "When the warden of one of the world's greatest prisons declares his opposition to capital punishment it is clearly not the opinion of a theorist but the view of what we like to call a 'practical' man."

Lawes was becoming hot copy. Speaking invitations flowed in. The *New York Times* asked for an interview on capital punishment, and reporters for the *World* and the *Herald* besieged Sing Sing. Lawes, savvy about the territoriality of the press, played one off against another, and got them all to write about him.

He took time off from his interviews and writing to welcome back Sing Sing's favorite yachtsman, tea mogul Sir Thomas Lipton, who had endowed the 1920 baseball cup and later returned, amid much jocularity, to be fingerprinted. This visit, he donated a purse of a hundred dollars for the ballplayers' families at Christmas and was saluted by the Mutual Welfare League Band playing a spirited version of "Yes, We Have No Bananas."

In New York, meanwhile, state supreme court justice Robert F. Wagner approved the incorporation papers of a new organization, the League to Abolish Capital Punishment, headed by Lewis E. Lawes.

16

Chapin was falling in love again. This time, too, it was a young pen pal, a magazine editor in Cleveland. Since the tapering off of his racy and abruptly censored correspondence with Viola Irene in Minneapolis three years before, and the loss of his beloved *Bulletin,* Chapin had found redemption in his flowers. He had become quite the horticulturist, bestriding the grounds in a natty white shirt, bow tie, and knit sweater. On the day he had begun his fifth year in Sing Sing—not long before Lawes would mark the start of his fourth—Chapin planted his first blue spruce, and he was so captivated that he often went down to the garden at five in the morning to admire it in the gaining light of dawn. At his plea, wealthy friends from his days on the *Evening World* sent him more seedlings, and he planted these in a row to the end of the cellblock—a line of trees, he mused poetically, that would serve their own life sentence at Sing Sing. Another friend sent him fifty dollars, and Chapin agonized over the florists' catalogs like a child with a penny pressing his nose to the glass of a candy store. Irvin Cobb, Chapin's ex–galley slave at the paper who had once likened the editor to a serpent, came to interview him and found him a changed man, given over to his love of plants, if not humans. How, Cobb wondered, did Chapin protect his fragile charges?

Chapin didn't understand the question. Protect them from what?

From being trampled by the prisoners, Cobb said.

Chapin stared in incomprehension. No man locked up in Sing Sing had ever touched one of his flowers. It was unimaginable.

Guards for the garden? Chapin snorted. There were twelve hundred of them at Sing Sing, every man in the joint.

Chapin had converted three old buildings into greenhouses, one filled with roses, one with carnations and chrysanthemums, and one with tropical plants. Nurserymen sent trees—more blue spruces, pines, firs, junipers, and Japanese maples. Birds arrived, an expensive parrot and a canary that Chapin christened Don. Even peacocks.

He had, by Lawes's indulgence, moved out of the cellblock and was living with a handful of other trusted prisoners in bigger and airier cells in the annex, with their own radio hookup.

"You may put chains on a man's limbs and set him behind steel bars, and you may take away his name and give him a number to go by," wrote Cobb later in prose to do his longtime chief proud, "but you cannot keep his intelligence jailed, not if he has any intelligence; it will somehow find a way to function."

In Cleveland, a woman named Constance R. had been editing financial trade magazines, looking for ideas, when an elderly acquaintance handed her Chapin's autobiography, saying: "This will tell you some things about editing. Chapin was the best city editor of his day."

She was transfixed. She had been reading Oscar Wilde and remembered the story of his trip to bankruptcy court. Wilde passed a friend and, deeply ashamed, averted his eyes. His friend doffed his hat in respect. Wilde never forgot the touching gesture. She resolved to do the same for Chapin. She would restore his humanity by giving him something to care for. She couldn't imagine anyone could just write to a prisoner, so she wrote George Putnam, Chapin's publisher, enclosing a letter for Chapin with one of her magazines, asking if he would critique it.

Chapin wrote back promptly. He was honored, he said, but his knowledge of banking was so limited that he could be of little use. Moreover, she didn't need much tutoring. "One who can write such a letter as this of yours that I have just read a second time needs only self-confidence to achieve the success she is reaching for. No one ever has expressed himself in a letter to me more clearly than you have."

He urged her to write again and she did, asking whether she should take a Columbia University correspondence course in short-story writing. No one who wrote as well as she needed such instruction, he responded. "Your last letter is the best literature that has come to me in a long time."

He would like to write another book, he confided, but it would have to await a hoped-for pardon. Then he would set sail on a windjammer for the Tropics, like his heroes Gauguin and Lafcadio Hearn. It might take a year or ten, but it would happen, he assured her. Meanwhile, he said, he had pored over the magazines she sent without finding the one picture he most longed to see.

Constance obliged and Chapin was transported. He was mesmerized by her long hair, which looked like it might fall below her waist. Did she know, he asked, that there was a rose named after her? The Constance, orange buds, streaked with crimson, opening to a glorious yellow of many shades.

Lawes had a miserable year's end as 1924 approached. He was felled by a mysterious bug, confined to his bed even as Thomas Mott Osborne, the ousted reform hero, made a rare return visit to Sing Sing, showing the governor of Colorado around as a prelude to Osborne's survey of prison conditions in Colorado.

Lawes recuperated slowly over Christmas while Feodor Chaliapin, the great Russian basso, sang a holiday program of "Ave Maria" and other favorites for the prisoners. Anna Buzzi and eleven other convicted slayers in the death house had to limit themselves to phonograph records.

By late January, Lawes had recovered enough to keep a speaking engagement at the University Club at Grace Church. Invitations went out in the form of a mock grand jury subpoena which amused its recipients. "Failure to obey this summons," it warned, "will cause you serious regret." He received a twenty-five-dollar honorarium, which he pledged to donate to a released prisoner.

Then came welcome news. Superintendent Rattigan, Lawes's longtime nemesis in battles over the *Bulletin* and prisoner coddling, was being replaced by his deputy, state senator James L. Long.

Early in the new year, Lawes wrote the chairman of the State Senate Finance Committee, lobbying for restoration of his twelve-hundred-dollar automobile allowance. Who had stricken it from the budget? How could he be without his transportation?

Lawes proved he knew how to play the political game. If the distinguished senator could restore the allocation, Lawes wrote, "I shall consider same a personal favor and will be glad to reciprocate at any time." What legislator would alienate the warden of a huge penal institution where constituents and their influential friends were bound to land? Lawes got his vehicle.

He soon traveled up to Albany to testify for another bill to abolish capital punishment. More than a third of the state's 458 convicted murderers had never gone to the chair, he noted. In Massachusetts, fewer than one out of four won pardons or commutations, and in Pennsylvania, a mere 3 percent. So much, Lawes said, for the scientific certainties of the death penalty.

In April 1924, the figures still at the tip of his tongue, he debated a capital punishment proponent, state senator William L. Love of Brooklyn, on WEAF. Afterward listeners voted. Lawes won, 568–501.

By midyear, he had more fuel. Anna Buzzi, still on death row, won a new trial. In court, she implicated her brother-in-law in Schneider's murder and was acquitted.

But Lawes's satisfaction was short-lived. He was losing one of his most faithful allies. It was Father Cashin's turn to leave. The chapel was jammed with prisoners and the altar bedecked with Chapin's roses. Outside, the band blared Irish favorites, though bereft of two of its stalwarts. Herman Hippelhauser, the tuba master, had recently waddled off on parole, and Pidge Hoolahan, the piccoloist, had also gone, clutching the instrument bought for him by the state as a farewell gift.

The men had come to say good-bye to Father Cashin, who was departing Sing Sing after twelve years, many times the term of ordinary inmates, for the parish of St. Andrew's in the shadow of New York's city hall and of newspaperdom's Park Row, where far more souls than the prison's needed saving.

The boys planned their own elaborate farewell, persuading Lawes to let a jewel thief called Spare Ribs Cohen travel down to the city with funds from the welfare league to pick out a suitable gift. To no one's surprise he returned, and that night in the crowded chapel he made the presentation to Father Cashin. It was a new gold crucifix to replace the one so worn down by the kisses of the condemned that the Christ could barely be recognized. Cohen had it inscribed: "To the Bishop of Sing Sing, from the Saints of Sing Sing."

In his farewell mass and sermon, conducted with the aid of an altar boy lifer and a white-haired organist who had murdered his sweetheart, Father

Cashin apologized. "I had hoped to make my work here among you my life's task. I am sorry to leave you all. Give to my successor the same loyalty you have given me. There is more loyalty, sympathy, and understanding inside these walls than in any other place of equal area in the world. Bring out the good in you. It is there and I have worked here long enough to see what others cannot. Be square with yourselves and you'll be square with God."

And then he was gone.

Without Father Cashin, Dr. Squire grew increasingly despondent. He dwelled on the macabre details of each execution and harangued Lawes about the horrors of the electric chair, as if he needed reminding. When newspaper stories extolled a new method of humane killing in Nevada—poison gas—Squire obtained an official report and read Lawes the sickening details. The condemned, a Chinese immigrant from Canton implicated in the notorious tong wars, was locked in an airtight room sprayed with two quarts of hydrocyanic acid. "Gee Joh turned his head slightly, then jerked it violently backward and forward. His body heaved, strained at the straps and then his whole frame twitched. These movements of his head and body continued for six minutes by stop watch." It took almost three hours before the room was opened and doctors in gas masks pronounced the man dead.

Nevada officials called the experiment an unqualified success, but Squire said it sounded grotesque.

Lawes shook his head in consternation. "The electric companies won't like it."

17

Nothing revived Lawes more than his sweet domestic routine. Cherie was now three years old, a bubbly tyke who adored being cuddled by her father on a rocking chair on the broad veranda of the warden's house. He smoked cigars and gave the paper rings to her. She alone called him "Daddy." To Crystal, a frail and precocious brunette of fourteen, and Kathleen, a robust fifteen, he was the more formal "Father." Yet he doted on them all, often throwing back his head for a good hearty laugh that set his deep blue eyes afire.

When they misbehaved, he didn't have to say much. Just a hard look communicated his message. Once, but only once, he swatted Cherie, after she crawled under the table at a restaurant and kept hammering away with a knife.

Cherie wore boys' clothes, not dresses. Not just because the Laweses had wanted a boy to go with their girls but because boys' clothes were more practical around the prison.

Lawes himself almost always wore a suit. He kept his jacket on at dinner. When they went swimming, the girls put on their bathing suits, but he stood by in his wool suit. He even played golf in a suit. He was especially proud of his shoes. "It pays to buy good shoes," he told the girls.

The house was full of staff, trusted prisoners speaking a gaggle of tongues who did the chores and watched over the girls and sometimes joined them at the dining table. Lawes took it for granted that the men would take good care of his children, and his trust carried more weight than any threats. Once, playing on the prison grounds, Cherie mischievously hid from her prisoner "nursemaid," who grew frantic with worry, finally shouting that if she did not come out immediately, he would escape. She came running.

Cherie liked to perch herself atop a pile of old clothes in the prison laundry, chew on a bacon strip, and watch the men feed linen into the ironing rollers. Her nurse for a time was a gentle black man everyone called Old Black Joe. He and another house servant argued one day and came to blows. Lawes ordered them both thrown into solitary. Cherie was inconsolable. "Li'l miss, you be quiet," Joe soothed. "I'll be back." But he wasn't. Cherie demanded his return, and Lawes sat her on his knee and explained why that could not be.

Lawes's daughter Cherie on the porch. (JOAN L. JACOBSEN)

Lawes was shaved each morning by a prison barber who had once slit a man's throat. He laughed off Kathryn's concerns and lay back, presenting his lathered jowls to the glistening blade. A visiting judge of the general sessions court once sat in the neighboring chair and looked up into the eyes of an Italian he had sentenced to twenty years. Then he suddenly remembered an important engagement and exited, soapy-chinned.

Being a prisoner at Sing Sing, Lawes told the girls, did not make someone a bad person. Prisoners, in turn, flooded Lawes with letters, asking for jobs on his household staff. Sundays, visiting days, he welcomed back former boys who arrived with their families, proud to show them off. Broadway actors came too. They knew lots of people inside.

Kathryn befriended prisoners as well, including Owney Madden, the small, dapper bootlegger king and New York gangster boss, whom she called "Owen." She often visited the death house on missions of comfort, once taking Cherie to see a woman who sat in her cell sewing something for her own daughter. But Kathryn was anything but a weeper. If an inmate betrayed her, she'd berate him: "You lied to me. I'll do anything to help you, but I will not be lied to." Still she'd forgive him. She kept their secrets too, even from her husband. Telling her something, the men said proudly, was like burying it in the sea.

To Cherie, their hundred-year-old house was magical with secrets. Dumbwaiters mysteriously delivered food and goods between floors. On the ground floor was Lawes's intimidatingly large office, with its ornate wood-paneled fireplace, heavy paneled ceiling, diamond-patterned carpet, gnarled claw-

Lawes and Cherie. (JOAN L. JACOBSEN)

footed desk, and chair with an eagle-carved backrest. Opposite the office were the large Victorian dining room and the kitchen, with gaping chutes to the laundry below.

Upstairs, Crystal and Kathleen shared a bedroom and sitting room, Cherie had her own nursery, and Lawes and Kathryn slept in their own large bedroom adorned with a big framed magazine picture of a factory worker and the message "Man Is Good." There was a green brocade armchair where Lawes liked to read, four or five books piled up beside it. Outside, along the second floor, was a porch that Kathryn had screened in for sleeping on sweltering nights. On the third floor were guest bedrooms, and above that was a staircase to the girls' favorite refuge, an octagonal glass cupola with a panoramic view of the prison grounds.

Kathryn got up early, going downstairs to supervise the kitchen and get the staff going. Lawes came down about eight. She still didn't like cooking much, but she made pot roast and vegetable soup and chocolate cake, three of his favorites. He appreciated commonplace pleasures like freshly picked vegetables that delighted him when he came to the table. "Oh, look! Wonderful corn and tomatoes!" But he didn't much like chicken. "What's the point? They're so small."

Rather than cook, Kathryn preferred sewing and dressmaking, following patterns from *Vogue*. She liked buying hats and shoes. Otherwise she roamed the prison inquiring into the men's cases and, on holidays, putting fresh flowers on the unmarked graves of potter's field. In the house, she did what she had to and left the rest to the staff.

Before dinner, Prohibition notwithstanding, Lawes and Kathryn sipped scotch and sodas in the bedroom.

Earlier in 1925, he had had to execute one of death row's more charming denizens, Patrick Murphy, a thirty-year-old Buffalo man convicted of murdering a woman in the

Prisoners who took care of Cherie. (JOAN L. JACOBSEN)

holdup of her husband's drugstore. Murphy was a famous joker who brought laughter to the condemned cells. But he turned mirthless as his final hour approached. Terrified, he begged Lawes for a favor, a stiff bourbon to rally his spirits as he walked his last mile. Spirits were kept in the infirmary, for medicinal uses. It was strictly against the rules, but Lawes had a prescription written up for three ounces in a small bottle, and delivered it to Murphy, who clutched the precious libation as he told his last joke. Then, just before uncapping the bottle, he looked at Lawes and handed it back. "You need the shot more than I do, Warden." Lawes drank it down, gratefully. At peace, Murphy walked stoically to his fate.

Music usually filled the house. Deprived of her own musical education, Kathryn bought no fewer than three pianos for the house and arranged lessons for all the girls. Crystal, in addition, studied the violin. With some of his first extra money, Lawes had asked Kathryn what she wanted. A subscription to the Metropolitan Opera, she had said, and he had bought it for her. She

Old warden's mansion. (OSSINING HISTORICAL SOCIETY MUSEUM)

Lawes's sumptuous office in his old Sing Sing mansion, before 1930. (OSSINING HISTORICAL SOCIETY MUSEUM)

went alone to the matinees, which was fine with him. "I don't know what I'm hearing," he confessed.

She gave away his clothes to the needy. Once in Ossining he saw a derelict wearing a familiar hat and confronted Kathryn. "It was my hat, wasn't it?"

She laughed it off. "Oh, don't worry, Lew, you'll have lots of hats."

Killing days were the hardest at Sing Sing. The warden's house fell silent. The phone line was left open for last-minute calls of reprieve from the governor, calls that rarely came. Lawes brooded. He never talked about the cases, but the family knew. They knew, too, that he never watched the moment of death, averting his eyes at the last moment.

He worried most in midsummer, when the prison sweltered and men seethed, sullen, in their cells.

Alone with the young Cherie, he questioned her. What did prisoners look like?

She didn't know; they looked like everyone else.

It was the right answer.

If she saw someone do something wrong, what would she do?

Nothing.

Right again. She must never be a squealer.

If she herself did something wrong?

She didn't know.

Admit it, Lawes said. Confess.

18

Father Cashin's successor, the Reverend John P. McCaffrey of Our Lady of Victory in Mount Vernon, not too many miles south of Ossining, was an athletic six-footer with a wavy brown pompadour topping his round, boyish face. He was barely thirty when he was called upon to escort his first prisoners to the chair eight days into the new year of 1925. It was to be a double execution, nineteen-year-old John Rys and twenty-three-year-old John Emieleta, both from Reading, Pennsylvania, convicted of killing a Chinese laundryman on Long Island.

Rys was a singer. He had come to New York from the coalfields of Pennsylvania hoping to follow in the footsteps of his idol, the Russian-born singing waiter Israel Beilin, later Irving Berlin. Looking for singing jobs in saloons, Rys had fallen in with Emieleta, an ex-convict, and accompanied him to the laundryman to collect what he thought was a debt. It ended with the laundryman dead. Emieleta had vouched for Rys's innocence, but now both were slated to die. Rys, with fifteen cents to his name, had not had a visitor in his seven months on death row.

Lawes found Rys pathetic and vented his outrage to a reporter: "Johnny is being crushed by the realization that the world has no heart and will not lift a finger to help him because he is poor. I have been ordered to kill in the chair this child of poverty and misfortune. If he were rich and could have engaged first-class counsel he might have escaped this, somehow. He might have been acquitted and served no time at all or, to satisfy the State, he might have been guided to plead guilty to the second-degree charge. He might now be working in the prison shops under a light sentence. But because he was penniless, he was railroaded to fatten a District Attorney's list of convictions. His poverty is the only reason for his plight. Did you ever see a rich man go the whole route through to the Death House? I don't know of any. Have you ever seen the sons of the rich in Condemned Row, no matter what they do? I don't know of any."

But by then Rys was dead. Emieleta had gone first, walking to the chair arm in arm with Father McCaffrey. Then it was Rys's turn, walking with the priest who read from his prayer book. His lips quivered as he tried to look brave. He was saying he would try to bear up when the current cut him off.

Squire had had enough. After signaling for the death of 130 prisoners, he was through, he told Lawes. His thinning hair was now plastered down off a near-center part, and his eyes had sunk in their sockets. He looked like a skull. He had been called upon to certify the killing of a prisoner he was convinced was a helpless lunatic. A panel of alienists had gravely pronounced the man sane, but he was so violently distraught he had to be confined in a straitjacket. Squire wrote Governor Smith appealing for a reexamination but heard nothing back. On the day of the execution, desperate for an answer, Squire, Lawes, and Father McCaffrey took the train to Albany to find the governor. Smith was not there. And no one knew anything about Squire's letter. It had been lost. Two hours later—an hour before the execution—the governor was tracked down by telephone and gave the order for a reprieve. The prisoner was reexamined and this time found to be, after all, demonstrably insane. He was sent to an asylum. The execution was canceled.

The close call spooked Squire as nothing had before. He took to his bed and stayed there a month. When he returned to duty in the death house, he stood as usual on the rubber mat to give the signal—and suddenly felt a wild desire, just as the switch was thrown, to step off and reach out fatally to touch the electrified body. He managed to restrain himself and later underwent rigorous self-analysis according to the latest theories of Dr. Sigmund Freud, telling himself that his suicidal impulse was aberrational. But it wasn't. At each subsequent execution, he inched closer to the chair, longing to lunge forward and embrace the deadly current, finally forcing himself, by digging his fingernails into his palms, to hold back. When he thought he could no longer resist, he confided in a friend. The friend told Squire's only child, his grown daughter, Evelyn. She climbed into his lap as she had when she was young, looked into his eyes, and asked him if it was true. Yes, he admitted. Then, she begged him, it was time to leave. He finally agreed, telling Lawes he was putting in his papers.

Lawes felt a pain in his chest—he was getting them now and then. Squire was his closest ally. Desperate to keep him, Lawes asked if a vacation would help.

It was too late for him, Squire said, but Lawes had to continue fighting for the cause. "You'll have to stay," he said, "and keep shouting and keep killing."

Chapin, meanwhile, was in ecstasy. The luminaries who paraded through Sing Sing made it a practice to stop for an audience with the world's most famous wife-killing editor. Two of the latest had been the actor Tommy Meighan, star of some eighty pictures, and Meighan's good friend, the novelist Booth Tarkington. Chapin's postal romance with Constance, furthermore, had entered a torrid phase. Lawes had presented Chapin with his own radio set and many a night he sat up late trying to tune in Cleveland, imagining it was bringing him close to his beloved. "Sweet of you to put on the black, square neck gown to write to me in," he answered one of her letters, "a becoming costume, I am sure, but, honey it is not the gown you usually wear when you come to me on a moonbeam to visit me." And soon she did visit in the flesh.

It was a June day in 1924. She spent anxious, precious minutes getting processed and fidgeting on a stool in the waiting room—the clock subtracting time from the regulation two-hour visit. Then a door opened and he was there, carrying a yellow Constance rose. He embraced her and they kissed. He hadn't slept all night. "If I'd waited any longer," he said, "they'd have had to put me in a straitjacket."

Constance pinned the rose on her dress. The minutes flew. They whispered endearments. From now on, Chapin said, they would call each other Captain and Mate—she would be Captain.

His eyes kept darting despairingly to the clock, and all too soon a patrolling guard with a chart in his hand ordered, "Time up." She laughed it off. Surely he of all people could arrange some extra minutes. No, Chapin insisted, suddenly sanctimonious, prison morale was crucial. "Please, honey, go."

She left for luncheon with the Laweses, including little Cherie. Then she went on a tour of Sing Sing and its gardens and was taken to see Chapin once again in his office, stacked with gardening books and magazines and so close to the Hudson that but for the fence she felt she could dive in. Flowers bloomed on the windowsill, and Chapin's prize canary, Don, serenaded them.

The guard who escorted her cleared his throat and discreetly turned his back, but Chapin just walked to his rolltop desk and busied himself with some letters.

The guard shook his head. Chapin was some stubborn cuss, the guard muttered. "You won't even take your inch."

Chapin ignored him and, picking up a copy of *Candide*, his mother's favorite book, presented it to Constance.

She wanted to see his cell, which, he had proudly told her, was not really a cell because it was never locked, and she was escorted there next. She stood alone by his cot and stripped the petals from her rose to use them to form three words she spelled out on his pillow: "I love you."

She returned to the Laweses to say good-bye and was presented with a bouquet of sweetheart roses from Chapin with a card.

> *The sweetest flower that blows*
> *I give you as we part*
> *For you it is a rose*
> *For me it is my heart.* . . .

By prearrangement, Constance stood on the top deck of the Hudson steamer *Washington Irving* as it slid past the greenhouse heading up to Albany. Chapin paced the river's edge, his jacket off, so she could spot him in his white shirt. He bit his lips in sharp pain, stifling tears.

She visited him again the following month on a detour from a business convention in Baltimore, bringing, of all imaginative treasures, cherries, for Don the canary. But then she was gone again and they were back to their steamy letters, Chapin writing cryptically of a "fountain pen"—a hoped-for pardon that would set him free to sail the seas with his Captain.

With his fifth anniversary in Sing Sing, Lawes had been there longer than many of his predecessors. The prisoners chipped in to present him with a gold charm, and the Elks gave him a gold ring. That five years in the job would set a modern record testified to the mess Lawes had inherited.

In November 1925, he traveled to Jackson, Mississippi, to the congress of the American Prison Association. He was crossing the lobby of the Edwards House, where the congress was being held, when he heard himself being hailed. He looked up to see B. Ogden Chisolm, the prison reformer who had first sounded the alarm on the censorship of the *Bulletin* and had always supported Lawes, and who had since been appointed by President Calvin Coolidge to be the nation's delegate to the International Prison Commission. Chisolm, beckoning from the top of the stairs, was with an attractive young woman. Lawes started up and they met halfway.

"Lewis," Chisolm said, "I've just been telling my young cousin that I want her to meet the best mind in the field of penology today." Chisolm introduced her as Elise Chisholm—her family spelled the name slightly differently. She was covering the congress for the *Jackson Daily News*. They exchanged pleasantries, Lawes smiling at the unfamiliar cadences of her southern inflection and struck too by the intensity of her gaze, which made him think she was searching for something, or someone.

19

Wallack's Theater on West Forty-second Street was packed with close to a thousand people, drawn by the topic of discussion—death—and a quartet of noted speakers. With the legislature about to receive a new bill to outlaw the death penalty, the program that night in January 1926 was a mass meeting called by the newly formed League to Abolish Capital Punishment. Peculiarly enough, less than a year before in the same theater, an actor looking for a prop had picked up the wrong pistol—a loaded one belonging to the stage carpenter—and shot a fellow actor through the arm, barely missing the star, Shirley Booth.

Now, leading the discussion were Lawes and the renowned criminal lawyer Clarence Darrow, famed for his defense in the Scopes monkey trial in Tennessee the year before and his lifesaving representation of the teenage thrill killers Nathan Leopold and Richard Loeb the year before that. Darrow's dashing associate Dudley Field Malone, as debonair as Darrow was rumpled, was also on the program, along with the elegant Kathleen Norris, prolific novelist, campaigner for women's rights, and sister-in-law of the muckraker Frank Norris.

Lawes was in fighting trim. Just weeks before, the *Brooklyn Daily Times* had printed the comments of the county judge Franklin Taylor accusing Lawes once again of coddling prisoners and running an institution where prisoners with money hired valets and purchased their meals from a caterer and where convicts actually "slap the warden on the back and call him 'Lew.'"

Indignant, Lawes had fired back with a letter to the editor. Convicts were as likely to slap him on the back and call him Lew as prisoners in the judge's court were likely to slap him on the back and call him Frank. As for the claim that Sing Sing was a preserve of the criminal aristocracy, it was as ridiculous as the judge's other misapprehensions, and Lawes invited Taylor to come to Sing Sing and see for himself.

Now his crusade against capital punishment was taking on a high new visibility in a Times Square theater.

When society took a life, said Norris in the evening's first address, it brutalized itself, shocking the finer feelings of the civilized. Crime, she said, should not be punished as much as treated like disease. She was getting a hundred letters a day from women opposing capital punishment—almost none supported it. Following her, Malone, a superb orator whose "duel to the death" speech at the Scopes trial had evoked the most thunderous ovation of all, called legal slaying barbarous. Two wrongs, he argued, could never make a right. Lawes spoke from his experience at Sing Sing. State killing was worse than wrong, he said, it was futile. The only effective deterrent to crime was the certainty, not the severity, of punishment.

Then Darrow, a lank strand of hair falling over his furrowed brow, rose to speak, to a roar of approbation. Twenty years Lawes's senior, he was a particularly forceful foe of the death penalty. Growing up in Kinsman, Ohio, son of the village undertaker and coffin maker, he had always been repulsed by death. But he was also an independent spirit, always ornery. As a progressive young lawyer in Chicago, he quit representing the railroad to defend the railroad union leader, Eugene V. Debs, "the bravest man I know." He had successfully defended Big Bill Haywood and other miners accused of assassinating the governor of Idaho, had helped Leopold and Loeb escape the noose for the admitted murder of fourteen-year-old Bobby Franks, and had "won" the Scopes trial with a daring admission of guilt, drawing a mere hundred-dollar fine.

Many knew his epigrams:

"The state doesn't punish for protection but because it gives men pleasure to know that others suffer."

"When governments prepare for war the first unit they mobilize is the liars brigade."

"I have never killed anyone, but I have read some obit notices with great satisfaction."

Everyone was a potential murderer, Darrow told the spellbound crowd. He himself did not kill, he said drolly, because it was not his "habit." It was society's task to remove the causes of bad habits, like faulty education. Murder, he said, was generally committed for two reasons: to escape apprehension after a burglary or robbery, or to vent hatred in a love affair gone wrong. Capital punishment was no deterrent in the first instance, though education was. And absolutely nothing would deter killing in the throes of thwarted passion.

After the Wallack's rally, Lawes and Darrow left for Washington to carry their case to the House Judiciary Committee. The District of Columbia had an electric chair but no funds to operate it, and Lawes and Darrow meant to keep it that way.

Two months later, Lawes and other allies were up in Albany lobbying for a bill to abolish the death penalty. "Murderers may fear death," said Lawes, "yet we have to watch them day and night to prevent them from doing what the state will do in a few days." He ran through his statistics: the last five years had brought almost 2,200 homicides, yet only 63 convicted killers went to the chair. Where was the certainty or deterrent effect in that?

The legislature, however, was not only disinclined to outlaw the chair, but was also on the rampage against lawlessness. In July 1926 it passed a package of criminal laws named for its sponsor, Caleb Howard Baumes, an austere and mustachioed Republican from the Hudson River city of Newburgh. The measures, one newspaper rhapsodized, "cemented the crevices in the Penal Code through which every artful lawyer sought to draw to freedom those depredators whose purses could be sapped." The Baumes laws provided for a bureau of criminal identification to help catch offenders, and collective trials for accomplices. Convictions not appealed within thirty days and argued within ninety days were irreversible. Sentences for armed burglary and robbery were increased to fifteen years from ten. And, in the most radical new provision, anyone convicted of a fourth felony was deemed a habitual criminal with an automatic sentence of life in prison.

It was everything Lawes abhorred—removing all discretion from judges, parole boards, and penal officials—and there was nothing he could do but hope that it wouldn't quickly jam Sing Sing beyond capacity.

Baumes insisted he was a man of compassion. "I wouldn't want the public to think I was a cruel, hard-hearted individual," he told the *New York Herald Tribune* Sunday magazine. "I'm not. I think I have as much mercy as the average man. In fact, I think I have more. But, after I began to investigate the laws, I found they were woefully weak, and their administration woefully lax."

The Baumes laws soon created havoc, filling the prisons with lifers and falling most harshly on the shoulders of blacks, who had disproportionately high felony convictions, albeit often for nonviolent offenses like gambling. One of the first ensnared was a black man fond of drink and taking rides in other people's automobiles. After his fourth conviction, he went to prison for life. The sentencing judge felt awful. "You do not seem to be of a vicious nature," he said. But his hands were tied.

Judge Taylor, who not long before had accused Lawes of coddling criminals, accepted the guilty plea of a black truck driver who had admitted to pocketing $116 he had collected for his employer, the large sum proving too great a temptation. His boss had accepted his apology and offered to overlook the theft, but the judge sentenced him to three years. Upon the prisoner's arrival at Sing Sing, he was found to have three previous convictions for stealing small sums and was returned to court to be resentenced to life.

As it happened, Sing Sing's executioner chose then to announce that he had retired. John Hulbert, the electrician at Auburn who had had presided over Sing Sing's electric chair since 1913, pulling the switch on 140 death row prisoners, gave notice that he intended to seek his pension. "I got tired of killing people," he said. He was only the state's third electrocutioner since 1891. His immediate predecessor, Edward Davis, had resigned after the state cut his fee from $250 to $50 per execution. The first electrocutioner, R. S. McNeal, dispatched five men and a woman for $100 before dropping dead himself in Auburn Prison.

The identity of Hulbert's successor, paid $150 per execution, was a mystery. Clearly someone had been hired, because the electrocutions went on, but his identity remained secret.

The *Brooklyn Eagle* smoked him out. He was somewhere between forty and sixty, mild-mannered, gray-haired, cadaverous and lanky like Abe Lincoln, and lived with his wife and four children in Queens. The paper learned his identity but agreed to keep it quiet, as long as "Mr. X" answered questions.

Yes, he was an executioner, in New Jersey, Pennsylvania, and Massachusetts as well as New York, though he wouldn't be a hangman. "That's too brutal. Electrocution is as humane as the thing can be done. It's over in an instant." He snapped his fingers.

"I didn't ask for the job and I would pass it up now if someone came along who was qualified," he said. "But somebody has to do it and it has to be done right."

Didn't it make him nervous?

No, he had good nerves. "A nervous, excitable man could never do it. I have to attach the electrodes to the skin and the top of the head and I have to get everything just right. It has to be done quickly, too, and I have to make sure that all the other officials are clear of the chair when I throw the switch."

"Does it bother you afterward?" the reporter wondered.

"It hasn't yet."

Bad dreams?

"No, I've always been careful what I ate."

But what if, the reporter persisted, the man he executed turned out to be innocent?

"Well, I would feel pretty bad, of course, but I would know that it hadn't been my fault."

He believed in capital punishment, he stressed. "People who don't believe in it forget the man the murderer killed."

Stung by the *Brooklyn Eagle*'s scoop, other papers quickly exposed Mr. X as Robert Elliott, a pipe-smoking, banjo-playing, Bible-reading family man with a little fox terrier.

The invasive coverage stunned him. Until then, his fifteen-year-old daughter didn't know he killed for a living. Now, he feared, her life might be ruined. He begged the papers not to print his photo.

As if it were all too much for a reform-minded penologist, Thomas Mott Osborne, the towering progressive who had triumphed over scandal, collapsed and died at age sixty-seven on the street in his native Auburn, where more than twenty years before he had served as mayor. After his ordeal at Sing Sing, he had commanded the naval prison in Portsmouth, New Hampshire, and retired in 1920.

Given the uproar he had aroused in life, his end was fittingly byzantine. At first no one recognized his body, and he carried no identification. But beneath the false whiskers, a set of false teeth cleverly fitted over the real ones, and a milky glass eye, the dead man was eventually determined to be Osborne. Precisely why he was so disguised no one ever knew, but friends said he always liked dressing up, from his days on the amateur stage and his undercover forays among the hoboes and in the dives of Auburn.

Was that to be his fate as well? Lawes wondered. In darker moments he fantasized about leaving Sing Sing and starting anew somewhere else, where Kathryn and the girls could live a normal life. But what would he do? Somehow, the insurance business had always appealed to him. He enjoyed talking to people, and helping them secure their future was a worthy endeavor, perhaps not too far afield from protecting society from the scourge of crime. He had run into a congenial insurance broker, Monroe Flegenheimer, in the business since 1912, and they had talked about it. Lawes was tempted.

20

By the fall of 1925, the wheels had come off Chapin's roller-coaster romance with Constance.

His privileged standing at Sing Sing had long included the indenture of Larry, a fellow prisoner and manservant who cooked for him, handled secretarial chores, and pressed his clothes. It was Larry who furbished an aerie for Chapin in a greenhouse in the rose garden, hanging Don's cage and clearing a space in a bower Chapin called the Roserie where the great man could partake of his meals far from the rabble in the mess. Larry, who had pored over cookbooks to study the French culinary arts, adorned the table with Chapin's own roses and orchids and prepared hors d'oeuvre and terrapin, asparagus, strawberries and sorbets with petits fours. After dinner, as strutting peacocks enlivened the view, Larry served coffee and cigars, supplied by Chapin's many well-placed friends on the outside.

After Constance's two lovelorn visits in 1924, she made a third the following year after hearing he had been hospitalized with the grippe. "Oh, honey," he had written, "I'm so tired and lonesome—so sick and sad." Constance, frantic with worry, borrowed a hundred dollars from a friend and caught the next train from Cleveland. She spent a few hours at his bedside, then rushed back home.

Larry, meanwhile, had received news of his impending discharge. His first thought was of Chapin. Who would catalog his library and prepare his crêpes suzettes? Chapin was cavalier. "Don't be a fool, Larry." The warden would soon supply him another man.

Larry stopped by the prison tailor shop to be issued a cheap suit, collected ten dollars at the front office, and stepped through the open gate to be re-sprung on an indifferent world. Several weeks later, he had found a job as a clerk in a small summer hotel on Lake Erie. But rather than feeling lucky, he was down. He had enjoyed serving Chapin but hated working for hotel guests. He knew of only one person he could call, and he did. Perhaps she would remember him, he said. He was a friend of Chapin's.

Constance thought she recognized the voice and invited him to her bank office in Cleveland. There she remembered all the care Larry had lavished on Chapin and sought to reciprocate. She found him a room, gave him money for clothes, lent him a hundred dollars, and found him a tutoring job. Things were looking up for Larry.

Somehow, without either of them telling Chapin, he heard about it and leaped to a furious conclusion. Insanely jealous, he fired off a letter to Constance demanding an explanation and quoting, ironically, Othello: "I had rather be a toad and live upon the vapors of a dungeon than keep a corner of the thing I love for others' uses." If he saw her as guilty as Desdemona, he had grievously misread his Shakespeare.

Constance dropped everything and rushed once more back to Sing Sing. Chapin refused to see her.

She took a room at a nearby inn and returned to the prison, insisting he see her. They met in the warden's office, where she told him she had only be-friended Larry to please Chapin.

He chewed on a mangled cigar and ranted, "The young pup! I'll have his ears cut off!" He shouted down her protestations until she turned on her heels and left. Back at the inn, she sent a note asking again that she be al-lowed to explain. She said that if she did not hear from him by the next day she would leave and never return.

By morning she had not heard, and she called Kathryn, asking if she'd had any word from him. Kathryn had not. "He's hard as nails," Kathryn re-ported. It was like when he first arrived.

"And there's nothing I can do?" Constance pleaded.

"Nothing, my dear. The man's beside himself and there's no use talking."

Still, Constance—true to her name—persevered. From Cleveland, she barraged him with letters and books and a short story about a faithful love that would not be quenched.

He grudgingly answered after a month. "Very interesting," was his reaction to the story—it was, he noted dryly, fiction after all. He added a sour P.S.: "Has it ever occurred to you, my dear, that Jealousy is the very cornerstone of affection? When Jealousy flies out the window it usually takes love along with it for company."

Their correspondence resumed, sometimes even with a spark of passion. Once, in the spring of 1926, she made plans again to visit Sing Sing, but she fell ill in Boston and canceled the trip.

Fellow prisoners knew little of Chapin's heartbreak. Indeed, the Sing Sing aristocrat sparked envy or contempt in many, among them a twenty-five-year-old Brooklyn hustler renowned for an impressive but obviously imperfect career of relieving merchants of excess cash and jewels. His name was William Francis Sutton Jr.—Willie for short—and he had arrived in Sing Sing for a prison stay of five to ten years for attempting an unauthorized withdrawal from the safe of the Ozone Park National Bank.

Sutton, henceforth no. 84599, took one look around Sing Sing and decided he didn't like it very much. They shaved his head and distinctive pencil-line mustache, had him strip, painted his body blue with delousing disinfectant, and issued him itchy wool clothes. His dim and airless cell was so narrow he had to enter it sideways. The jagged rock of the walls stuck out like daggers. But accommodations could be made, Sutton soon found. The visiting rules were fairly lax and could be made more relaxed by discreet deposits of five dollars on the guard's desk. The prison tailor did a good business in custom uniforms, lighter and better-fitting than the crude issued clothing. Officially everyone ate in the mess hall, but in practice, the commissary did a brisk business, and many prisoners feasted on delicacies prepared in a cookhouse and consumed in the rec hall, where the inmates had created a more convivial clubhouse with their own utensils and comestibles. Sutton was certain Lawes knew all this—how could he not?—and allowed it as a way of easing the harsh prison regimen. Hadn't Lawes given his blessing, too, to the Mutual Welfare League that governed the prisoners through the two-party system, the Democratic Party and the Cheese Party? Exactly how much Lawes knew of the cronyism that might have made Tammany blush, Sutton wasn't sure. Lawes was away a lot making speeches, leaving Sing Sing in the hands of distracted or crooked deputies, so there were payoffs and gambling and, if you had the clout of a Brindell, off-site visits with your family. The good part of it, Sutton reflected, was that he didn't have to worry about getting killed in a prison riot. The leaders were not about to sanction a riot. They had it too good.

And no one had it better than Chapin, who still had the run of the prison, where he played host to celebrity moviemakers and former newspaper colleagues like Irvin Cobb, and took trips outside the walls with Kathryn Lawes to buy plants and nursery supplies. Sutton had quickly sized up the situation, made the right friends, and landed a job in the four greenhouses under Chapin, one of a landscape army of thirty that now planted shrubs and manicured the grounds as slavishly as the reporters once sweated for Chapin in the newsroom. Sutton puzzled over the strange hold Chapin seemed to exercise over Lawes and Kathryn and thought he understood. He decided Chapin must be ghosting Lawes's books and articles. Sutton labored for Chapin for three months and then got the bad news. Sing Sing was overcrowded. He was being shifted upstate, to Dannemora.

21

Sutton was right about one thing—Lawes was often away or distracted. He had flirted with the insurance game but had decided, fatefully, to stay at Sing Sing, where he installed a hardwood floor, constructed in the prison shops, spelling out *Humanum Est Errare*. To Err Is Human.

Lawes was out of touch on the July Fourth holiday in 1927 when three boys, canoeing in the choppy, wind-whipped Hudson just off the prison, ran into trouble. A wave slapped the flimsy green craft and it overturned, spilling the boys into the river. They screamed for help.

A thousand prisoners exercising in the yard before lunch sprinted for the fence.

Two of the boys clearly couldn't swim. They grabbed wildly for the canoe, pitching and bucking in the waves. The third boy struggled to reach the shore, but he was tiring fast.

One prisoner started to scale the fence. "I can swim!" he screamed. "For God's sake let me help them!"

A guard ran forward, aiming his rifle. "Stand back! I'll shoot the first man who tries to climb that fence."

The men fell back. Then—a collective gasp. One of the boys gripping the canoe lost his hold and slipped beneath the water.

"One's gone!" a prisoner shouted. "You've let one of them drown!"

More guards had trotted up, fingering their rifles. "Get back there—back," said one. "Or we'll shoot."

The men were hysterical now, cursing and leaping up and down in horrified frustration as the boy trying to swim disappeared and then the last boy flailing for the boat sank out of sight barely five yards from the end of the Sing Sing dock. Men ran over the grounds trying to find Lawes.

The din faded to a stunned and awful silence. Lawes was soon located, but it was too late. The boys were lost.

For the holiday, a chicken dinner—a rare treat—was laid out, but it went untouched. No prisoner would eat.

Lawes, grim-faced, said the guards were technically right. No one but he had the authority to let prisoners out. And there had been too many occasions when prisoners took advantage of a distraction to escape. But this, he added, was a case of common sense and humanity—he would never have disciplined a guard who allowed men out to save the lives of three struggling children. "The right kind of man," he said, "would risk his job to save a human life."

The prisoners were the heroes, the press decided. The villain was the system.

The macabre episode threw the spotlight once more on Sing Sing, already a major sight-seeing attraction. Some days as many as three thousand visitors streamed in for tours, giving Lawes a prominent showcase for his progressive penal policies but distracting him from his duties. Many visitors were celebrities, very important people, whom the prisoners had been calling VIPs since the days Charlie Chaplin and Harry Houdini came to visit. Just recently, after Houdini's untimely death from an unexpected punch that ruptured his appendix, his widow, Beatrice, had sent Lawes a rare treasure, thirty of her husband's books on magic.

Often the visitors came to see the ball games, which Lawes enthusiastically hosted. Warden William H. Moyer, his most immediate full-time predecessor (Brophy and Grant together having lasted less than a year), had promoted baseball at Sing Sing, as he had previously at the Atlanta Penitentiary, and Lawes had eagerly exploited the opening. He had groomed the field and built the grandstands, and on most weekends teams representing Sing Sing's various workshops played for a cup, to the delight of the VIPs, visiting family members, and tourists. Elsewhere, prisoners played handball and, on a miniature course, wielded sticks to coax small white balls into holes, confounding one visiting prosecutor. "I'll be goddamned," he said, "they're even playing golf." And why not? Lawes retorted. Squire had recommended it and the men had built the little green themselves. Older, out-of-shape prisoners needed their exercise too.

Cartoonists chuckled and went to work. *What? No caddies?* Lawes shrugged. They could laugh. At least society was getting a new view of prisons. Besides, he had long since come to appreciate the value of publicity, even negative publicity—if there was such a thing.

He had created a clipping department at Sing Sing, subscribing to various services that scoured the nation's newspapers and magazines for articles on him, Sing Sing, other prisons, and crime and punishment around the world, especially capital punishment. He recruited a literate staff to organize the clippings and paste them into large scrapbooks by topic—lynchings in the South, suicides, executions, and "potentials," capital crimes likely to land their perpetrators in the Sing Sing death house. The project was put under the capable direction of a newsman serving a stretch for rape.

The scrapbooks were precious to Lawes. He could see how his work was being perceived and how crime was trending nationwide. This was crucial because, along with his speeches and articles, he was working on his second book, this one for Doubleday Doran and Company, for a handsome advance of fifteen hundred dollars. If Chapin or anyone else was helping him, it was a well-kept secret.

Meanwhile, too, he kept turning out magazine articles heavy on facts. Since the state had adopted electrocution for murder in 1889, he wrote in *The Survey*, 409 men and six women had been sent to Sing Sing for execution. Of these, 261 men and one woman had actually been electrocuted. The convictions of 53 men and two women had been reversed, resulting in thirty acquittals. Eighteen others had been reconvicted but on lesser charges. How many others, Lawes wondered, might have been spared with better lawyers? It was largely common sense, he argued. Fifty years before, the foreign-born Irish had led in murders, with Germans and Italians next. Then the Italians took the lead, with Irish second and Negroes third. Italians still led, but Negroes had dropped to second. "In other words," he wrote, "the typical murderer of any given period comes from that race which is making a place for itself in a new environment."

His new book, *Life and Death in Sing Sing*, carried a foreword by philanthropist and reformer Adolph Lewisohn. Lawes's first book, published three years earlier, had focused on the death penalty, but the new one was broader, on crime in general—the theme of more books, Lawes noted, than perhaps any other subject but love. Yet although everyone talked about crime, little was known about it, despite the fact that the nation's prison population was about 125,000, the same size as the army. No fewer than fifteen million Americans had spent some time behind bars. Yet amazingly, no one could agree on the cause or causes of this stupendous amount of crime. There had been books written from the so-called front of the problem by sociologists, from the back by jurists, and from the bottom by prisoners themselves. This was to be a book written from the inside by someone who really *knew*.

Lawes began provocatively. Crime was relative, subjective, and ancient. Anyone who read the Bible knew that Cain murdered his brother, Abel; Abraham married his half sister and fathered children with his wife's maid-servant; Lot committed incest with his daughters; Jacob conspired with his mother to defraud his brother; Solomon was a polygamist; and David committed adultery with Bathsheba, wife of Uriah the Hittite. More recently, George Washington bootlegged his own beer and whiskey, Thomas Jefferson traded in slaves, General Grant trafficked in liquor with General Sherman, Grover Cleveland caught fifty-seven bass, and Teddy Roosevelt shot more than a hundred ducks in a day—none of which were crimes when they were committed, but all of which were when Lawes was writing.

You could keep all Ten Commandments and commit a hundred crimes or violate six commandments and commit no crime.

Before the Civil War, to help a slave escape to Canada was a crime but not a sin. To fish on Sunday was a sin but not a crime. How many people knew that it was a federal crime to write a check for less than a dollar, punishable by up to six months in prison?

A burglar in New York could get fifteen years in prison, a rapist one year. In Texas, the rapist could get death, the burglar two years. In New Jersey, the adulterer was a felon; in New York, a misdemeanant.

So what was crime? Just acts that violated the law.

And what was law? Whatever a bunch of legislators bullied by small-minded merchants and farmers said it was. The laws they passed were often so ambiguous that it took the Supreme Court of the United States to decide what they meant—and even then the justices were often split.

Who were the criminals? According to one New York judge, anyone with a receding chin, protruding jaw, wide stare, left eyelid droop, low and bumpy brow, thick hair, and ears jutting perpendicularly to the head. Lawes could think of a university president, a great English preacher, a Russian states-man, a leading Spanish writer, and a world-renowned inventor, not to speak of many of the judge's fellow jurists, who exhibited many if not all of those traits. The criminal, Lawes concluded, was Everyman. Goethe himself had written that he had never heard of a crime that he could not imagine com-mitting. Even the bluest of blue bloods could not trace his ancestry too far back without encountering a prison or a gallows.

He analyzed the Sing Sing population, highly representative, since the prison in its first century received almost three-fourths of the felons locked up in the state, drawing from an area with roughly one-twentieth of the na-tion's population. New York–born whites committed far more than their proportional share of robberies. On the other hand, whites born outside the city committed far more than their expectable share of forgeries and sex crimes. Blacks born outside New York committed staggeringly high rates of burglaries, assaults, and homicides—far more than city-born blacks. So the crime problem was hardly a simple matter of race.

Youths committed far more than their proportional share of robberies. Illiterates committed more than three times their proportional share of as-saults, homicides, and sex crimes. The highly educated dominated in forger-ies and larcenies.

Policemen and preachers committed a disproportionate share of sex crimes.

Was crime the willful resort of the lazy? More than 80 percent of those in for assault or murder were willing workers with jobs.

Were repeat criminals a major cause of the crime problem? Yes—for lar-ceny, forgery, and burglary. No for sex crimes, robbery, assault, and murder.

Did crime pay? Based on the illicit gains and the time he served when caught, the average robber's enterprise earned him $1.30 a year.

Escapes? Eighteen men had gone over the wall since Lawes took over in 1920, but only three were still at large. One long ago had died in his hiding place inside the prison. His skeleton was found years later. Another had con-structed decoy ducks attached to rubber tubes, made it over the fence to the Hudson, floated the ducks on the surface, and, swimming underwater and breathing through the tubes, made his getaway, although he was soon recap-tured. In a feat worthy of Houdini, two other prisoners seemed to have van-ished into thin air.

"Discipline" was a word derived from "disciple," Lawes wrote. It did not mean harsh treatment. Harshly treated pupils didn't learn. The object of prison was not to chop the hands off a pickpocket so he would forever be a burden on society but to teach him to use his hands to earn an honest living.

But for all the theorizing in his book, Lawes sometimes guessed wrong. Christmastime brought the return to Sing Sing of a jolly and familiar face, that of Pidge Hoolahan, the piccolo player released just three years before as Father Cashin was retiring.

Back again! Lawes scolded, secretly ashamed at his delight at seeing Pidge again, whatever the circumstances. Lawes asked what happened.

It was like in the Bible, Pidge said. "I fell in among thieves," sax players to be precise. As an alumnus, he skipped many of the admission formalities. His prints and photo were already on file. He received a new number and ritually surrendered his piccolo to the guards, rejoining his cheering bandmates. Lawes made a ceremonial gesture of restoring Pidge's piccolo to him and soon the strains of "Good King Wenceslas," with piccolo variations, were enlivening the holiday preparations.

22

Nineteen twenty-eight rolled in with death in the rumble seat. Waiting in the execution cells were the adulterous lovers Ruth Snyder and Judd Gray. Their last date, with the chair, was imminent.

Blond and light-blue-eyed Ruth Brown had been a nineteen-year-old telephone operator at *Cosmopolitan* magazine in 1917, the year America went Over There, when she met Albert Snyder, a rugged-faced artist for the women's monthly. They courted and married, living well in Queens, sailing on Jamaica Bay and raising their baby daughter, Lorraine. But Ruth, a fleshy beauty, had a roving eye, and in June 1925 she met a thirty-three-year-old married New Jersey corset salesman, Henry Judd Gray, handsome and sensuous with an intellectual's high forehead, curly black hair, and bookish horn-rimmed glasses. He fitted her for a girdle, and then took it off.

They pursued their illicit romance for almost two years, until the spring morning young Lorraine came upon her mother bound and gagged, and frantic beyond words over the fate of her dear husband Albert, who was soon found quite dead under a pile of bloody bedclothes. He had been bashed in the head with a heavy object. Picture wire constricted his throat and chloroformed cotton filled his nostrils. He had taken a ghastly long time to die. All Ruth Snyder could remember, she told the police, was that she had been seized by intruders evidently bent on burglary. Her gems and a fur were missing.

But strangely, there was no sign of forced entry, and the loot was soon found under her mattress, where thieves were unlikely to have stashed it. It further emerged that Snyder had taken out a fifty-thousand-dollar life insurance policy on Albert, with double indemnity in the event of a violent death. And little Lorraine remembered an Uncle Judd who visited when her father was away. It was ridiculously easy for the police.

Snyder soon turned against her paramour, blaming him as the mastermind. Gray, tracked down in Syracuse, offered an alibi, but detectives found a shredded train ticket from New York in his trash. Arrested and escorted back to New York, he tried to swallow poison but was restrained. Then he admitted everything. He and Snyder had jointly plotted and carried out Albert's murder.

She denied it, blaming Gray. But who, if not she, detectives wondered, had unlatched the door for the supposed interloper to enter? And why had she not come to her husband's aid as Gray was pummeling Albert to death with a sash weight? And, worst of all, as Gray had alleged, hadn't she tried to kill her husband with poison and other means at least *eight times* before the fatal attack?

Less than a month after the killing they were both on trial. The jury took less than two hours to find both guilty, and they were quickly sentenced to death.

Sing Sing had not executed a woman in nearly three decades, not since Alfred Conyes had gallantly escorted Martha Place to the chair as its first female victim. Auburn had electrocuted Mary Farmer in 1909 for killing a neighbor, but executing a woman remained a rare sensation, and now the frenzy of the yellow press knew no bounds. Lawes's scrapbook squad scrambled to keep up with the screaming black headlines, and even the stray mutts, chickens, parrot, and goat that roamed the Sing Sing grounds could not escape the relentless coverage. The papers printed photographs of the creatures as the supposed playmates of the doomed lovers.

From the moment the pair arrived in mid-1927, reporters descended on Sing Sing clamoring for interviews. Lawes's phone rang incessantly, and two low-flying planes with photographers nearly collided over the prison. The hoopla was manna for eager commentators: the Baptist hellfire preacher John Roach Stratton, who had championed the Bible in the Scopes monkey trial; moviemaker D. W. Griffith; the zany physical culturist and inventor of the tabloid, Bernarr Macfadden; the brainy philosopher Will Durant; and the master scribes Ben Hecht, Damon Runyan, and James L. Kilgallen, father of a fifteen-year-old budding journalist named Dorothy. Many recalled other femmes fatales in eras past who had yielded their lives to the hangman, and recounted their lurid crimes, or supposed crimes, for some of them had been quite possibly innocent. Outside the walls, meanwhile, the roads to the prison were clogged with curiosity seekers, balloon sellers, and ice-cream vendors.

Lawes was repulsed by the circus; the prisoners more so. It was all right somehow to fry a man, but a woman? Their rage boiled over one day in the mess hall, when the beans seemed particularly inedible. There were cries for a strike as the men filed out, plates untouched, to return to their work. Lawes toured the shops, declaring work halted for the day, hoping that the men would remember his efforts against capital punishment.

But in the mattress shop he found himself encircled. From the back, a voice rang out. "You killer! You son of a bitch!"

Lawes turned scarlet. He stood his ground and put up his fists. "If the man who said that has any guts, he'll step up and repeat that to my face." Forget he was the warden, he ordered. They would settle it man to man.

No one moved. Then there was a rumbling murmur, and the circle parted, offering him a path out. He took it.

As Snyder and Gray waited in the death house, executions continued like the drumroll before a particularly spectacular high-wire stunt. William Wagner, a twenty-four-year-old convicted murderer from Brooklyn, went to the chair in July confiding that Wagner was not his real name. He didn't want his relatives in Germany to be disgraced. As he passed in the corridor, Gray reached through the bars and patted him on the back, saying, "Keep up your courage."

Snyder shunned everyone, preferring to remain in the rear of her cell, eyes averted. She had hoped that Governor Smith's political ambitions would keep him from executing a woman, certainly a woman as prominent as she, but she was fast losing hope.

The next to go, Peter J. Heslin, twenty-eight, convicted of killing a patrolman during a holdup, maintained his innocence and politely refused a farewell handshake with Snyder and Gray or any other of the condemned. "They are feeling badly enough without me making it worse by saying good-bye," he said. Then came Charles Albrecht, a thirty-three-year-old child-killer who said he had been "crazy drunk" and just wanted to scare the child's mother. Again, Gray was the last to say good-bye. In December, Peter A. Seiler, twenty-two, also convicted of killing a policeman during a robbery, and George Ricci, thirty-three, convicted of killing his boss, a wealthy

Brooklyn contractor, took their final hand-shaking tour. Gray pumped their arms encouragingly but said nothing. He was tired of seeing his words in the paper the next day. Oddly, their appointment with the chair was delayed two hours to allow guards and prisoners to watch an eagerly awaited Sing Sing revival of a 1924 Gershwin show, *Sweet Little Devil*.

Finally, Seiler stood before the chair, gazed at the witnesses, and read a brief statement beginning, "Gentlemen, you are about to see an innocent man die." The appeals court had recommended a change in the law that had convicted him, he said. That didn't do him any good but perhaps it would help someone else. Minutes later he was dead. Ricci followed without a word.

In early January, two upstate men, twenty-four-year-old Louis Mason and twenty-five-year-old Charles J. Doran, convicted in separate robbery-murders and claiming they had been double-crossed by their co-defendants, took their long last walk, once again shaking Gray's hand.

Then came January 12, the day set for Gray and Snyder to die.

Snyder's priest and lawyers were her last visitors. They didn't know what to say, so they mostly said nothing.

She told them not to feel bad and then began sobbing. "I am ready to die. Oh, my poor baby Lorraine. And my dear, dear mother. Please tell them I forgive everybody, that I hold no malice against anybody in the world."

The great James Kilgallen was in the chamber for William Randolph Hearst's International News Service. In the blindingly white room at precisely 11:01 p.m., there was a rap at the door under the sign that read, ominously, "Silence."

In walked Father McCaffrey reciting the Litany, followed by Snyder supported by two matrons and a guard. She wore brown felt slippers, a brown smock over a knee-length black calico skirt, and black cotton stockings, the right rolled down to the ankle to accommodate the leg electrode. Even from a distance, her light blue eyes glittered. Her strong chin trembled, though she struggled to hold it high, and her delicate lips quivered. Her blond hair was bobbed in the latest flapper fashion and in the light it looked slick, perhaps pomaded. But in the back a naked patch of scalp showed where the hair had been shorn for the head electrode.

As she dropped into the chair with its thick oaken arms, straps, and buckles she broke down and wept, clutching a crucifix and crying in a high-pitched and tremulous voice, "Jesus have mercy on me, for I have sinned."

There was no other sound.

Quickly, guards pulled a horizontally slit black mask over her face, the top covering her forehead and bridge of the nose, the bottom her chin. They pressed a leather football helmet over her head, securing the top electrode. One of the matrons stepped aside, holding a handkerchief to her face and sobbing.

The guards nimbly buckled the straps across her ample chest and trembling knees.

She was still weeping. "Jesus have mercy."

Robert Elliott, the executioner, gaunt and expressionless, stepped into an alcove to the side of the chair. Nearby stood the physician, Dr. C. C. Sweet, with one of Chapin's white roses threaded through his buttonhole.

Lawes stood by the rear door, looking away. Earlier he had summoned the press to his office to go over the rules. It went without saying, of course, that there were to be no cameras. He was sure they knew how to conduct themselves with dignity, although the histrionics of the last few days had been beyond all imagining, with one paper printing the fantastic notion that after her execution Snyder would be revived with adrenaline to appear on the stage for a million dollars. Hearst's *Daily Mirror, American,* and *Cosmopolitan* had even begun competing to sign her to exclusive postmortem contracts. The facts were, Lawes said, that she had entrusted him with some last letters for her mother, and that Gray had asked that his Bible be sent to his mother. He answered a few questions, saying that neither of the two had asked for or would receive a sedative, since it was against the rules. He would be in the room but would not watch, he told them. He never did.

One strange fellow no one recognized conspicuously clutched a pad and pencil and declined a chair, insisting on remaining standing. Then Lawes said, "The hour has come," and escorted them to the chamber.

Snyder had stopped crying. The room was frighteningly still. A matron stood in front of the chair, blocking some witnesses' views, but she suddenly swooned and was carried out by the guards.

A bell tinkled. Elliott threw the switch.

A crackle of electricity sizzled through the masked form. Snyder's body lurched forward, straining against the thick straps, then fell back. The mask had slipped and below it her forehead glowed bright red, the same crimson hue as her bare right leg.

There was another ferocious sizzle and sputter. Then a third. The body was limp.

Sweet stepped forward, unbuttoned her smock, extended his stethoscope, and listened. "I declare this woman dead," he said.

Kilgallen looked at his watch. It was nine minutes past eleven.

Snyder's body was released from the restraints and lifted onto a porcelain-topped gurney. An attendant held up a towel to block the witnesses' views of her bare leg, but not quickly enough to hide the dripping perspiration and an angry coin-size burn mark on her shapely calf. Her arms hung limply, her mouth was agape, her eyes were shut. She was wheeled away for autopsy, the 167th victim of the Sing Sing chair.

Five minutes later, there was another rap on the door. Gray shuffled in on gray slippers, preceded by a Protestant chaplain intoning the Beatitudes. He wore a gray suit with the right trouser leg slit from the knee down. A hand-kerchief spilled debonairly from his breast pocket. He was not wearing his glasses. His blue eyes were clear. His black hair was neatly combed.

He seated himself resolutely in the chair, raising his eyes to the ceiling and moving his lips in an inaudible prayer. He let the mask and helmet be attached and sat stoically as the straps were fastened.

Once again Elliott stepped to the alcove and slammed the switch home.

Gray's body went rigid, his chest heaving. An unnerving puff of smoke curled from his head, and a blue spark crackled wickedly where water from the soaked electrode sponge dripped through the slit pant leg. There was an-other jolt of electricity, then silence, and then once again a sizzling—this time from the steam radiator.

Gray was pronounced dead, and his mask was peeled off to reveal a face suddenly bleached of color, with swollen throat and jaws, and teeth clenched in macabre resistance to his fate. Then his body, too, was carted off for autopsy.

Not all the gentlemen and ladies of the press had abided by Lawes's admonitions. A month before the execution, in fact, the headstrong publisher of the New York Daily News, Captain Joseph Medill Patterson, a war hero whose family had sold its Chicago Tribune, had summoned his managing editor for another strategy session on getting "that picture." They would, of course, have to betray Lawes and violate every standard of taste and decency. But the *Daily News*, locked in a circulation war with Hearst's *Daily Mirror*, wasn't about to miss the greatest scoop of modern times.

For weeks now, Tom Howard, a photographer for a *Daily News* syndicate in Chicago and therefore unknown in New York, had been secluded in a hotel room practicing with a one-shot custom miniature camera strapped to his left ankle under his pants cuff and activated by a cable running up his leg to a rubber bulb in his pocket. He had positioned himself approximately where he might be sitting on the witness bench in the death chamber and pointed his left toe toward Patterson sitting where he thought the electric chair would be, and when the prints were rushed through development, they showed what they were supposed to. Still, there was no way of knowing whether the scheme would work when the time came.

Howard had joined the crush of newsmen at Sing Sing, passing himself off as a *Daily News* reporter. He had the fresh pad and pencil to prove it. He nervously chewed aspirin and stepped so gingerly on his left foot that the *Graphic*'s man asked if he had the gout. When the throng filed into the death chamber, he was right behind Lawes and took a front-row seat. For long, terrifying minutes, his view was blocked by a matron, but when she suddenly fainted, he had his clear shot, dramatically from below at floor level.

Lawes had come down to breakfast the next morning and was beginning to go through the papers, the *Times*, as ever, on top, when Cherie reached underneath to grab the papers with the comics. Suddenly she stopped and screamed. The front page of the *Daily News* was black with a huge photo of Snyder in the chair and the headline

DEAD!

Kathryn had to be helped upstairs to the bedroom. Lawes, overcome by a sense of betrayal, was so distraught that the house staff sent urgently for Squire. The doctor prescribed a ten-day rest for both of them in Palm Beach. Lawes checked his list of pending executions. He had a month and a half before the next one.

Kathryn had one final chore before they left for the train. She put all of Snyder's letters, entrusted to her, in the fire.

23

Capital punishment had gotten its most indelible image, one that portrayed the death penalty with hideous specificity. The public no longer had to imagine what legalized killing looked like. It was what opponents like Lawes had been trying to convey all along, that state-sanctioned killing was no abstraction. It was a nauseatingly mundane process of buckling straps and attaching electrodes and standing carefully aside on a rubber mat while electricity boiled a living human brain and cooked the flesh.

Two days after the by-now world-famous execution, with the Laweses recuperating in Florida, Samuel Untermyer, the prominent lawyer who had battled Lawes over the Westall parole bill, took his side against capital punishment in a debate with Senator Love, whom Lawes had bested four years before in a similar radio contest over WEAF. This debate, at the University Club in Brooklyn, had been booked before the Snyder-Gray execution, but now it took on a new immediacy.

Had the pair been given life, Untermyer said, no one would have cared about their fate and the public would have been spared the sordid spectacle of their deaths. It proved anew, he said, that the motive of the state was not to protect society but to exact a "vicious" retribution, the way colonial Puritans danced around the stake where women and children were being burned alive. If the purpose of the death penalty was to strike terror, then restore public hangings, he argued, as Lawes did so regularly. Otherwise, he said, if death was to be retained as the ultimate penalty, let the doomed commit suicide, open his veins and bleed to death in the privacy of his home, as was done in civilized ancient Greece and Rome.

Senator Love fell back on familiar arguments, that prison life was too soft and that only the prospect of death deterred criminals. There was nothing wrong with retribution, he said; "retribution prevents repetition." Nor, Love said, was there anything deliberately brutal or uncivilized about electrocuting or hanging murderers. Did a surgeon desire to inflict pain when he excised a cancer? Besides, if opponents of the death penalty were so concerned for human life, why didn't they protest the truly horrendous number of automobile fatalities?

As revulsion over the excesses of the Snyder-Gray debacle spread, Dean George Kirchwey of Columbia Law School, who had replaced Osborne at Sing Sing, denounced the executions as "an orgy of cruelty and sensationalism." The time would come, Kirchwey prophesied to the Council of Women at the Astor Hotel, "when our children and grandchildren will look back and wonder how we lived under such conditions of savagery."

No less an American icon than Henry Ford had rallied to the abolitionists' banner, hinting darkly that the forces behind the death penalty were "the same crowd of financiers" who had dragged the world into global war a decade before. Given Ford's blatant anti-Semitism, it was not hard to read "financiers" as "Jews," and it was they, he insisted, along with the "ministers and editors," who had perpetrated the propaganda for war and were rooting for capital punishment. "They want to harden the sensibilities of the people, for it serves their ends to have war," Ford declared. As ever, he mixed his paranoia with the down-to-earth practicality of an industrial genius who had put the entire country on wheels. Now, he said, he wouldn't mind giving a man a licking when he needed it, but he drew the line at killing. Killing a man was simply wrong. It did no good to the man or society. Capital punishment was the wrong cure for crime, just as charity was the wrong cure for poverty.

Like Lawes, he took a progressive economic stance toward crime. "If the finances of the country were properly adjusted," he said, "there would be plenty of work for these boys who are committing crimes, and it is my opinion every one of them would work if there was work to do."

John P. Hulbert, the pudgy longtime state executioner who had pulled the switch on Gordon Hamby and had relinquished his post to Robert Elliott two years before, registered his own strong statement on capital punishment. He was found shot to death in the cellar of his home at Auburn. His own .38

revolver, with two bullets mysteriously expended, lay nearby. The coroner somehow ruled it suicide. The executioner's hands had taken their last life.

As Lawes approached his tenth year in Sing Sing (the *New York Herald Tribune* speculating he would soon retire with his pension), he watched the last stages of the prison renovation with impatient satisfaction. It would be finished, he figured, in less than a year, surely by early 1929. Then finally, perhaps, he could persuade the legislature to build him a new house, outside the walls.

From his office in the old prison he could see, crowning the rocky cliff above, the new redbrick cellblock with its twenty-foot-high windows. Those windows would be a godsend for men who had long passed their time in Stygian gloom and had to be sent into the yard as much as possible to get them out of the foul contagion of their wet stone cells. Some lucky fellows—if he could call anyone here lucky—were already housed in the new quarters, high above the damp riverbank. He could see the new chapel, divided inside by removable partitions to accommodate three denominational services, and the hospital with its surgical ward, laboratory, and even a psychiatric clinic. Prisons had too long been viewed as giant holding pens for criminal animals. Now his Psychiatric Department of seven, under Sing Sing's new official psychiatrist, Dr. Amos Baker, would evaluate each man individually and decide on a course of mental and social rehabilitation to prepare him for the day he and almost all his compatriots would surely see, the day they would walk out of the gate and back into so-called normal society.

Ninety percent of the Sing Sing population was cooperative, Lawes told the *New York World*. Traditionally, security and discipline had been dictated by the 10 percent of troublemakers, to the detriment of the good ones who had to conform to the harsher standard set for the difficult minority. But now the troublemakers could be singled out and helped, the others could be treated more maturely, and those found truly insane could be sent to the state hospital at Dannemora.

The evaluation process was constant. At that moment, in fact, Lawes was trying to figure out what to do with a stooped and derelict old-timer making a less-than-triumphal return visit behind bars. George C. Parker was now sixty-eight, a graybeard by Sing Sing standards, although not the most senior—Chapin was seventy. Parker's record went back to the 1880s, when,

as a dapper confidence man with half a dozen aliases, he all but defined the
unbridled metropolis and its wicked ways. It was indeed Parker who had sold
the new Brooklyn Bridge to a gullible visitor from the West for fifty thousand dollars, and four choice lots in City Hall Park to another westerner for
twenty-five thousand dollars. He had recently been arrested in New Jersey
on a forgery complaint and had been wanted on other larceny charges. Convicted as a fourth offender under the Baumes laws, he was packed off to Sing
Sing for life, which in his case promised to be a mercifully short sentence.
Lawes doubted he would prove troublesome.

Life and Death in Sing Sing was out, garnering fine reviews and winning
Lawes more of the publicity he relished. He wanted the attention for his
ideas and his program, but he could hardly deny the healthy share of vanity
that came out in his fastidious tailoring, his eagerness to see his name in
print, and the close attention he gave to the entire business of publishing
and marketing his books. Like all avid authors, he made sure his celebrity acquaintances received autographed books personally from him, so he sent out
copies to Charlie Chaplin, columnist Irvin Cobb, retired Tombs warden
John J. Hanley, the writer Edward Hale Bierstadt, his old mentor Katharine
Bement Davis, and the Ossining newspapers. No fewer than seven copies
went to prison reformer B. Ogden Chisolm.

Davis, retired as parole commissioner and finishing her own book, was
particularly touched by Lawes's inscription crediting her with nurturing his
career. She did indeed take pride in her ability as a "picker" she told him,
and Lawes had more than justified her early faith in his talents. What he had
written about lawmaking, crime, and sentencing, Davis wrote, was so like
what she had always said "that I might have written it myself!"

Hanley too responded warmly. "Without any desire to flatter, permit me
to say, that you have placed your name amongst the immortals." Bierstadt
was only slightly less effusive. He was reviewing the book for *Outlook*, he responded, and before his notice would run, he wanted Lawes to know "that
you have done a sane, fine and courageous piece of work."

For eighteen months, Bierstadt reminded Lawes, he had been Osborne's
liaison to the press at Sing Sing, and now he confided that his loyalty to the
"old regime" had made him suspicious of Lawes. But Osborne had told him:
"No. Lawes is a good man." As usual, Bierstadt went on, he found that

Osborne was right, and he added: "In fact, after all these years, it is probably safe to say that you are a better man for the job than Osborne was. It is seldom safe to leave the pioneer too long in the saddle. The man who breaks the trail needs different qualities from the man who carries the load." Lawes saved the letter, forwarding it with the others to Doubleday's publicist for blurbing in the newspaper and magazine ads.

He also liked to check his displays and sales in various bookstores, indignantly calling his agent, Hamilton Thompson of Service for Authors, when he did not see his book in the Doubleday Doran bookshops in Pennsylvania Station in New York. Doubleday was after all his own publisher. Thompson reminded the store manager that he was dealing here with the warden of Sing Sing Prison and was assured that a full and immediate investigation would follow.

Still, Lawes and his agent grumbled that Doubleday was not doing enough to push the book. After an initial magazine excerpt—a five-part serial in Doubleday's own magazine, *The World's Work*—second serial rights were going unsold, to Lawes's frustration. Thompson was struggling to get *Real Detective Tales* in Chicago to buy a spinoff article by Lawes called "The Death Penalty."

Kathryn often asked Chapin if he had heard again from Constance, and each time he had to admit that no, he had not had a letter for years, although she had sent him some articles on gardening. Chapin occasionally wrote her, though in a more distant way than before. He told her he had suffered a hernia from lifting something too heavy and so was now harnessed in a truss. The doctors had wanted to operate, but Lawes, who had gone through a similar operation himself, counseled Chapin to skip it. Chapin agreed and told the doctors to wait for the autopsy. Don the canary sent his regards to her, and there was more news from the birds. Chapin's feathered family, augmented by gifts from newspaper readers, now numbered 127, necessitating a new aviary he was building near the old morgue. He was especially fond of macaws, whose picky appetites kept him combing his gardens for special grubs. He also fed them egg whites. An interior decorator who appreciated Lawes's sense of humor sent in a parrot, a fearful swearer that filled the prison grounds with squawks of "Goddamn joint! To hell with this place!"

Chapin had been burned again by a woman, he confided to Constance. He provided no clue to her identity but said she had been a frequent visitor until she committed the indiscretion of showing one of Chapin's letters to a reporter and intimating they had plans to wed. That was enough for "the slimy little tabloids" and was the end of that pen pal.

In the spring of 1929 he wrote Constance again. He had been bedridden five weeks with the flu, delirious some days with fever. But he was on the mend. Kathryn, however, had suffered a mishap. In Elmira to visit her mother-in-law, she had stepped out of an automobile and fallen to the street, breaking an ankle. She would be months in a cast. He wrote Constance one more time, when it looked like she might be coming east and could make a stop at Ossining. It would be, he was sure, her last visit to him. He was, he said, already hearing the distant notes of the trumpet summoning him to Glenwood, where Nellie, by his hand, had lain at rest these last ten years. But Constance later wrote from Boston to say she had rerouted herself, skipping Ossining to enjoy the New England scenery.

24

From the relative tranquillity of Sing Sing in the sweltering July of 1929, Lawes read the dispatches with alarm. Up at Dannemora, the bleak Siberia where he had started his career some quarter century before, where he had learned his first practical lessons from the demented Frenchy Menet and wise Old Chappleau, and to which he had dispatched the retrograde Willie Sutton, the thirteen hundred inmates were in revolt, smashing and burning the factory shops and storming the walls to break out. Three Clinton prisoners had been shot dead and a score of others wounded before guards drove them back to their cells with machine guns and shotguns, hand grenades and tear gas. That didn't sound like a revolt to Lawes. That sounded like a war.

He grimly remembered the harsh conditions there, starting with the fierce Adirondack cold and the impossible remoteness—twelve hours or more by rail and road from New York. Did the men ever get visitors? Sing Sing was twenty years older than Clinton, but Sing Sing had been modernized. Most Clinton prisoners were still confined to their cells of seven feet deep, four feet wide, and six feet high. Those were the bigger cells. More than five hundred of the oldest cells were half a foot narrower. And it was the lucky prisoners who had cells. Nearly four hundred overflow inmates had to be housed in the corridors and the tuberculosis hospital. And most of these men were lifers, thanks to the Baumes laws, four-time losers who no longer had any hope of ever leaving prison alive.

Six days later, Lawes was sickened to hear, the violence had leaped closer, erupting at Auburn, where many of the seventeen hundred prisoners fought guards for five hours. Four of the ringleaders made it over the wall, two others were shot dead, and eleven others were wounded.

The news stunned New York's new governor, Franklin Delano Roosevelt, elected the previous November as his predecessor, Al Smith, fell to the forces of reaction in his historic bid for the White House. Roosevelt was only too well aware of the political volatility of the issue. He had barely taken office when he, along with Smith, had been attacked by the Republicans for prison conditions.

But now Roosevelt took charge. Rushing up to view the carnage at Clinton and plainly annoyed at his commissioner of correction, Dr. Raymond F. C. Kieb, who had yet to visit either of the now secured prisons, the governor scratched out a statement in pencil on a borrowed memo pad. "The first thing to do about these outbreaks is to stop any others before they happen. Therefore I am calling on Dr. Kieb, the Commissioner of Correction, who is charged with the safe keeping of prisoners, to report to me at once on how the Dannemora and Auburn outbreaks occurred." He kept writing for a moment, adding, "And whether any one was at fault and how any recurrence in these or other prisons may be definitely prevented." Then he angrily crossed that out and wrote simply, "And where the responsibility lies."

Kieb, a holdover from Governor Smith and formerly superintendent of the Matteawan State Hospital for the Criminally Insane in Beacon, had seemed paralyzed, saying there was no way to stop the rioting and blaming the unrest on the Baumes laws. Roosevelt also criticized their severity but asked pointedly whether the problem might not have stemmed from Kieb's inability to control the prisons. At any rate, Roosevelt said, Clinton and other state prisons needed to be rebuilt to reduce overcrowding. This would take time, he said, but was vital to the morale and well-being of the prisoners.

From the first violence at Clinton, Roosevelt, unlike Kieb, had acted decisively, mobilizing army troops by getting the postmaster at Plattsburgh to certify that federal property was in danger and thereby sparing himself the distasteful chore of asking President Herbert Hoover for federal aid to put down insurrection in his state. Hoover had already taken notice of the crime problem, proposing in his inaugural address to name a federal commission to study crime and criminal justice and especially the rampant racketeering linked to Prohibition. In May he had appointed a prestigious eleven-member panel under George W. Wickersham, a former attorney general. It was getting organized when Clinton and Auburn erupted.

Roosevelt arrived at Clinton hours earlier than expected and shortly before Kieb, catching the staff off guard. After his inspection, he sped south to Lake George and the Great Meadow Prison in Comstock, a model low-security facility more like a farm than a penal institution, where he admired the fireproof buildings and modern sanitation and the hundreds of inmates working constructively in the open air. Now that was his idea of a progressive prison.

Senator Baumes meanwhile protested that his laws were not responsible for the uprisings; rather, the cause was the laxity and special privileges the prisoners enjoyed, along with the undeniable overcrowding. But Roosevelt had clearly seized the initiative. It was, Lawes could only think, a masterful performance.

Sing Sing, by contrast, was peaceful, although Lawes had received troubling reports of ferment. Days after the eruptions at Dannemora and Auburn, Lawes had all prisoners searched and confined to their cells, and the arsenal moved to a secret redoubt outside the walls. The flammable factories were shuttered. There had been an earlier scare in March, when Lawes was off to Elmira on a one-day visit to comfort Kathryn with her broken ankle. Tipped off by a prisoner, the acting warden, Principal Keeper John Sheehy, checked the vegetable cellar under the dining hall and found an iron gate to an underground conduit ajar, with the lock broken. Suspicious, Sheehy, a six-foot-four, 250-pound giant with fists like Westphalian hams, forced his bulk into the four-foot-square opening and crawled to its end under the bathhouse. There, to his amazement, he discovered a freshly dug tunnel jutting off the conduit at a right angle toward the prison wall five feet away.

It was an ingenious construction job, Sheehy and other guards quickly agreed, with supporting timbers and a reinforced roof where the tunnel ran under a heavily trafficked prison road. The tools, discovered at the unfinished dead end, consisted of six flashlights, two claw hammers, and two mason's trowels. No less than 640 cubic feet of dirt had been removed, they calculated but there was no sign of it. The ingenious diggers may have thrown it into the furnace or dribbled it out on the grounds in pocketfuls.

The prisoners were closely questioned and all denied any knowledge of the escape scheme. Sheehy then combed prison records to see if any of the inmates, past or present, had been sandhogs in construction of the New York City subways, for the work was that professional. Lawes had a prime suspect in mind, a prisoner who had recently been transferred to New Jersey to stand trial for murder. But he couldn't prove anything. It took nearly eight truckloads of earth to refill the tunnel.

Lawes had been lucky. And yet, as the saying goes, he made his own luck. It was no accident that Sing Sing had escaped mayhem, said Frank Tannenbaum, a longtime aide to Osborne. Lawes, like Osborne, knew how to treat men. At Lawes's Sing Sing, men walked, not marched, to dinner, arms thrown comradely around each other's shoulders. Whether it was the modernized plant or Lawes himself or the combination, it was working. At almost forty-six, he projected confidence as an authoritative figure with still-penetrating blue eyes and brown hair that showed no trace of gray. Lawes had few illusions about the men. "I don't maintain they are going to pick a daisy and say, 'she loves me, she loves me not,'" he told a writer for the *New York Times* Sunday magazine, which was courting him for ever more interviews and original articles, "nor do I believe that they will grow wings. But, after all, they are not very different from the rest of us."

The boys were right to grumble about the food, Lawes said. The daily meal allowance worked out to twenty-one cents each—less than half the amount in 1868, when the dollar bought twice as much. Canada spent twice as much to feed its prisoners. He had his own complaints, as he wrote Albany once again. "The failure to approve the recommendation, made last year, for a new residence for the Warden was disappointing. The Warden's family is now as securely locked within the walls as any of the prisoners. Six times daily, almost two thousand men march between the old and new prisons, pass directly in front of the Warden's house. There is no sense of privacy and, with the present conditions which need no elaboration, the desirability of a safer location for the Warden's family should be apparent."

Yet things were looking up. Days after the battles at Clinton and Auburn, all eighteen hundred modern cells in the new part of Sing Sing were occupied for the first time, leaving just 168 overflow prisoners in the original 1825 cellblock by the river.

Replying to a questionnaire from Roosevelt seeking advice for a State Crime Commission inquiry, Lawes urged construction of special quarters to take up the overflow so that no one would have to be housed in the dank old cells. The guards needed a day off—they now worked seven-day weeks, with two weeks' vacation—and he needed twenty more men to cover all the posts. He asked for an increase in the food allowance and an expansion of prison shops and outdoor construction jobs so that more men could work and be trained in healthful surroundings. The men should be paid more, up to twenty-five cents a day instead of the existing penny and a half, with repeal of a provision requiring prisoners to repay the state thirty cents a day for their maintenance before they could start earning even their measly cent and a half. Lawes urged, too, restoration of a highly popular incentive, eliminated by the Baumes laws, that allowed prisoners with indeterminate sentences to earn ten days off their time for every thirty days of good work. To the men, time off was more alluring than money and went a long way toward encouraging good behavior.

As for the Baumes laws, they accomplished the opposite of what had been intended, Lawes said. More robbers used guns, to stave off a fateful fourth arrest. Juries hesitated to convict four-time offenders, knowing they would go away for life. For the same reason, prosecutors often accepted misdemeanor pleas rather than seek a fourth felony conviction. A second-degree murderer fared better than someone convicted four times of burglary. The men even joked about it, Lawes told Roosevelt—to get a break, you had to kill. The prisons should be classified by severity, he went on. Sing Sing for those most open to rehabilitation, Auburn for intermediate cases, and Clinton for the most recalcitrant, along with drug addicts and sex perverts. Prisoners who showed improvement could be reclassified to an easier institution, "thereby keeping hope alive." That system, with Great Meadow as a kind of minimum-security halfway house, and the excess capacity to be provided by the new Attica Prison under construction, should take care of the state's penal needs, Lawes concluded.

A month after the riots in Clinton and Auburn, all Sing Sing was agog, the men thronging the corridors and doorways and peering from every window to catch a glimpse of the godly visitor. He arrived in full plumage—white golf shirt and black tie, white knickers, black stockings, and black and white shoes. Used to the stares and adulation, Babe Ruth waved and growled to one and all, "Hello, kid."

The New York Yankees with Ruth and Lou Gehrig had come up to play the Mutual Welfare League team, the Sing Sing Orioles, at Lawes Field. Like the Giants and other teams that periodically visited, they began with a lunch at the warden's house, and then were given a tour of the prison, Sheehy making even the biggest players among them look like midgets. Then the Yankees were whisked away, to reappear moments later on the field in their dazzling white home uniforms. Practice was delayed while the prisoners clustered around, thrusting forward baseballs for autographs. Lawes sat patiently in his tarpaper box behind home plate. Outside the walls, on a hill overlooking the grounds, hundreds of townspeople had gathered, hoping to snare one of the Bambino's blasts.

He didn't disappoint. In his first trip to the plate for batting practice, he drilled one over the right field fence, a feat last accomplished five years before by the Giants' Bill Terry. In the game, he doubled to right and smacked three more over the walls and high over the heads of guards standing with machine guns, one a swat that might have been his mightiest ever—six or seven hundred feet, no one ever measured it—that vaulted the eight tracks of the New York Central Railroad and thudded into the cliff under the new administration building.

Up on the hill, fourteen-year-old Tony DeAngelis of Ossining saw the ball hit and scampered down to retrieve it, pocketing it reverently.

Ruth played first base for seven innings, then pitched the last two. "Can you hit a hook?" he asked the first prisoner to face him.

The man nodded, swinging at the Babe's curveball and smacking it foul.

"He can," Ruth announced respectfully. He tried a fastball. The batter belted it to center for a single.

Ruth paid his respects. "I should have pitched him a knuckler."

The next Sing Sing batter scored with a smash over the left field wall.

Ruth feigned dismay. "Hey," he yelled, "are you eligible to sign a contract?"

"He's got one now," came a shout from the stands. "He's a ten-year man, Babe."

The final score was Yankees 15, Sing Sing 3.

Clutching his precious Babe Ruth home run horsehide, young Tony DeAngelis ran to the parking area outside the main gate, where the baseball gods smiled yet again. There, getting into his Packard, was Ruth. Tony rushed up and gave him the ball to sign. Ruth took it, scratched his signature, and handed it to the man next to him to sign too. Tony DeAngelis went home that day in September 1929 with a record home run baseball signed by Babe Ruth and Lou Gehrig.

But elsewhere the news was grim. The rash of prison uprisings persisted. In Canon City, Colorado, an attempted breakout by two long-term convicts in the state penitentiary set off a riot that killed seven guards and five prisoners, wounded a score more guards, inmates, and civilians, and caused half a million dollars in damage. The federal prison at Leavenworth was also rocked by unrest. And violence was at the very gates of Sing Sing. Two weeks after October's Black Friday stock market crash, Lawes announced that Sing Sing had thwarted a dangerous plot by an unlikely inmate, a brilliant twenty-four-year-old former Columbia University student, Roy H. Sloane, who had been serving ten years for auto theft. He was suspected of having stolen more than twenty cars—each one a Nash, for some reason—to put himself through college, although he came from a wealthy family. He had argued his own appeal, winning a new trial and acquittal—but then was resentenced to seven years for having been found with brass knuckles and attempting an earlier escape.

Now, Lawes learned, Sloane and two confederates, one with a series of killings on his head, had schemed to cut the lights in the old cellblock and open the cells, loosing a growing count of the now nearly two hundred most dangerous prisoners. A search had uncovered a letter from Sloane ordering various implements for an escape, a wooden model of the keeper's master key that could open all cells, and a set of tools that could short-circuit the prison's electrical system. Lawes ordered Sloane and two confederates moved to the death house for safekeeping.

Then on a chilly December afternoon, as the prisoners started filing out of the recreation yard to return to their cells, seventeen-year-old Reuben Kaminsky of Brooklyn, who had arrived several months before for a seven-to-fifteen-year robbery sentence, staggered out of line and collapsed, bleeding from five slashes in his chest, underarm, and cheek. Known as the "kid convict" of Sing Sing, he had been tagged as a squealer. Stony-faced prisoners, eyes fixed straight ahead, saw nothing. But if Kaminsky was a squealer, he gave no information on his deathbed. He never regained consciousness. Lawes knew the problems he faced in finding the murderer. Whoever talked would surely meet the same fate. But he ordered a lockdown and canceled the night's perfor-mance of the annual prison

Time *magazine cover featuring Lawes.* (TIME LIFE PICTURES/GETTY IMAGES)

show, *Good News.* Within two days informants angered by the cowardly attack fingered two men, black prisoners with a grudge against Kaminsky.

A week after Roosevelt's crime commission issued its report giving weight to many of Lawes's recommendations, Auburn exploded once more in violence, the second time in five months. Sixteen lifers, deeming death preferable to perpetual confinement, fomented a riot, killing the principal keeper and holding Warden Edgar S. Jennings hostage while demanding that the gates be opened. With Roosevelt away in Chicago, Lieutenant Governor Herbert H. Lehman in Albany demanded unconditional surrender by the rioters. Roosevelt, reached aboard the train speeding home, endorsed the judgment. Jennings was finally rescued in a gas attack by state troopers. Eight convicts were killed and a dozen guards were injured in the six-hour melee.

In a bitter season, Lawes was widely credited with keeping Sing Sing peaceful. Even before the latest outbreak, he had drawn the admiration of one of the nation's most influential news titans, Henry R. Luce, whose innovative weekly magazine, *Time*, was now reaching more than 250,000 readers. Lawes's opposition to the death penalty and his other ideas were perhaps a bit, well, advanced, but Luce liked Lawes's independence. He put Lawes on the cover of *Time*'s November 18, 1929 issue, along with the caption "The state . . . has not enslaved my opinions."

25

Eight-year-old Cherie with her blond ringlet curls and tomboy ways was the darling of the family, daddy's little girl. She was his constant companion, often accompanying him on trips to New York for radio broadcasts and other business, during which Lawes telephoned the prison hourly to make sure everything was all right.

Now, finally, she wore dresses and bounded though the gates each morning to attend school outside at the Ossining Seminary. She had her own pony, Beauty, and a groom to accompany her around the grounds. She skated and swam and tap-danced, and never missed a movie at the prison. She had the run of the grounds, often popping into the commissary in the evening to have a chat with the boys—as even she called them—or turning up at the ball field to watch baseball practice and be instructed in how to pitch a ball or steal a base. The boys were good at stealing. Some ex-burglars tried to teach her tennis, but for some reason, she found, burglars made terrible tennis players. Lawes liked to throw a ball around with her too, but the last time they played catch, he tripped and fell and broke a wrist. He was not a natural athlete.

If Lawes doted on Cherie, clearly twenty-year-old Crystal was Chapin's favorite. Something in her fragility seemed to evoke his protective instincts, and he often insisted on safely escorting her the half mile to the train station when she left Sing Sing to return to the University of Vermont. At the station, he bought her magazines and candy for the trip.

Lawes had no qualms about Chapin. But his confidence in his family's

Cherie saying good-bye to Keeper John Sheehy before leaving for Hollywood in 1930. (JOAN L. JACOBSEN)

security was tested when a prisoner tipped off Kathryn to a plot by another inmate, a sex criminal, to kidnap Cherie and break out. Lawes, shaken, called Cherie in to gently tell her of the scheme.

"Oh," she said, "I know."

Lawes, stunned, said it couldn't be. "You don't know. You couldn't possibly know."

"Well I do," she said. She had heard it from the boys, but hadn't said anything because her father told her never to squeal.

Lawes went away shaking his head, muttering, "My God . . ."

The Laweses were upstate one day heading to Elmira for a family visit when they suddenly came upon a crowd of white-hooded figures around a burning cross. It was a frightening scene, the more terrifying for its isolation in the countryside.

One of the hooded men moved into the road to block their car. Ed the chauffeur looked around helplessly. "What do I do?"

"I'll talk first," said Lawes.

The hooded man peered through the windshield. "Any Catholics here?"

"Yes," Lawes said. "We're all Catholics, and if you don't get the hell out of the way we'll run you down!" He signaled Ed to gun the engine, and the big Buick shot forward, forcing the man aside. They sped off in shocked silence until Lawes spoke again. "You see what ignorant people can do?"

Cherie asked how her father had known what to do. You don't always know, Lawes said, but you try something. But, she asked, what if it doesn't work?

Crystal. (JOAN L. JACOBSEN)

"If it doesn't work," Lawes said, "you have to live with it."

Fox Studios had come to the prison in the spring of 1930 to shoot a short picture, *A Day in the Life of Sing Sing.* Lawes, a great fan of the movies,

Cherie on Beauty. (JOAN L. JACOBSEN)

Cherie and her father with director John Ford, left, on Hollywood set of Up the River. (JOAN L. JACOBSEN)

hosted the filmmakers, including a thirty-five-year-old son of Irish immigrants who had been born Sean Aloysius O'Feeney in Cape Elizabeth, Maine, and who now went by the name of John Ford. He had broken into Hollywood doing set construction, props, and stunt work and had played one of the Klansmen extras in D. W. Griffith's *Birth of a Nation*. Since 1917 he had made seventy-one movies.

At Sing Sing, Ford caught sight of a startling blond moppet parading among the prisoners and asked Lawes, "Who is that?" That, Lawes said, was his daughter Cherie. Ford squinted though his owlish glasses and pipe smoke and blurted, "How'd she like to come to Hollywood?"

Ford found Cherie to be a bright little thing. She pointed out the men who could best portray the convict characters and project their voices for the new kind of movies with sound. Truly, the production team said, she deserved billing as assistant director. So Ford asked Lawes if Cherie would be available for a part in his next feature, a prison movie called *Up the River*. She could play little Jean, the warden's daughter and the prison's little ray of sunshine. She wouldn't be the only one light on film experience. Two of her fellow cast members would be making their movie debuts—a lovely ingenue, Claire Luce, and a new Broadway star, Spencer Tracy. Another male lead had already appeared in two films. His name was Humphrey Bogart.

Up the River was a comedy set behind the walls of Bensonata, a prison not unlike Sing Sing. Tracy was St. Louis, a jailbreak artist who arrives in Bensonata just in time to become a winning pitcher for the baseball team. Bogart was Steve, a convict doing time for accidental manslaughter and in love with Luce as Judy, also behind bars, taking the rap for her stock-swindling boss. There was an escape, a sentimental homecoming to Bensonata, and a triumphant baseball victory for the prison nine.

Lawes already admired Tracy, then starring on the stage in *The Last Mile*, a stark death house drama written by the actor John Wexley and based loosely on the riots in Auburn and Colorado. Lawes had even written a preface for the Samuel French edition of the play, and the *Evening Post* had reprinted excerpts.

And so they were off to Hollywood. Sporting a hammered silver ring and leather makeup bag and other farewell gifts from the boys, Cherie and her father left by train at the end of May 1930. All Sing Sing turned out to see them off, the hulking Keeper Sheehy posing for a formal good-bye shaking Cherie's hand gravely at the gate. Chapin had cabled the head of Fox, Winfield Sheehan. "My dear Winnie:—My little pal Cherie Lawes is leaving for Hollywood tomorrow. Please do all you can for her, as we all love her here and will miss her much."

When they stepped off the Union Pacific's Los Angeles Limited days later, Ford himself was there to escort them to the set. He asked Cherie what she thought of it. She was not impressed. There was something wrong with the look of the far wall, but the south gate looked all right, she decided, and made her feel right at home.

She and other minors had to appear before a judge to have their contracts approved, and then she was officially on the payroll at $250 a week—more than her father was earning as warden of Sing Sing, as Cherie excitedly chattered to everyone she met.

They shot the movie all summer. Crystal and Kathleen, home from the University of Vermont and from Cornell, came out to relieve Lawes so he could return to Sing Sing, although he made a special trip back to see Cherie for her ninth birthday in June and deliver a gift doll that Cherie named Patsy.

In August, Ford cabled Lawes.

DO YOU WANT CHERIE BACK IMMEDIATELY
STOP NOW THAT PICTURE IS FINISHED
I'LL TELL YOU SHE WAS GREAT.
REGARDS JACK (JOHN FORD)

A week later, the three sisters returned home, Cherie now a diva of the silver screen. After the train pulled into Ossining, they stopped at the depot restaurant for lunch and Cherie posed for a photographer before returning to the prison. "Hollywood's nice and I love making pictures," she announced grandly, "but after all Sing Sing is home, and there are the boys."

They were personally invited to the premiere by the movie palace impresario Samuel Lionel "Roxy" Rothafel at his extravagant Roxy Theater, the nearly six-thousand-seat "Cathedral of the Motion Picture" on West Fiftieth Street, and they could bring as many guests as they wished. People said nice things, but *Up the River,* Tracy and Bogart notwithstanding, soon sank ignominiously beneath the waves.

Still, Hollywood had taken note. As *Up the River* was being made, Metro-Goldwyn-Mayer asked Lawes to help sway the censors in favor of its prison riot film, *The Big House.* Lawes found it raw but not likely to incite violence and said so, gaining an invitation to the opening at the Astor Theater and an offer to visit the MGM lot and meet Louis B. Mayer and production head Irving Thalberg.

The real Sing Sing, meanwhile, continued to provide drama aplenty. In August, as Cherie was across the continent approaching a wrap, twenty-two hundred prisoners were taking their exercise in the yard when two men and two women in a rowboat just off the prison dock began to scream and flail frantically. The boat was filling with water. It was an eerie reprise of the disaster just three years before, when the three young canoeists drowned as the caged prisoners clawed helplessly at the fence, held at bay by guards threatening to shoot. Now, once again, men scrambled to volunteer as rescuers, but this time a self-confident guard sergeant picked four short-termers and swung open the gate for them.

From inside the fence, every pair of eyes followed them. The four sprinted

Poster from Up the River. (JOAN L. JACOBSEN)

to the dock. Two plunged into the Hudson, swimming for the rowboat, while the other two, wielding firemen's hooks, positioned themselves at the end of the dock. The two in the river pushed the water-filled boat with the four desperate passengers toward the dock until the other two with their grappling hooks could pull it closer, allowing the two women first and then their escorts to step onto the dry planks. The four boaters and their rescuers were then quickly escorted back within Sing Sing's walls. The boaters, it turned out, were the chief of police of the New York Central Railroad Lines, his brother-in-law, and their wives.

Some of the prisoners were disgusted. Others insisted a railroad cop wasn't really a cop and was okay to save. Lawes hailed his four Sing Sing heroes, one a career larcenist with eleven arrests, in prison since 1910 serving two five-to-ten-year terms for forgery. Another was serving time for robbery and assault. The third was in for carrying a pistol and robbery; the fourth for grand larceny. It proved again what he always said. There was good in every man.

The euphoria was short-lived. Less than three weeks later, three rioters in the fatal uprising at Auburn the year before marched to the chair. Security was stepped up amid rumors that one would try a desperate bolt for freedom. The first to be led in was twenty-year-old Jesse Thomas. He shook off his guards. "I can walk through and die like a man," he insisted. He seated himself, glared at the witnesses, and said: "See you all in hell. Let's go." Four minutes later he was dead. Next to go was William Force, twenty-eight. He goaded Elliott, the executioner. "What are you so nervous about? Take it easy. I'm in no hurry." He started to address the witnesses, "You came to see blood—" when the current cut him off. The last was Claude Udwin, twenty-nine, the coolest of all. "I'm going on an exploration trip," he announced. "The good part about this thing is that they carry you out and you don't have to walk." Minutes later he too was dead.

The new Sing Sing now rose triumphantly on the crest of the cliff over the railroad tracks that bisected the prison. Below the vibrant redbrick battlements, far down along the Hudson, the anemic old white cellblock was largely abandoned, but the factory shops hummed with work and the pathways between the ball field and death house were ablaze with Chapin's rose hedges and banks of irises. Then one day, a giant steam shovel lumbered in through the high main gate and clanked steeply downhill toward the lower prison. It mowed down a bed of madonna lilies and cut a swath through the bachelor buttons before starting to dip its claw-toothed bucket into the bloodred roses.

Men came running from all over, waving their arms and shouting "Stop!" over the din of the machine. A worker with a blueprint clambered out of the cab. He had his orders, he said, from the superintendent of prisons. New pipelines were coming in, and he was digging the trenches.

By now Chapin had been summoned. He stood there uncomprehending at first, reaching out to touch the shuddering iron monster as if to make sure it was real. The operator waved him out of the way and started up again.

The men lunged to storm the cab, but Chapin, shoulders sagging under his white knit sweater, called them back in a low, strangled voice. It was no use. Nothing was of any use.

The bucket clawed into the rosebushes.

Cherie, riding Beauty along the fence by the river, saw the commotion and galloped over. When she spotted the pirouetting machine mowing down the flowers, she jumped down and ran toward it with tears of rage. One of the men caught her and held her back as she kicked to break free.

Keeper Sheehy strode up, his colossal bulk for once dwarfed by something bigger. "I'm sorry, Chapin," he said. "It was ordered from Albany." He added as an afterthought, "I liked the flowers too."

On his sickbed on the second floor of the death house, Chapin lay listlessly. He had been confined for weeks with an undiagnosed ailment after all but collapsing under the advancing steam shovel that had mowed away his flowers. He had no more visitors. His last correspondent had been Beatrice Houdini, widow of the magician. There were rumors that they were sweethearts and would wed upon his parole in 1934, if he lasted that long. But then her letters stopped too.

Across the prison, in the warden's house that November Saturday night in 1930, Lawes and his family were dining with guests when one visitor chanced to remark on the surprising peace. "Yes," Lawes foolishly assented, "we have had good luck here." Then came the crackle of gunshots.

In his tomb–like cell, Chapin heard the shriek of the prison siren, trampling feet, and snatches of frantic orders.

In the chapel, two prisoners had gone to confession with Father McCaffrey. Suddenly in the corridor they and two confederates whipped out smuggled pistols and seized a guard, grabbing his keys that opened a gate to the prison yard, taking his coat as camouflage, and locking him into a cell. Coming upon four more guards, they overpowered them and locked them up. Next they came across four privileged prisoners, trusties with the run of the prison, whom they corralled in the cell with the guards. Then they bolted for the yard.

They might have made it, but one of the locked-up guards carried a secret key. He freed the group and sounded the alarm.

The four escapees dashed across the open expanse to the north wall under an unmanned watchtower and tried to hurl a makeshift iron hook with a rope over the thirty-foot wall. It was too heavy. They dropped it and ran, just as Lawes appeared in the yard sweeping a hand-held electric torch. The four saw Lawes before he saw them. They turned on their heels and darted back toward the new cellblock, but soon found themselves facing four well-armed guards. One guard called on the escapees to surrender. He didn't finish his demand before one of the prisoners fired, wounding an officer. The guards answered with a flash of submachine-gun fire. One of the escapees, hit twice in the chest, shot himself in the right temple. Guards bombed the yard with tear gas, and in ten minutes it was over.

Chapin sank in and out of consciousness to the wail of the prison siren.

Lawes was horrified. Where had the four guns come from? How many other weapons had been smuggled in? He remembered a gift box that had come in one year to a prisoner. That night the man, who owed him a favor, brought it back to Lawes—his gift to the warden. Lawes presented it to Cherie to open. She found doughnuts and candy and under them, a .38-caliber pistol. She excitedly brought it to her father. This was beyond snitching. Once he recovered, Lawes thought it was his best Christmas gift ever. But clearly, not all prisoners were surrendering their weapons.

How had the four guns slipped in? Everyone was always searched, everyone but . . . *him*. The more Lawes thought about it, the more he realized it must have been him, or rather his car. It was often parked unattended outside the prison. Someone must have figured out how to hide guns in the undercarriage and remove them once the car was back inside the gates.

When calm returned, Lawes addressed the prisoners on the radio. "I realize that talk is cheap and I am therefore going to speak to you briefly, but frankly." As in baseball, boxing, football, and other sports, he said, the best clue to the future was the record of the past. And what was his record? The new Sing Sing had risen in his time, he said. Before him, inmates had never performed shows for a visiting public. Since he took over, they had staged eleven shows. Now, in the wake of the deadly shoot-out, he said, the latest show was canceled. "I would be a complete nitwit to permit it." The Mutual Welfare League accused him of turning authoritarian, but Lawes called that nonsense. "Is it likely that after twenty-five years of liberal prison administration, I should suddenly become 'hard-boiled'? I have always been criticized for being too lenient."

He reminded the men of his arrival more than a decade before. "I then said, when asked to talk from a platform which had been specially erected, 'No, I am standing on the level and I hope to stay that way.'" He had tried to be fair, he concluded, but in the end one man was in charge at Sing Sing and that was the warden. "I have no intention of delegating this responsibility to any man or set of men."

Two weeks before Christmas, Lawes stopped by Chapin's bedside. "Do you need anything, Charlie?"

"Yes," Chapin said. "I want to die. I want to get it over with."

And so he did, at age seventy-two, officially of pneumonia. At his wish, he was buried beside his devoted Nellie in Washington's Glenwood Cemetery in a zinc-lined hardwood box inside the least expensive black-cloth-covered casket, never to be opened, sealed for all eternity.

26

Lawes could see it coming. Another sensational multiple murder. Another notorious death row denizen. Another sickening press circus. In early May 1931,
hundreds of police officers, including Commissioner Edward P. Mulrooney
(who as a young rookie had taken bodies off the burning *General Slocum* as
Chapin excitedly tallied the toll), besieged a rooming house on West Nine-
teenth Street. Inside, nineteen-year-old gunman Francis Crowley, his sixteen-
year-old girlfriend, and another crony had been cornered. Crowley, a slight,
wavy-haired youth of only five feet three known as "Two-Gun" for the twin
automatics he packed, had been hunted for days in the killing of a patrolman
on Long Island.

The trail of blood had begun weeks earlier when Crowley and a moon-
faced trucker named Rudolph Duringer stole a car in Ossining and made the
rounds of speakeasies, picking up a taxi dancer, who spurned Duringer's advances in the backseat. Her bullet-riddled body was soon found dumped at a
seminary in Yonkers. As the manhunt spread, Crowley and his teenage girlfriend, Helen Walsh, were sitting in his parked car in North Merrick when a
suspicious officer drew a gun on Crowley and asked for his license. Crowley
pretended to reach for his wallet and drew his own pistol. The cop pulled the
trigger but the gun misfired—twice. Crowley shot the officer three times in
the arm, then grabbed the policeman's own gun and finished him off, also
wounding his partner running to the scene.

The chase was on, ending at the top floor of an Upper West Side rooming
house where Crowley, Duringer, and Walsh were holed up, facing an army
of police. As ten thousand curiosity seekers thronged the war zone, and

neighbors, heedless of the danger, hung from windows and fire escapes, the police poured fire into the building from batteries of rifles, shotguns, and machine guns. Crowley blazed back while Walsh and Duringer cowered under the bed. The police lobbed in tear gas bombs. They were hurled back into the street. Finally, emergency crews chopped holes in the roof and dropped the gas bombs through while Mulrooney and a detective smashed down the door with an ax.

Crowley, dazed and running low on ammunition, had been shot three times in the legs and once in the left arm. Duringer and Walsh had been grazed by flying bullets and falling plaster. Surrounded, Crowley, said, "I'm shot, I give up. Anyway, you didn't kill me." He said he had thrown away his pistols, but they were found in his trouser legs, the barrels thrust into his socks and the butts clasped by his garters.

"What do you mean by that?" a policeman demanded.

"What do you expect me to do?" Crowley snarled. "I'm going to the chair anyway."

Love had undone him. The apartment he had holed up in was an old flame's, and when she found him with a new sweetheart, she tipped off the law.

Quickly convicted and sentenced to death, Crowley entered Sing Sing a small, angelic-looking youth of borderline intelligence—a pathetic spectacle, Lawes thought. But he was found to be concealing a long-handled sharpened spoon tucked into a sock. He regularly cursed the guards, and when fellow inmates cheered him on, he settled into his part. In his cell, he removed a bedspring from the mattress and wrapped the sharpened coil around a rolled-up magazine to improvise a fearsome weapon. When that was found and confiscated, he asked a guard for a cigarette and a light—he didn't smoke—and set fire to his bed. Then he smashed everything in his cell and used his clothes to stuff up the plumbing. He was sent to isolation, where he again plugged the toilet, flooding his cell. Lawes, remembering his success with his Boob Squad at New Hampton, ordered Crowley stripped naked in the cooler, and there he stayed.

He spent his time luring flies with sugar and killing them. Then one day a starling flew into his cell. Unaccountably, he fed it and didn't kill it. It kept coming back.

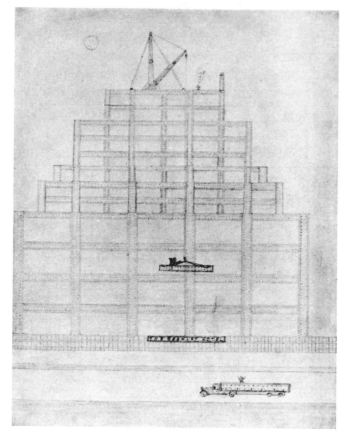

Drawings by Francis "Two-Gun" Crowley, done at Sing Sing, from Lawes's book 20,000 Years in Sing Sing. (OSSINING HISTORICAL SOCIETY MUSEUM)

Lawes heard of the episode and went to visit Crowley. Naked and primitive as a caveman and for the first time subdued, Crowley asked if he could keep the bird. Lawes said yes and gave him his clothes back. Soon, Crowley asked for paper and pencil and began drawing. He showed a surprising artistic aptitude. He sketched the Empire State Building and the interior of the death house, engineering projects like aqueducts, and a fanciful Crowley Hotel under construction with cranes. He asked for wood and built models of his architectural visions, populated with cockroaches he had captured.

Crowley hadn't tamed the bird, Lawes thought; the bird had tamed Crowley. And if Crowley could be redeemed, who could not?

Slowly Lawes learned his story. His loathing for the law went back to the cradle. His father, a policeman's son, had abandoned the family when Francis was born, and his mother placed the month-old baby with a woman named Anna Crowley. The boy, abused or neglected, suffered blows on his head when he was a child and had trouble learning. At fourteen he was found to have a mental age of ten. It was then he learned from a visit by his real mother that he was adopted. About the same time, his troubled elder stepbrother, John, was killed by a policeman he had tried to ambush. Francis was arrested for car theft—framed, he insisted. After that, all cops were his enemies. He set out on his criminal career in earnest, stealing automobiles for joy rides with girls. Arrested in the Bronx, he was put on probation. After a shoot-out in the Bronx, he armed himself with pistols, blackjacks, and brass knuckles. Soon after that he met up with Duringer and their murderous crime spree began. "I knew when I bought that gun," he told Lawes, "that it would land me in the chair."

It was classic, Lawes thought, foreordained.

Some parts of the country were resisting the clamor for death. Michigan, which had outlawed the death penalty, was considering restoring it, and Lawes traveled to Detroit with one of his strongest speeches to try to sway the debate. In the end, Lawes asked his listeners, if executions were restored, would they personally pull the switch? The death penalty was rejected by fifty thousand votes.

There was some other good news for Lawes. Maud Ballington Booth, the socialite from the Volunteer Prison League of the Volunteers of America, who with Lawes had reached out to help the destitute wife of Howard Baker, one of the first prisoners he had had to execute, wrote to say that she had kept in touch with Mrs. Baker and continued to help her. She had become a wonderful mother to her three fatherless boys, Booth said. The boys, close enough in age to look like triplets, were doing well in school, frequented the YMCA, swam and skated, and attended summer camp on Staten Island. "They are fine examples," she said, "and prove that a criminal's children, if given a chance, can be just as straight and honest as any other children."

Of course, Booth added, they know nothing of their father's sad fate. "They think he was killed in the war."

Sing Sing's scrapbook squad was feverishly cutting and pasting, archiving the stories Lawes was collecting for his speeches and another book he was writing. One large marbled-cover scrapbook in the archive was peculiarly labeled.

FOOTBALL CLIPPINGS
& SUICIDES

The title's second part said it all. As bad as it was inside the walls, for many it was worse outside, as the clips recounted. The nation, on the long downhill slide into the Great Depression, was suffering an epidemic of self-annihilation. The year 1930 had broken all records in the state, as 2,345 people had taken their own lives. One poignant news filler, cabled from coast to coast, told the sad tale a desperate down-and-outer, A. S. Larmie, who actually applied to be electrocuted. He was tired of standing in breadlines.

Others took matters into their own hands.

John P. Bowman, a seventy-year-old law partner from Rochester, threw himself to his death from his third-floor window of the Hotel Commodore on East Forty-second Street. His body was identified by his partner, the new state superintendent of insurance.

Samuel E. Robertson of the United Cigar Stores Company visited a tobacco executive at Madison Avenue and Thirty-fourth Street, asked for a glass of water, and jumped out of a seventh-floor window.

Ruth Hesmas, a penniless and unemployed nineteen-year-old dance-hall hostess, flung herself out of her fourth-floor room on West Sixtieth Street.

Helen Pabon, thirty-one, hurled her wailing five-year-old daughter from the window of their fifth-floor apartment in the Bronx, then climbed to the sill and followed her to the pavement.

Harry J. Koerper, dismissed as manager of an apartment building on Riverside Drive, fired a bullet into his heart.

A police sergeant under investigation in a rum-running case shot himself to death in the precinct house locker room.

A Staten Island doctor's wife and her nineteen-year-old daughter turned on the gas jets and stuffed a pillow under the doorknob to keep the lethal fumes from escaping through the keyhole.

Some died by ways of their own making, if not by their own hand. Roy Sloane, the felonious Columbia prodigy, had finally argued his way out of Sing Sing, winning an acquittal at retrial and, as a first offender, gaining release for time served. Five months later, in May 1931, he met three companions at the Mad Dot Boat Club at the foot of Dyckman Street on the Hudson, and was

Lawes in 1930s with inmates at picnic at his new Sing Sing house. (OSSINING HISTORICAL SOCIETY MUSEUM)

gunned down from a passing car. He may have been planning to testify for the state in a jewel heist. In any case, Lawes thought, he was always a little too slick for his own good.

In Sing Sing, by contrast, law and order ruled. There was safety from crime. There was food. There was shelter. Indeed, Lawes and his family would finally be getting a new home. The legislature appropriated twenty-five thousand dollars for a new warden's residence, blessedly outside the walls. And now, there was football.

Lawes, who had broken protocol to introduce catches between prisoners and guards at Elmira, knew what was plain to everyone in prison. The biggest loss was freedom. But sex wasn't far behind. A woman had once written Lawes asking "what you give your prisoners to repress their sex instincts."

"Prison does not give prisoners anything 'to repress their sex instincts,'" he responded. "It takes no notice of sex instincts. In the very nature of things, it must ignore them. But it is concededly a disturbing factor. Self-

Football game at Sing Sing, from Lawes's book 20,000 Years in Sing Sing. (OSSINING HISTORI-
CAL SOCIETY MUSEUM)

abuse, particularly among younger prisoners, is practiced more widely than
prison administrators are frank to admit." There was also homosexuality, he
acknowledged, which was why he no longer doubled up the men in cells.

Some had suggested allowing prisoners to return home periodically to
their families and conjugal pleasures. But Lawes said a man who was trust-
worthy enough to be sent home from time to time was undoubtedly eligible
for permanent release.

No, he concluded, "the only practical answer to this problem is to keep
the prisoner busy physically and mentally for as many hours as is possible
with the facilities at hand." That meant, above all, sports. "The wholesome,
stimulating effect upon the men cannot be overestimated; they look forward
eagerly to these weekend contests."

Teams from the various factory shops had scrimmaged on the field for
years, but in October 1931 Lawes had scrounged some professional red
leather helmets and red-and-blue jerseys and organized two squads to face off
against visiting teams each Sunday under the careful eye of Keeper Sheehy.
All games, of course, would of necessity be home games, and the circuit

would be known, aptly enough, as the Big Pen Conference. There would be, alas, no traveling, no road, no away, and visiting players would have to be thoroughly searched. Still the men were ecstatic, swarming the field eagerly to practice plays and kicking. The prison eleven were soon known as the Black Sheep, and a coach with some promise of longevity agreed to helm them—George "Red" Hope, a forty-five-year-old convicted kidnapper serving a sixty-year sentence. He had abducted two Broadway mobsters to squeeze them for ransom, but the scheme went awry when he crashed his car into a police booth in Columbus Circle. Everything Red knew about football he had read in the papers, but he sounded impressive when he said he was using "the Hope system." He immediately laid down the law, underscoring his words with a slab of a fist. "No slugging in the scrimmages."

For quarterback, Red pinned his hopes on a twenty-year-old six-footer with a mop of corn-colored hair, Edwin Colline Pitts from Opelika, Alabama, who had arrived in Sing Sing the year before. His grandfather had been chief of police in Opelika. His father had died when Pitts was six and his mother moved the family to Peoria, Illinois. At fifteen, but looking older, he enlisted in the navy, where he played his first football. Discharged in New York at the end of his service, he struggled to find work. An older navy buddy who was hungry with him said if Pitts had any guts he would quit dreaming about money and go out and get some. Pitts took the challenge. The pair embarked on a crime spree that lasted all of two months and ended in a chain grocery in New York. They had just held up the owner for $76.25 when the police walked in. His partner stuck a gun in Pitts's hand. He could shoot it out or surrender. He surrendered. On his guilty plea, Pitts was sentenced to eight to sixteen years in Sing Sing. "Alabama," as he was quickly dubbed, was put to work as a coal passer in the powerhouse. But he showed great aptitude on the baseball diamond and the gridiron.

From his flag-draped tarpaper shack in the grandstand, Lawes gazed out at the rectangle of chalk-lined, hard-pounded turf that narrowed as it stretched into the distance to the thin white H of the opposite goalpost. He felt the chill breeze from the river and caught a sour whiff of prison sewage that cut through the sweet woodsmoke from the fireplaces of houses up on Spring Street. Off in the distance, beyond the far goalpost, the tracks of the New York Central Railroad sliced through the prison, affording passengers who craned their necks a flickering view of the death house. The ground was flat and muddy and brown—not a blade of grass could survive the trampling footfalls of hard men in leather armor. It was airless in the shack, where Fred, the erudite inmate scorekeeper, compulsively smoothed his tally sheets. But if Lawes regretted his tweed three-piece suit and snug Hoover collar, he gave no sign of it. Behind him, and the haze of smoke from his panatela, flowed the river, a plate of dark and viscous water sliding by under a gray November sky. It seemed temptingly close to many, he knew. But watchful eyes peered from the turreted watchtowers that poked up along the walls where photographers and film cameramen jockeyed for a good view of the action and where a radio announcer stood by to broadcast the play-by-play to the unfortunates in hospital beds or lonely cells in the death house.

For the Sing Sing squad's opening match against the Ossining Naval Militia that damp and mild November 15, two thousand inmates crowded the stands, along with five hundred privileged visitors who each paid 50¢ to sit in a secure section, swelling Ossining's unemployment relief fund by $250. Two hundred lesser entities were turned away. As the tension mounted, the Sing Sing band took the field, led by its spirited saxophonist and clarinetist, Bob Gooding, who had played for John Philip Sousa. At the last strains of "Throw Him Down, McCloskey," the 1890s popular Irish fight song that spurred vaudeville audiences into throwing anything at hand onto the stage, the crowd roared its welcome to the home team mascot, a pony painted in zebra stripes, carrying a demurely waving Cherie Lawes.

Sing Sing opened strong, inspired no doubt by a toss of the coin that pointed the Black Sheep toward the far goal—in the direction of the prison gate. They mowed down the Ossining militiamen for two touchdowns in the first period and another two in the second, gaining a few extra points on the kicks. They might have scored a fifth time in the third quarter when, far back in their own territory, they handed off to an end who broke clear and was galloping away unchallenged until he was unexpectedly dropped from behind. When the tackler brushed off his mud-smeared uniform, it was Sing Sing red and blue. He had incomprehensibly felled his own teammate. The stands erupted in fury. "Slug him!" "Gang him!" On the field, Captain Pitts forestalled a lynching and rallied the team to a final touchdown in the last quarter, for a decisive opening triumph, 33–0. Lawes was exultant, pronouncing it the finest, cleanest contest he had ever seen.

There was little time to celebrate. The following Sunday, Sing Sing would meet a more daunting foe, the Port Jervis Police Department from across the Hudson. A rematch with the forces of law and order, this time on the playing field. How better to even life's score? If the outlaws could beat the lawmen, then there was hope for all of them inside the walls. There were rumors that the Port Jervis team was under strength, that even with part-time and special officers the departmental roster of thirty could field a squad of only five, but commanders denied they were secretly recruiting ringers. The Black Sheep shrugged. It wouldn't be the first time the cops hadn't played square. They sharpened their cleats and dreamed of revenge. Lawes, well aware of the stakes, doubled the visitor admission to a dollar.

This time seven thousand spectators turned up—the inmate population in the grandstand, plus seventeen hundred visitors who bordered the field, another two thousand on the roadway leading to the field, and almost as many who were unable to get in and perched on hilltops outside the walls. Among the many distinguished guests were state prison officials and Mayor Frank "I Am the Law" Hague of Jersey City. Three thousand of the well-frisked outsiders were the Port Jervis cheering section, garbed in the team's black and orange. They brought their own fife, drum, and bugle corps, and three hundred cars bearing placards reading "You Can't Win, Sing Sing," an insulting twist on a popular police anticrime slogan.

The visitors took the field, orange helmets and jerseys ablaze in the blinding sunshine. Hisses were drowned out by good-natured cheering. Then Alabama Pitts and the Black Sheep lumbered out, to a far greater roar. The Sing Sing band followed, pumping out "That Wonderful Mother of Mine." The captains huddled with the referees and then a prisoner ran out with megaphone, bellowing numbers. The Port Jervis players looked around nervously, wondering if this was a coded Sing Sing strategy. When some inmates in the stands clambered hurriedly over their fellows to get out, all became clear. They had visitors in the waiting room.

Pitts kicked off and the field echoed to the thud of clashing leather and the grunts of the armored legions hammering each other's lines. After each scrimmage the intertwined bodies had to be pried apart. It was an even match, and neither side could score. Inmates in the stands kept up a raucous clamor, demanding, "Smear them babies."

Then as the last minutes of the second quarter ticked away, a Port Jervis quarterback streaked for the goal line, tailed by a lone Sing Sing pursuer. The convict made a flying leap and fell short by a yard. Port Jervis scored, and even convicts in the stands cheered the feat. The half ended with the cops ahead 7–0.

The Port Jervis band in blue and buff took the field, led by Bill, the team's goat. The prisoners clapped and hooted, vowing with knowing smiles that Sing Sing would indeed get their goat. When the Black Sheep's turn to entertain came, Bob Gooding stepped forth with his clarinet and trilled a plaintive melody. As the men caught on to the tune, laughter rocked the stands. It was the new Bing Crosby hit, "Just One More Chance."

> *Just one more chance*
> *To prove it's you alone I care for*
> *Each night I say a little prayer for*
> *Just one more chance. . . .*

> *I've learned the meaning of repentance*
> *Now you're the jury at my trial*
> *I know that I should serve my sentence*
> *Still, I'm hoping all the while*
> *You'll give me*
> *Just one more word. . . .*

The third quarter started off badly for the Black Sheep. The cops scored again on a forward pass, and after the kick was blocked, the score stood at 13–0.

With growing desperation, the Black Sheep tried to smash through the Port Jervis line, but the cops held fast, once coming close to bloodshed. A convict drew back a fist to deck a runner he had downed, then thought better of it and pulled the punch. A young Sing Sing ballcarrier ran for forty yards before he was dropped hard and had to be carried off in a stretcher. With time running out, Red Hope himself entered the fray, by far the oldest player on the field. He fared no better against the daunting Port Jervis line. When the clock ran out, Sing Sing had been blanked. The tally stood at cops 13, robbers 0. The Black Sheep immediately smelled a rat. It quickly came out that the visiting team was made up of former Port Jervis high school football stars and other hulking men who were not cops, at least not until the Port Jervis police chief deputized them the week before. Two, moreover, had played under aliases. The hometown was humiliated. The victory parade was canceled and the menus for the celebratory banquet were torn up. Lawes, sensing an advantage, was gracious. "We'll play them again within two weeks if they are willing," he said, "and we'll beat them even if they bring the same lineup."

Sing Sing savored one small triumph. Port Jervis's Bill the goat stayed behind, hostage of the prison.

That night, Lawes took over the microphone in the cabin housing the prison broadcasting studio and addressed the inmates on radio. "We lost today, but make no apologies for our defeat. The boys in the team played a good, clean game." He could not help but feel a sense of pride in observing the two camps that faced each other in the yard, he said. He wasn't talking about the contending teams but the denizens of Sing Sing and the spectators. The first were doomed to life inside the walls. The others could come and go. Yet there were no incidents. It vindicated his faith in his boys. There would be more games and a lot more work for the prison staff. But he wouldn't begrudge it as long as the boys lived up to their responsibilities. In the end, he was sure that all who attended went home convinced that prisoners were human beings entitled to the full respect due their compatriots outside the walls.

The cellblocks were silent; then came shouts: "Good speech all right!"

"The warden puts it across!"

But an angry voice cut them off. "So what? I bet there wasn't two men in that crowd'd give a guy a job so's the board could okay him to get out."

The following Sunday, Lawes reinforced his message in an article in the New York Times, where he had become something of a regular correspondent and a great favorite of the imperious Sunday editor, Lester Markel. Earlier in the year, Lawes had written an article for the Times Sunday magazine on the psychology of prisoners that Markel had called "the most eloquent piece on crime I have ever read." The year before, for an article on society's changing attitudes toward crime, Lawes, citing his busy schedule, was emboldened to ask for $200, but ended up settling for $150. Now, with Sing Sing's football team the subject of amused and outraged commentary by editorial writers and cartoonists, Markel had ordered up another magazine piece by Lawes on the significance of football behind the walls.

"Football in Sing Sing!" Lawes wrote. "Surprising isn't it? How we are coddling those fellows!" Prisons were peculiar places, he said. Whenever anything funny happened, it seemed ten times funnier if it happened inside prison walls. But there was nothing comical about the realities. For decades past, Sing Sing had been the toughest prison in the country, a place where inmates languished in airless cells and lockstepped silently to slavelike labor. Prisoners were lashed into conformity, yet wardens feared to cross the prison grounds, and the convict population kept growing. There was this paradox too: those convicted of a crime were to be segregated from the rest of humanity, yet eventually returned, rehabilitated, to society. The prisoner had to reflect on his crime, but that reflection was morbid, blocking the mental healing that would hasten his recovery. And so, Lawes said, the men were offered relief in work and hobbies and sports like football.

"They have a big fight ahead of them—the fight against despondency. It is a tough fight. In order to retain society's confidence it must be a clean fight. Football has all the essentials that encourage men to strive for accomplishment."

There were some 2,400 prisoners in Sing Sing, with 2,400 individual goals, Lawes concluded. "Every one of our prisoners has to make his own fight. As warden I am willing to help them reach it, provided they play fair and clean and with common purpose." During the Great War, he recalled, British troops ordered to attack the German trenches punted a football ahead and chased it into battle. The same spirit imbued his boys. Each, he said, "must make his own play, whether it takes him one year or fifty years."

27

Francis "Two-Gun" Crowley was set to die weeks into the new year of 1932. The pint-size killer had rejected a visit from his young sweetheart, Helen Walsh, who had won a court order to see him for a death-cell kiss of forgiveness. Crowley refused. It would be a Judas kiss, he insisted to Lawes. "All she wants is to sell a story to a New York newspaper." Lawes, who finally gave up trying to persuade him to see the girl, had his arm in a sling. He had fractured his right wrist in three places falling on the sleet-covered steps of his house, which was to be torn down as soon as the handsome new Georgian brick residence outside the walls was finished.

"Gee," Crowley said, "I feel sorry for you."

Lawes smiled indulgently. "And I feel sorry for you."

Duringer, Crowley's round-faced partner in the murder of the taxi dancer, had gone to the chair the month before. He had gained 40 pounds in the death house and was, at 260, perhaps the fattest man ever executed at Sing Sing. He shared his last meal of roast chicken and mashed potatoes with Crowley, who ate with gusto. "I'm in a great spot," Crowley gushed. "I get half the dinner."

The woman who had raised him came with her two daughters and sat in Lawes's office, struggling to understand where she and her son had gone wrong. "He was a thoughtful boy," she said. "He would bring home his pay envelope and give it to me." A news syndicate begged Lawes for a last interview with Crowley for a series on his life in crime, in his own words. Only court-approved visits were permitted the condemned, Lawes said. Then the syndicate sent a desperate telegram admitting that the articles had already been written. All Crowley had to do was sign his name to them. For this he would get half the proceeds, at least five thousand dollars. Sickened, Lawes told Crowley of the offer. Crowley laughed. "If mother had that five grand when I was a kid, maybe things would have been different."

With the clock ticking away Crowley's final hours, a package in brown paper arrived for him. A rosary and a note: "From your mother," the woman who had abandoned him at birth.

Crowley called for Lawes. They shook hands in farewell. "Try to see me again," Crowley said.

"Don't know if I'll be able to," Lawes said huskily.

"You come back or I won't go," Crowley said. As they spoke, a large water bug scuttled across the floor of the cell. "See that?" Crowley said. "I was about to kill it. Several times I wanted to crush it. It's a dirty-looking thing. But then I decided to give it a chance and let it live." Lawes smiled.

But he didn't go back to Crowley. Instead he sent some ice cream.

The guards came for Crowley at nine-thirty that night. Helen Walsh was still outside the gates, hoping for his change of heart over a death-house kiss. Crowley ignored her.

He shook off the comforting grip of guards and Father McCaffrey and walked unaided to the chair. He looked around at the room and said, almost to himself, "I don't mind." He unbuttoned his white shirt for the stethoscope. He caught sight of one of his favorite keepers and boomed out, "Hello, Sarge!" The officer answered in a whisper. "Hello, Crowley."

He sat down and, just before the guards slipped the mask over his head, said, "Give my love to my mother."

A foot strap was hanging loose and Crowley pointed it out. The guards obligingly tightened it. The priest droned a prayer. The switch was thrown.

Willie Sutton meanwhile had come back to Sing Sing, and he had vowed to leave on his own terms. Paroled out of the dread Dannemora after the 1929 riot, he had gone back to his old profession, relieving banks of excess cash. His favorite disguise was a police uniform. Then, betrayed by a jealous woman, he was cornered and arrested again. He got the full third degree, beaten bloody by detectives with blackjacks and rubber hoses. He refused to confess but was convicted anyway and sent back to Sing Sing in mid-1931, five years after his departure. Desperate to avoid a return to Dannemora, he told Lawes he needed to stay in Ossining to be closer to his lawyer, who was appealing his conviction. For the time being, Lawes ruled, he could remain.

Sutton immediately began planning his escape. Assigned to the shoe shop, he found a tunnel with pipes leading toward the powerhouse. But the pipes were too narrow for him to crawl though. Other escapees, meanwhile, tried their luck with poor results. One of Sutton's pals secreted himself in a sandwiched pair of hollowed-out mattresses being exported from the shop. He was immediately caught. "You know how many times that's been tried?" asked a guard.

Sutton brooded in his cell. Who said Sing Sing was escapeproof? He and fellow prisoner John Egan, serving ten years for assault and burglary, scoped out the possibilities. A friendly trusty told them which guard tower was un-manned at night and where they could find two ladders that could be lashed together. A prison buddy slipped Sutton two hacksaw blades, and another filched a guard's set of keys and made a quick impression with a slab of wax. Sutton and Egan bundled their blankets into sleeping forms and cut through the bars of their cells. With a wooden key made from the wax impression, they unlocked the first corridor door and opened the rest with picks. They surprised a trusty, tying him up with wire and tape, found the ladders, threw them up against the deserted wall, and lowered themselves down with a rope the guards used to haul up supplies. They were out. Sutton's Buick, by prearrangement, was idling on the road, and they bolted for it, Sutton stopping only to look down on the sleeping prison and say to himself, I beat you, you bastards!

A fellow prisoner with an equally enviable escape record remained behind on a lifetime sentence dictated by the Baumes laws. Reynolds Forsbrey, once called the nation's worst criminal, had been sprung by a commutation of Governor Roosevelt in the summer of 1931, after a decade in Sing Sing. He was hardly out when he was collared in Miami for a holdup in Manhattan. Now, at forty-six, he was back in prison for good. Forsbrey, a onetime ragged Brooklyn urchin and incurable romantic, had served time in a juvenile home, Elmira, and Sing Sing, all before his twenty-sixth birthday. Then in 1912 he met an adventurous young stenographer, Margaret Ryan, who was his kind of girl. They set a wedding date but had no money for the cere-mony, and when he should have been standing with Margaret in the aisle, he found himself in the Tombs, charged with murdering a Delancey Street jeweler to make the minister's fee. Margaret, who loved Reynolds, was beside herself. She smuggled him acid and hacksaws. They were found and he was sentenced to solitary, but no bars could contain their love. He escaped, only to be apprehended a month later in her arms in a Bronx apartment. This time he was sent to Clinton, where he was found to have a gasoline bomb big enough to level the cellblock. He went back into solitary, where he used a leg of his bed to pry apart the bars of his cell. He was then sent to Auburn, where he waylaid a guard, put on his uniform, and strolled out of the prison. Margaret was waiting nearby with money, fresh clothes, and food. They were bound for Canada but got lost and were discovered the next morning hiding in a haystack. He went back to solitary. He managed once again to saw through the bars of his cell and flee, only to be apprehended a third time. If only he'd been allowed to hear from Margaret, he explained, he wouldn't have escaped. But by now she had dropped from sight, despairing that he would ever be free. He went back to Sing Sing in 1921 for what looked like eternity, to a cell in solitary with his own guard posted outside the door day and night. Now, eleven years later, after a brief respite on the outside, Forsbrey was back behind Sing Sing's bars. Lawes was all for rehabilitation, but some men, he thought, belonged in prison, period.

It was all over for Forsbrey, but other fourth offenders would no longer be automatically sentenced to life. In April 1932, Governor Roosevelt signed a repeal of the Baumes laws, and fourth offenders faced a mere minimum fifteen years.

Lawes's third book, called, with dramatic hyperbole, *20,000 Years in Sing Sing,* came out the following month; a selection of the six-year-old Book of the Month Club, it was also an immediate best-seller in Sing Sing, where seventy-six prisoners and thirty-two guards snapped up copies. The title derived from the sentences of the prisoners, taken together, serving all their time for the dozen years of the Lawes administration. It opened dramatically: "I have been directed to kill lawfully one hundred fifty men and one woman." Roosevelt said he looked forward to reading it. At the FBI, the book was quickly digested for J. Edgar Hoover and disdainfully dismissed as a work "which is supposed to present the convict as a 'human being.'" It had no value for Bureau work, an aide decided, but suggested Hoover order a copy anyway for reference, and he did.

To celebrate its publication, Lawes threw a dinner for himself at the warden's residence following an exhibition of the drill squad, a baseball doubleheader, and tours of the prison. The guest list was heavy with press titans: H. L. Mencken, Henry R. Luce, Lowell Thomas, Jack Lait, Irvin Cobb, George T. Nathan, columnists O. O. McIntyre, Franklin P. Adams, and Heywood Broun, Henry Hazlitt of *The Nation,* Lewis Gannett of the *New York Herald Tribune,* and J. Donald Adams of the *New York Times* Book Review. Sending their regrets were the *Times's* Markel, Harry Warner of Warner Brothers, and the *Daily News* publisher, Captain Joseph Medill Patterson, who had masterminded the sensational photo of Ruth Snyder in the electric chair and whom Lawes, for the purposes of book publicity anyway, had clearly forgiven. Guests either drove to the prison gate or took the train to Ossining, where for twenty-five cents taxis ferried them the quarter mile to Sing Sing.

The book burnished Lawes's literary reputation, although rumors continued to circulate that others helped with the writing. The year before, the Broadway columnist Louis Sobol had alleged in the *New York Graphic* that at least some of the warden's magazine articles had actually been ghosted by Chapin. Lawes had strongly denied it, and Sobol issued a tongue-in-cheek correction. "Charles Chapin never wrote a single line for him. We apologize therefore but we wish we didn't have to. We still think that if Charlie Chapin didn't write some of Warden Lawes's stuff he should have been permitted to. If we were a busy warden and we had a newspaper man in our prison, darn if we wouldn't make him write most of our material. Wish we were a warden now and had someone to write this column for us."

Editors continued to clamor for Lawes's copy. The *Daily Mirror* bought reprint rights to Lawes's previous book, *Life and Death in Sing Sing,* and Lawes wrote managing editor Emile Gauvreau, a scrappy tabloidist and Walter Winchell's despised nemesis, to express his delight and assure Gauvreau that "every word is fact." Markel had chided Lawes over an article he had submitted in April for the Sunday magazine, "Young Criminals: The Rising Tide." He was annoyed to find that Lawes had reconstructed quotes or made them up entirely. Markel suggested that Lawes make it clear that while he may have spoken at length to prisoners like seventeen-year-old "Shorty," the words were his own. So after a long soliloquy by the young robber, Lawes now concluded his article: "Had Shorty been able to think clearly, I am sure this would have been his answer to my question." Markel was satisfied.

. . .

With the approach of Sing Sing's second football season, all the Black Sheep could think of was their rematch against the Port Jervis cops—"*Revanche,*" as Fred the scorekeeper kept muttering. This year the squad was in far better shape. During the summer, a candidate for the state Assembly, campaigning upstate with the Pawnee Democratic Club, had dropped in at Sing Sing for a game of baseball. Playing with the inmates, he figured, could draw attention and give his sagging political campaign a boost. Besides, one of the ballplayers was truly impressive, a natural athlete in for robbery who held varsity letters, or the Sing Sing equivalent, in baseball, football, basketball, and track. With players like Alabama Pitts, he thought, it might pay to stick around.

The visitor had been pretty good himself in his time. Captain of the un-defeated 1929 Notre Dame football squad, he had played for the legendary coach Knute Rockne, who complained that the alumni were always on his neck. Rockne wished for a place where he wouldn't be harassed by alumni, and Sing Sing fit the bill better than many.

Rockne would never get the chance, but his protégé would. He had re-turned home from Notre Dame to Yonkers and a coaching job at Manhattan College. But he was restless, and became a rental agent at Rockefeller Cen-ter. Then the political bug bit. He decided to run for the state Assembly, which was how he came to be with the Pawnee Democratic Club at Sing Sing. It was funny for convicts to be playing football, he thought. When he became coach, the joke was complete. His name was John Law.

A coach couldn't ask for a better setup, Law realized. The average age of the men was barely a year older than those who played college football, and he had a big pool to choose from. About 125 inmates each season tried out for the squad, of which he could choose the 35 strongest. He didn't have to worry about whether his players would meet scholastic standards. He also didn't have to worry about keeping his squad fit on the road. These men weren't temperamental, and they were used to taking orders. You could cor-rect them and they wouldn't take offense. And perhaps best of all, he didn't have to worry about replacing graduates. There were few departures, and those who did leave, often returned. For some reason Law couldn't quite fig-ure out, the best players were those serving time for robbery.

The football squad had special privileges. Players ate together in the prison mess hall so they could talk business. Training rules were bent to allow ciga-rettes in the locker room. There was no smoking elsewhere for the players, but if they lit up while changing after a game, everyone looked the other way.

Drawn by Law, other star recruits soon joined the coaching staff. Vic Kennard, onetime Harvard football coach, had been persuaded to do a good deed by visiting Sing Sing and instructing the team in the finer points of kicking. But Kennard was clearly nervous about being around criminals. Fi-nally he agreed to don a sweat suit and get out on the field. He took out his wallet and gold watch and asked if he could check them somewhere. No such place existed at Sing Sing, he was told; he should just leave them in the gym. Dubious and very unhappy, Kennard complied. He worked with the boys for a few minutes, glancing forlornly at the gym and his imperiled valu-ables, then suddenly broke off and said he had to be going. He rushed back to his clothes to find his wallet and watch where he had left them. "Hell," he said, converted, "I couldn't get away with that even at Harvard." Kennard signed on, joining John Law and visiting coaches like Lou Little of Colum-bia University and his former assistant, Herb Kopf of Manhattan College, and star players from Columbia and Harvard.

The 1932 season started under a cloud. As the team was holding its last practice before its opening game against the Clover Athletic Club of the Bronx, a holdup man who had recently arrived for a stay of ten to twenty-five years took advantage of the hubbub to escape, perhaps under a departing coal truck. The men agreed that was pretty unsporting.

Leading the Black Sheep onto the field was ten-year-old Cherie in a gray West Point–tailored uniform with a black Sam Browne belt. Behind her marched the band and then the drill corps, also in cadet uniforms, two com-panies inevitably segregated by race, a corps of blacks and a corps of whites. There followed stretcher bearers—fondly dubbed the Two Ghouls—carrying a dummy policeman and a banner inscribed "You Can't Win Because John Law Is on Our Side." And bringing up the rear was Sing Sing's new mascot, the Black Sheep, which was actually a goat. The Sing Sing squad made short work of their visitors, romping over the Bronxmen, 19–6, once Law imple-mented the daunting "Rockne shift."

The following Sunday, Sing Sing blanked the American Legion's Irwin Post from the Bronx, 12–0, thanks primarily to William "Jumbo" Morano, 240 pounds from Manhattan's bad East Side.

Cherie Lawes in her
West Point–tailored
uniform, as mascot for
the Sing Sing football
team. (JOAN L. JACOBSEN)

The season's third contest—the long-anticipated rematch against the Port Jervis cops—would be Jumbo's last. He was graduating, one of the few Black Sheep who made it out. Coach Law had found him a spot on a semi-pro team in Paterson, New Jersey, where the ex-con from Sing Sing was sure to be quite a draw. The Black Sheep had already lost another stalwart, William Egan, the left end, who had gotten his ticket out. Game or no game, he was leaving, never—or so he hoped—to return again.

The largest crowd in Sing Sing's athletic history assembled that October 16 to see the Black Sheep seek vindication against their blood enemies from Port Jervis, who this time were presumably playing with real cops. The contest was brutal. When an orange-clad figure was left on the turf after an early skirmish, the prison band played the Death March. "One cop down, ten to go!" came the cry from the stands. "The cops can't take it." Only five minutes into the action, the Black Sheep's quarterback ran the ball forty-one yards and slapped it down for a touchdown. Pitts kicked the goal for a 7–0 lead.

Jumbo's mother had come up to see him play and shouted from the stands: "Be careful and don't get hurt!" She needn't have worried. Morano kept crashing through the Port Jervis line, collecting clinging Orangemen like beads on a necklace. "Hold 'em, jail!" roared the stands. They screamed for Jumbo to be given five more years, just so he could stay and play.

At the half, Sing Sing's lead remained unchallenged. Cherie led the prison drill team onto the field. "B Company all present and accounted fo' suh!" shouted the sergeant of the all-black platoon.

"They'd better be!" answered someone in the stands.

The second half was as bitterly fought as the first. Six cops were carried off. When it was all over, the score held. Sing Sing had triumphed, 7–0. The vindication stood, but not for long. In a return bout just six weeks later, the cops turned the tables, beating the Black Sheep by the very same score, 7–0.

Between games, Lawes sat in a New York City courtroom, a defense witness in a lawsuit against the state by the family of Reuben Kaminsky, the seventeen-year-old youth knifed at Sing Sing three years before. Lawes at one point looked around mildly and said, "I could kill any man in this room now." When the uproar subsided, he explained that not even the court officer by his side could prevent a sudden act of violence by someone bent on evil. And so it was too, he said, at Sing Sing.

28

Long before Cherie had gone to Hollywood in 1930, Lawes had been mesmerized by the silver screen. He had staked his early career on using his boys to shoot the silent film *The Brand of Cowardice* at New Hampton in 1916. He had befriended Charlie Chaplin shortly after taking over Sing Sing and hosted him and other stars at the prison. He had brought in screenings and premieres, even in the death house. And now, in January 1933, while the state's other wardens were invited to a private showing in Albany—where his friend Franklin Roosevelt was preparing to be inaugurated as president—Lawes was escorting his veteran actress daughter, Cherie, and a hundred ex–Sing Sing inmates to the Manhattan Strand Theater in New York to screen the Warner Brothers version of his book *20,000 Years in Sing Sing*, starring (at Lawes's urging) Spencer Tracy, and a young belle from Lowell, Massachusetts, making her thirteenth picture, Bette Davis. Hollywood had taken some liberties with the book, as the breathless trailers made clear.

SEE

What Happens in the

CITY WITHOUT WOMEN

And to the Love-Starved
Women Locked Outside!

Tracy played Tom Connors, a tough con who goes head to head with an equally hard-boiled warden bedeviled by a jailbreak. Connors has a sweetheart (Davis) who visits him every day but then is critically injured in an auto accident. The warden allows him out to visit her and he gets into a fight with her lawyer. She shoots and kills the lawyer, but Connors takes the rap and goes to the chair.

Critics were less than wowed, and Lawes, who served as technical adviser, had mixed feelings about the picture. He picked it apart, pointing out that the warden wouldn't carry around a master key any more than he would carry a gun. And no prisoner would ever be sent off unaccompanied to visit his girl. But otherwise he liked the way it depicted prisoners harnessed to the rules. Turning critic, Lawes lauded Tracy's "marvelous performance" and promised it would make people think, which was all anyone could ever expect. And he said, "If it makes them think more about the inequalities of capital punishment it will have accomplished a great deal." Left unmentioned were the lucrative sales. With the help of the movie, the book had already sold nearly fifty-seven thousand copies and the publisher was rushing to print another five thousand.

Another boon came out of the film. With the state prohibiting payments to prisoners who played extras in the movie, Lawes got Harry Warner instead to put up money for a gymnasium at Sing Sing to which Lawes also contributed some of his earnings.

He diversified, turning *20,000 Years in Sing Sing* into a radio show as well. Sponsored by the William R. Warner Company, makers of Sloan's Liniment, the half-hour program of fictionalized crime stories narrated by Lawes himself premiered on the National Broadcasting Company's Blue Network Sundays at 9 P.M., shortly after the film's debut. For each of his performances, Lawes was soon receiving the princely sum of twelve hundred dollars, and two hundred for any rebroadcast, destined for the charitable Lawes Work Extension Fund and the purchase of radios for the prisoners. Lawmakers would have frowned on a state official's use of his position to enrich himself.

With Ben Grauer as one of the regular announcers reading an opening commercial ("Perhaps right now you've got a kink in your muscles, or your back is aching from overexertion, or you're all choked up with a cold; then by all means use Sloan's Liniment for quick relief . . ."), the shows often began with Lawes welcoming someone into his office for a talk that ushered in the dramatization of a crime and its inevitable punishment. Lawes had the last word, drawing a moral from the story. And listeners were invited to send in a Sloan's Liniment box flap for free gifts like a child's fingerprinting kit or an illustrated booklet about Sing Sing written, of course, by Lawes, who by now in 1933 was easily America's most famous warden and the nation's second most famous crime fighter after J. Edgar Hoover, although neither man was much a fan of the other.

From Sing Sing, it seemed hard to imagine that people outside were standing in breadlines and jumping out of windows, although Lawes, who never shied away from a stunt if it aided charity, joined the International Itinerant Workers Union—the Hoboes of America—on their silver anniversary, receiving a membership card and uttering the oath: "I pledge myself to assist all runaway boys and induce them to return to their homes and parents."

The Laweses meanwhile had finally said farewell to their dark and rambling hundred-year-old dwelling adjoining the old cellblock inside the walls and moved into a Georgian brick mansion the state had built for them just south of the prison on a bluff overlooking the Hudson. From the entrance hall, French doors led to the large living room with three exposures and an enormous fireplace. Six windows offered spectacular vistas of the river and broad expanses of lawns, gardens, and a tennis court. Across the entrance hall was a library with oak paneling carved by prisoners more than a century before and carried over from the old house, and a carved desk, also built by prisoners. The sunny dining room also overlooked the river and gardens. Upstairs were four bedrooms, including the master with two four-poster beds, and a music room. The third floor had yet another bedroom, a small office, Lawes's barbershop, a card room, and a game room with a pool table. In the basement was a tailor shop. The outlying grounds also accommodated a garage, a stable, a laundry, and a chicken house. They were living well.

For Lawes's fiftieth birthday that September, Kathryn indulged in a stunning extravagance. From Cartier on Fifth Avenue she bought him a platinum ring with a rectangular diamond and two baquette sapphires. It cost $1,825—more than two years of wages for an average factory worker in the pit of the depression. Lawes was donating his radio earnings to charity, but his movie royalties and speaking fees clearly left plenty more.

For the inmates there remained, above all, football. The Black Sheep had won their first three games of the 1933 season, but it was the next contest

The new warden's mansion, around 1930. (OSSINING HISTORICAL SOCIETY MUSEUM)

that really counted, the fourth engagement against Sing Sing's archrivals, the Port Jervis cops. Befitting the occasion, Lawes had introduced something special. Up in the south grandstand, where the inmates sat, a new refreshment booth sold hot dogs and soda pop. It was off limits to the guests, since no mingling was allowed between the resident population and the outsiders, but Whitey, a convict with privileges, made regular catering runs to the visitors.

The anticipation was nearly palpable, but in the end it was no contest. Led by Pitts and Moon Byrd, the large black fullback described by A. J. Liebling of the *World-Telegram* as "a born toter, who brooks no interference with his toting," the Black Sheep jumped out to an early lead. At 195 muscular pounds, Byrd, known as "the Black Express," teamed up with Pitts to steamroller the visitors, who were no match for Law's squad. The final score was 40–13.

A commentator for the *Syracuse Herald* was overwhelmed. "If we ever got a ticket to 'the place down under,'" he wrote, "we would like to be flanked by a couple of fellows like 'Alabama' Pitts and 'Moon' Byrd. . . . Those boys would walk right up to the door, kick it open, carry you through hell and bring you out the other side, and without even flinching."

29

Whatever the diversions at Sing Sing, death demanded its due. To Lawes's disgust, it next marked for sacrifice a pigeon-boned, dark-eyed, and raven-haired twenty-eight-year-old mother of two little girls and a boy, Anna Antonio of Albany, who in the spring of 1934 was marking her first year in the death house. Kathryn, also a mother of three, was particularly affected by her plight. Two years before, on Easter morning, Antonio's husband, Salvatore, a railroad worker with shady connections and, according to his wife, a weakness for dope dealing and wife beating, was found stabbed and shot to death on a road outside Albany.

The investigation led to two of Salvatore's associates, Sam Feraci and Vincent Saetta, who confessed to the murder but implicated the widow, saying she had commissioned them to kill her husband for $800 of the $5,300 she would collect in insurance money. All three were convicted the following year and quickly sentenced to die. Appeals, however, delayed the execution for a year, during which Antonio prayed and sewed, making, among other garments, a pink cotton dress trimmed with a white collar.

As the only woman on death row, she was attended by three matrons specially hired at a hundred dollars each a month, their duties to include standing in front of the chair to block any execution photos. Lawes was not about to be betrayed by the press again.

That Easter, Antonio received lilies and tulips from the Sing Sing greenhouses, a belated legacy of the long-departed Chapin. In May, as the only mother behind the walls, she received a Mother's Day tribute from her fellow prisoners. In June, her lawyer; her brother, Pasquale Capello; and her three children, nine-year-old Phyllis, six-year-old Marie, and three-year-old Frankie, traveled to the executive mansion in Albany to plead with Governor Lehman for a commutation. If anyone would sympathize with Antonio's plight, they thought, it would be Lehman, the liberal-minded banking scion and Roosevelt confidant known for his progressivism.

He turned them down the next day.

The execution was set for a night in late June. Antonio had shrunk to eighty-five pounds. She had made out her will, asking that Pasquale, a world war veteran, bring up her children. "He has been very good to them," she said. "If I could only live to comfort my children! It's them, more than myself, that I'm thinking of." A barber trimmed her hair. Her lawyer, Daniel H. Prior, came to visit, bringing Frankie, who kissed his mother through a screen and delightedly played with her pet kitten. Fifteen minutes before the first of the three condemned killers was to be led to the chair, Saetta called to a guard and demanded to see Lawes. He came quickly.

Saetta said Antonio was innocent. He and Feraci had planned and carried out the killing, he said, after they and Salvatore had argued over a seventy-five-dollar debt. He rambled on.

With the clock ticking toward the appointed hour of eleven, Lawes was aching to cut Saetta off and finish his manifesto for him. But he forced himself to let Saetta tell the story his way. Only when he was finally finished did Lawes bolt for the telephone to call Lehman and announce a two-hour delay. Antonio, stressed beyond all endurance in her overheated cell, collapsed in a faint. Precious minutes passed as Saetta's statement was dictated to a typist, signed by him, and then read to the governor. Waiting reporters chewed their pencils, agonizing over press deadlines. In their death cells, Antonio and her two doomed compatriots endured the excruciating wait.

After listening to Saetta's statement, Lehman granted a twenty-four-hour reprieve.

Antonio got the news in her cell. Still half comatose, she didn't know whether she was alive or dead. After asking if the report was true and being told it was, she burst into tears. "Oh! Thank God!" She knew after all, she said, that she would never be executed.

The next day, her agonizing wait began anew as the governor huddled with advisers at his Park Avenue apartment.

One hour before she was once again to go to the chair, the decision came:

Lehman had granted a ten-day delay, time for her lawyer to move for a new trial based on Saetta's statement. The prosecutor was enraged, branding the manifesto "an absolute fabrication of lies" at odds with everything brought forth during the investigation and trial. In her cell, Antonio burned candles alongside a crucifix.

As the days crawled by and the new deadline neared, the governor ordered a third reprieve, delaying the execution a month to allow the state's highest court, the Court of Appeals, to consider whether to order a new trial.

Antonio's hair, where it had been trimmed for the electrode, was growing back. She asked to be allowed to keep it. Lawes assented.

Days later the appeals court ruled. It would not intervene. No points overlooked or misapprehended had been presented, and new evidence could not be introduced on reargument.

Nevertheless, Prior, her energetic lawyer, grasping at new information—a priest's enigmatic call to the widow the night of the killing—obtained an order from yet another local justice requiring the prosecutor to explain why a new trial should not be granted. But then the same court quickly ruled against a retrial, finding that the new claims, however "eloquent and potent as they may be, at the portals of mercy," had "no proper place in the stern administration of justice."

Lawes was dizzied by the seesaw judgments of life and death.

An exhausted Prior was unable immediately to lay his hands on a copy of the order, but newspapermen showed him excerpts. He appealed to Lehman for clemency. He was running out of options.

Antonio's brother, Pasquale, visited with Frankie, while Phyllis and Marie stayed in an orphan home. "Anna is bearing up better than I expected," Pasquale told reporters. "When I said good-bye to her she called me back and made me promise that I'd take care of her children." He would keep Frankie with him in Schenectady. He'd like to take the girls, too, he said, but his wife was in ill health. If she got better, perhaps they could take the girls out of the orphanage.

A delegation of Brooklyn politicians traveled to Albany to beg Lehman for clemency. The governor listened, and pledged to give the case close consideration.

In her cell, Antonio was losing her last hope. She stared at a photo of Phyllis and read a letter from Marie, about to turn seven, to whom she had sent a box of candy and a dress she had made. If the news was good, Marie hoped to have a birthday party. Frankie played with a ball until it rolled away beyond his reach. His mother called to him. "Here, Frankie," she said, handing him an apple, "here's another ball for you; it won't bounce, but it's a nice ball just the same."

Frankie wasn't fooled, but he played with it anyway. Antonio hugged him farewell. "I hope you grow up to be a good man, Frankie!"

She was offered a last meal but rejected it. A matron brought her a cup of coffee and she drank it. She had eaten nothing for days.

The barber returned to snip her hair again. She submitted quietly. "It's going to be, I guess" was all she said. When the barber left, she put on a gingham dress she had made, blue like the keepers' shirts with white trimming at the front and sleeves. It had been starched and ironed by one of her matrons.

She donned her stockings, and one was promptly slit for the leg electrode. "I'm not afraid to die," she volunteered. "I have nothing on my conscience. I never killed anyone." She continued to ramble. Yes, she had heard that Saetta or Feraci had marked her husband for death, but she had shrugged it off. She didn't care. If she had wanted to kill him, she said, she could have done it easily. "There were always plenty of guns and dope in the house to do it with."

All afternoon she asked if any word had come from the governor. Told none had, she despaired. "Why doesn't he say something? He knows everything there is to know!" She was lost, she said. "God alone can help me."

Father McCaffrey called at her cell door. "Are you ready, my child?"

The priest and the principal keeper led her down from the women's wing to the circular arena of cells that the condemned, with sardonic humor, had dubbed "the dance hall" and along the fabled last mile through the brown door to a room ablaze with incandescent white light. Eyes stared at her. The witnesses. Then there was the heavy wooden chair. She stepped forward mechanically, paused, turned, backed up two steps, and sat down. Two matrons buckled the strap across her thin chest and held her skeletal arms while the guards tightened the leg straps and applied the hood over her head.

Her lips moved in prayer. The room was so quiet that her murmuring voice sounded thunderous. The matrons took up positions at the foot of the chair, deliberately blocking the views of the witnesses. The electricity crackled, followed by a crash as a news reporter toppled over in a dead faint.

After Antonio's body was wheeled out for autopsy and she was followed to the chair by Feraci and then Saetta, Lehman issued a statement. The case had received his most intense scrutiny, he said. It was so distressing that he had sought the slightest fact that would merit his intervention. He had granted delay after delay—and still found no reason to thwart the will of the people. The entire history of the state, Lehman said, afforded few instances where a capital case had received such scrutiny. The jury and all court reviews had found her guilty of murder. And after the most careful study of the record, he too, Lehman said, believed her guilty. As for the appeals for clemency on grounds of her sex, the law made no distinction between male and female. The crime was abhorrent. The administration of justice had to be fair. In this case, he was satisfied it was. As long as there was a death penalty, he was obligated to carry it out.

Not long after Antonio's execution, Lawes had Lehman to lunch at Sing Sing. Kathryn was particularly taken by the easygoing humanitarian who had launched his public career bringing relief to war-ravaged Europe and to whom they had looked to spare the life of the young mother of three. "If I knew you were such a kind man," she told the governor, "I would never have given up."

If Antonio's state-ordered death was supposed to deter murder, Lawes was more convinced than ever that it was futile. And the case that proved so was unfolding even as the papers bannered Antonio's last desperate efforts to escape the chair.

That summer, in the small upstate city of Oneonta between Albany and Binghamton, a hefty and exuberant forty-seven-year-old divorcée with the fetching name of Eva Coo was running a roadhouse and truck stop bordello coyly known as Little Eva's Place. Coo, born Eva Currie in Ontario, had drifted to Toronto in her teens and married a rail worker named William Coo. The marriage failed and she moved on to upstate New York, where Prohibition created a vibrant and illicit after-hours drinking industry.

One fixture at the bar was Coo's crippled handyman, a onetime farmer named Harry "Gimpy" Wright, who lived, and drank copiously, at the roadhouse. Coo also employed a twenty-eight-year-old mother of two, Martha

Clift, from Pennsylvania. One night in June 1934, Wright went missing. The police found his battered body in a ditch, the apparent victim of a hit-and-run driver. That might have been the end of it except that Coo soon turned up at an insurance office as the beneficiary of policies totaling as much as twelve thousand dollars on Wright's life. Suspicious investigators then discovered that Coo and Clift had been near the crime scene that night, and a search of Coo's home turned up dozens of insurance policies in the names of acquaintances. The women quickly confessed. They had taken Wright to an old farmhouse in the area, bashed in his head with a mallet, run him over several times with the car, and thrown him into the ditch. But each blamed the other as the actual killer. The sheriff, in a grisly bit of detective work, exhumed Wright's decomposing corpse and arrayed it in various locations, making the women explain how and where and when they had murdered him.

By August, just as Anna Antonio was meeting her end in Sing Sing's electric chair, Coo went on trial in the baseball shrine of Cooperstown, with Wright's poor remains exhumed yet again as evidence. The prosecution called no fewer than seventy-four witnesses over four weeks, including Clift, who fingered Coo as the instigator. The jury of farmers took barely two hours to find her guilty of first-degree murder. A judge swiftly sentenced her to death. Clift was allowed to plead guilty to second-degree murder and given twenty years to life. While she was shipped to the women's prison at Bedford Hills, Coo went to Sing Sing, to the death house cell earlier occupied by Ruth Snyder and Anna Antonio, previous man-killers whose dire fate had clearly not deterred her. "Well," she said, looking around, "I'm here at last."

30

Thirty-five miles south of Sing Sing, the gilded art deco ballroom of the Waldorf-Astoria Hotel on Park Avenue was aglow with spotlights and candle shine. On that March night in 1935, five hundred luminaries of the penal establishment, law, business, and politics turned out at a testimonial dinner sponsored by the Boys Athletic League, a unit of the Boys Clubs of America, to honor Lawes for thirty years of service to the state. A first-day cover issued by the Sing Sing Philatelic Association marked the occasion with an envelope bearing Lawes's image, the dates, and a legend: "In appreciation of thirty years service as a humanitarian and penologist."

Lawes was a literary celebrity by then as well. A recent newspaper column listing great dollar-and-under books cited *War and Peace*, *Les Misérables*, *The Hound of the Baskervilles*, *Tobacco Road*, *Lady Chatterley's Lover*, and *20,000 Years in Sing Sing*.

For the Waldorf banquet, Harry Warner flew in from Hollywood to join the likes of Mayor Fiorello H. La Guardia, Father Cashin, and Corrections Commissioner Walter Thayer. "This is a bad time for any man with vision to be mayor of the city of New York," piped the scrappy La Guardia, who had inherited the mess left by the fugitive Jimmy Walker. "Not until you are able, Warden Lawes, to put a sign in front of your institution—'Going Out of Business'—will government and society have done their duty. There must be something wrong with society if we have so many prisoners."

From Washington, President Roosevelt wired: "Your devotion to the objective of a square deal for the man in prison has had an effect wider than the confines of our own state and a profound influence on the solution of a

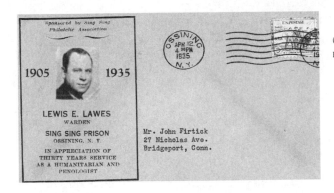

vexing social problem." Charlie Chaplin cabled congratulations, adding: "However, speaking for the good of society, I think it would be a mistake to release you from Sing Sing even after doing thirty years there and if I had my way I would insist that you remain."

Mounting the podium, Lawes, his oratorical skills polished in dozens of speeches to civic forums and radio listeners, professed puzzlement over why he was being celebrated. Indeed, he said, he should be lionizing his worthy guests. Words of thanks being inadequate, he asked that his audience merely gaze at him to sense his innermost feelings of gratitude. The crowd was captivated.

In sharp and practiced rhetoric, Lawes ranged widely over the inequities of a justice system that favored the rich, the unnecessary complexity of rules of evidence, the benefits of parole, and the social origins of criminality.

Their difficult era of history, Lawes wound up, was laying the groundwork for the America of the future, a country where youth might find a new deal—he had worked the phrase in deliberately—to grow into law-abiding citizens. It was really quite simple, he said. All the energy put into conferences on criminality should be channeled into developing community centers for young people. It would put wardens like him out of business. "Prisons exist," Lawes concluded, "only because conditions which send men to prisons exist."

The widely publicized event and Lawes's speech projected his name and cause before the public as little had before. In Albany, an Assembly Democrat boosted Lawes as a candidate to succeed Lehman as governor in 1936. But with Lawes averse to politics and Lehman inclined to run for a third two-year term, Lawes quashed the effort. His first loyalty, anyway, was to his boys.

Two months later, Lawes had his textbook case of the pitfalls facing ex-cons. Alabama Pitts, having served five years of good time, won state parole at age twenty-four. It was a bittersweet day not only for Sing Sing's sports teams but also for its menagerie. In addition to his feats on the gridiron and the diamond, Pitts had been taking care of Sing Sing's captive foxes, Chinese pheasant cocks, hens, turkeys, ram, and goats. In the 1934 Big Pen football season, the tall blond quarterback had carried the Black Sheep to an 8-3 record, including a decisive 41–0 shutout of the despised Port Jervis cops. Now, the following spring, Pitts was batting a phenomenal .500 for the baseball squad and was being scouted by several big-league clubs and some minor-league teams, including the Albany Senators of the International League, the oldest of the minors, where Babe Ruth had gotten his start with the Baltimore Orioles.

Senators general manager and erstwhile second baseman Johnny Evers, pint-size cornerstone of the immortalized Chicago Cubs double-play combination Tinkers to Evers to Chance in the century's first decade, offered Pitts a two-hundred-dollar-a-month contract to play outfield. Lawes urged him to take it. Pitts, awaiting release, signed, triggering jubilation in the state capital, where the home team was in the cellar.

A rival club owner denounced it as a publicity stunt, saying that at least Pitts should have changed his name. More ominously, the International League refused to approve the contract and was backed by Judge William G. Bramham, president of the National Association, baseball's first organizing body, who called the contract against "the interests of baseball."

But public support for Pitts was strong. When he walked out of Sing Sing with his mother on June 6, imposingly dapper in a double-breasted suit and rakish hat, a hundred newsmen and fans greeted him. He said he didn't blame Bramham. "Baseball is a business," Pitts conceded, and the judge was just looking out for the game. But Pitts said he was sure he would justify any faith placed in him.

He was particularly grateful to Lawes. "The principal thing I have learned here is how to make good as a citizen," he said. "I came here when I was young and foolish. I did what I was accused of. I had a different view of life then." He had learned, he said, to be happy without money. But he wanted to be able to support his struggling mother. Lawes returned the praise, calling Pitts "a man in every sense of the word." Judge Bramham's ruling, he said, effectually restored the long-despised prison stripes for those who left the walls, forever tagging them as ex-cons, and he urged the International League to reconsider.

The reply was disheartening. "It is not a question of the individual," the judge replied by wire, "but the case presents a question: Shall the ranks of organized baseball be opened to ex-convicts?" It was his duty, he continued, to answer in the negative. But he was willing to be overruled by the association's executive committee and the commissioner of baseball.

The next day, at a night game in Syracuse, the Senators had a former police chief introduce Pitts from home plate and the crowd roared. Evers stuck by Pitts, deploring the rejection of his contract and saying the club would honor it even if Pitts never took the field. Pitts's mother joined in, begging Bramham to let her son play. Lawes added to the clamor, attacking Bramham's stance as "narrow" and "reactionary." It was hard to fathom, Lawes said. "It seems to me that if a man is able to do any legitimate work, he should be allowed to do it, not discouraged."

Others also leaped to Pitts's defense. A Manhattan radio station sought him for a sports announcer. Manager Jimmie Wilson of the Philadelphia Phillies offered to sign him. "I need a good-hitting extra man. If Pitts can fill the bill, there's a suit waiting for him at the clubhouse. I don't care what he did. He's paid his debt to society and that is finished. He should not have to pay any interest until he dies." Dizzy Dean and Pepper Martin of the St. Louis Cardinals cabled Bramham in support of Pitts. A sports columnist for the *Buffalo Courier-Express* called the ban on Pitts "Un-Christian, un-American and un-sportsmanlike." Two pro baseball teams, the New York Giants and the Brooklyn Dodgers, offered to give him a tryout. Fans circulated petitions backing Pitts. Lawes was swamped with telephone calls and telegrams, eight hundred in a few days.

Less than a week after Pitts's release, the executive committee ruled. It backed Bramham's ban. Pitts was driven to tears, calling it "the hardest blow of my life." Evers was also distraught. If Pitts couldn't play, said the diamond legend whose mastery of the baseball rule book equaled his storied fielding, then he too was prepared to quit the game.

Support for Pitts continued to build. Even the store manager he had robbed in 1930 rallied to his cause. If it was safe enough to let Pitts out, he wired the team, then it was safe enough to let him play baseball.

Baseball commissioner Kenesaw Mountain Landis had the final word. Landis, a craggy-faced, white-thatched federal judge appointed to the bench by Theodore Roosevelt and named for the Civil War battle that had cost his father his leg in Georgia, had saved the new national pastime in 1915, when the Federal League sued, challenging organized baseball's monopolistic character. Landis delayed a ruling until a negotiated settlement could be reached, avoiding a potentially disastrous court test. So he became the natural choice to restore confidence in the sport after the "Black Sox" World Series–fixing scandal of 1919, shortly before Lawes took over Sing Sing. Now the Pitts case was in his hands.

As they waited tensely for his verdict, Pitts and Evers visited Lawes and later, with fourteen-year-old Cherie, drove down to the Polo Grounds to see the Giants beat the Cardinals. After the game, Pitts stopped at radio station WEAF to talk about the case. A reversal, he said, "would do much to help Warden Lawes build up the self-respect of the men at the prison."

Two days later, on June 17, Landis ruled. He recalled the armed robbery that had landed Pitts in Sing Sing, and at least five others he had never been charged with. Landis said he was in complete agreement in principle with Bramham and the executive committee. Like the military and public service, baseball could adopt standards to disqualify criminals. The policy could stand.

And yet, Landis continued, "a new situation has arisen." Pitts had been pronounced reformed, and denying him a chance to play would thwart his rehabilitation. "Solely for these reasons," Landis concluded, "Pitts will be allowed to play." He had to sit out the exhibition games but could join the team when the regular season started.

Pitts, who got the news first, triumphantly telephoned Sing Sing, reaching Kathryn. "They told me I can play!" he shouted. Kathryn ordered the news announced on the prison loudspeakers. The men broke into cheers.

Lawes was jubilant. "The decision speaks for itself and shows intelligence," he said. "Nobody can add to it."

Evers too was beside himself. "I've had many thrills in baseball," he said, "but this is the greatest thrill I've ever had in my life."

Lawes savored the victory, but the business of death soon intruded. Eva Coo, the buxom roadhouse madam who had bludgeoned her crippled handyman, walked her last mile to the chair in a flowered blue print dress. Lawes had monitored the final details but absented himself from the execution. He couldn't bear it.

"Good-bye, darlings," she breathed to the two matrons who stationed themselves decorously between her and the twenty-two witnesses, before the crackling current rendered her limp. She was quickly followed into the death chamber by a twenty-seven-year-old upstate gangster, Leonard Scarnici, who had killed a detective during a bank holdup in Rensselaer. He came in chomping gum and puffing on a cigarette. Lawes had reappeared. "Okay, Warden?" Scarnici asked. Lawes nodded. The mask was applied. A priest proffered a crucifix and the condemned man kissed it. "Okay, pard," he said. Then he too succumbed to the current.

Afterward Lawes talked to reporters. "I don't know if she was innocent or guilty. But I do know that she got a rotten deal all around." To pay a lawyer, she had signed over her rights to collect a debt owed her. "She gave them everything to defend her," Lawes said. "I suppose I ought not to say anything. My job was to kill that woman, not defend her." But he couldn't hold back. She might be guilty as hell, he said, "but she got a raw deal." What galled Lawes most was a letter from her trial attorneys. "Do you know what they did to help her lately? Know what? One of them wrote to me saying he'd like four invitations to her execution. That's the kind of defense she had."

But Lawes had other things on his mind. In a flurry of activity, he was teaming up with a publisher and a socialite to start up a new monthly magazine called *Prison Life Stories*, with grand ambitions of distribution "throughout the entire English-speaking world." He was also contracting for $2,000 with *True Story* magazine for a four-part serial of one of his prison stories. At the same time, he was negotiating with Warner Brothers to film a story he had written, called "Over the Wall," based on the exploits of Alabama Pitts. And he was also talking to the Edison Film Corporation about an option on one of his crime stories, "Beating Back," with himself as on-screen narrator, for $2,500 plus 10 percent of the net.

In the middle of it all, he was rushing to prepare for a grueling if deluxe European trip that would take him, Kathryn, and the girls across the Atlantic, first-class to London on the French Line flagship *Normandie*, the largest and fastest ship in the world. From London they would head to

Window display of Lawes's magazine. (LAWES COLLECTION FROM SPECIAL COLLECTIONS, LLOYD SEALY LIBRARY, JOHN JAY COLLEGE OF CRIMINAL JUSTICE)

Dublin, Killarney, Paris, Cologne, Baden-Baden, Lausanne, Florence, Rome, Venice, Vienna, and finally Berlin, the Nazi capital of Hitler's young Third Reich, to attend the Eleventh International Penal and Penitentiary Congress in its first meeting in the German capital since the group's founding in 1872. The family would then return to New York on the German vessel *Bremen*. All this in just twenty days in July 1935.

Just then, as if there weren't enough to think about before leaving, their daughter Crystal, twenty-four and a social worker at the Westchester County Department of Child Welfare, revealed that she had eloped. She and her beau of two years, Jack Stratton Douvarjo, a florist from nearby Mount Vernon, had been secretly married at St. Patrick's Cathedral in May. Lawes and Kathryn had had no idea. It only came out now, nearly two months later, when the young couple returned from a three-day honeymoon in Atlantic City. Lawes was mortified. He had no trouble controlling more than two thousand criminals but couldn't keep track of his own daughter. And he was undoubtedly hurt by her decision. Perhaps she wasn't his special darling, like Cherie, but he had doted on her nonetheless, detailing Chapin to escort her to the train when she left Sing Sing to return to college, and painstakingly coaching her himself through her civil service exam. Nevertheless, any pain he felt he kept to himself, and he took the inevitable ribbing with good grace. Lawes invited the newlyweds to live at the warden's residence until they could set up housekeeping on their own.

As they readied for their departure to Europe, the Edison Film project "Beating Back" was going nowhere, but Lawes hurriedly signed a contract with Warner Brothers for "Over the Wall." It paid him ten thousand dollars, a fabulous sum in the depression. If any of the proceeds were to be shared with Pitts, the contract made no mention of it.

Later that day, Lawes, Kathryn, Kathleen, and Cherie boarded the *Normandie* with a passenger list of notables including Samuel Untermyer, the investigative lawyer who had locked horns with Lawes a dozen years before on the Brindell case, as well as the jeweler Pierre Cartier, Treasury Under-secretary Dean Acheson, the wife of publisher Max Annenberg, George Gershwin's sister, and the daughter-in-law of former French wartime prime minister Georges Clemenceau. To the Laweses' stateroom came a round hand-painted card with the image of a ship and the message "Bon Voyage!" It was signed, "The Boys."

Approaching England, Lawes gazed with awe at the embarkation point of the *Mayflower* and at Lady Astor's grand seaside mansion. In Europe, they were thronged by reporters who called Lawes the governor of Sing Sing and questioned him incessantly about his rehabilitative methods and the electric chair. Kathryn gave some of her own interviews, and the *London Sunday Post* gave her a byline under the headline "All 'The Boys' Know Me as Mother."

Berlin was their last stop, and Lawes, through an interpreter, told the *Berliner illustrierte Nachtausgabe* about life at Sing Sing, Alabama Pitts, and the death house. The paper photographed him with Cherie and gave him lots of space.

CELLS WITH RUNNING WATER—
PRISONERS' MUSIC CHORUS—
25 EXECUTED YEARLY

At night from their room in the sumptuous Adlon Hotel, they stared out aghast at the goose-stepping brownshirt hordes, hellishly illuminated by flaming torches. But Lawes was most chilled by the welcoming address of the congress's host, Reich Justice Minister Franz Gurtner, a decorated veteran of the Great War and fervent German nationalist who had helped Hitler

escape retribution for his abortive uprising in Munich in 1923, a decade
before he ascended to power.

Germany took a lively interest in the congress's proceedings, Gurtner
said, particularly questions regarding juvenile offenders and sterilization.
The Reich was maligned in the world press, he declared. This was a chance
to set the record straight. Germany had been trying to reform its penal law
since 1909, but, Gurtner said, "It was not until after the National Socialist
government had got rid of party quarrels that the basis for the successful
achievement of the great work of reform was secured." Now that the führer
had entrusted him with the task, a new criminal justice system was dawning.

They all knew, Gurtner said, the bedrock principle of the penal code expressed by a Bavarian criminologist in 1801: *Nulla poena sine lege, nulla poena
sine crimine.* No penalty without law, no penalty without a crime. The law
had to precede the crime and the punishment. But what, he said, if by legislative oversight or some other lapse, there was no prescribed penalty for a
crime? Was a judge still obligated to let the offense pass? It was at this point,
he said, that National Socialism sought a new formulation: *Nullum crimen
sine poena,* No crime without penalty. "The future German criminal law,"
Gurtner boasted, "will release the German judges from being closely bound
by the text of the law."

Lawes couldn't believe what he was hearing. The judges would make their
own law?

Gurtner, oblivious of the consternation in the hall, was continuing. National Socialism replaced the concept of a "formal wrong" with a "material
wrong," that is, "any attack on the interests of the national community and
any offense against the demands of the national life.

"Hence," he said, "a wrong is possible in Germany in future even when no
law threatens it with punishment." Even when there was no threat of punishment, he went on, "every infringement of the *vital aims* adopted by the
national community is a wrong." The law would no longer be the only de-
terminant of right and wrong.

Gurtner anticipated an objection. Would not uncertainties arise if judges
ruled not strictly according to the law but other lights? Not at all, he was
happy to add, "for National Socialism has presented the German nation
with a uniform view of life dominating the whole nation." It was hardly a
new concept, he argued, pointing out that England and America recognized

common law. Germany was no different. "We thereby empower the judge not only to find the law within certain limits, but also to create the law." Yet the judge was constrained by the principle of leadership of the National Socialist state, "which reserves the entire leadership of the people, and hence also the legislation, for the führer."

Lawes had heard enough, but Gurtner was working himself into a frenzy. The new Germany was bent on punishing criminal *intention*. Of course, he conceded, if a potential offender kept his intention secret and took no steps to carry out his crime, he could not be charged. But the slightest sign of an intended violation was the same as a completed act. One need not even be conscious of committing an offense, as under the old law. One need only have a sense "that he is acting contrary to the will of the national community and to the general feeling of what is right." And who would decide when an individual had contravened this general feeling? The judge, naturally. He would weigh the *personality* of the accused. And not in the old way, in which to understand everything is to pardon everything, as the French proverb had it. "The National Socialist criminal law will not make this mistake." It emphasized "the transgression against the community." And the further the transgressor had deviated from the views of the community, the harsher the punishment. Severity was prescribed "so that the punishment may be an appreciable evil" to deter future transgressions. The aim was not to inflict suffering, but rather to induce "order, subordination, and obedience." Indeed, it was to be accompanied by a spirit of humanity but not by any weakness "alien to the German character" that allowed "evildoers" to live more comfortably than their law-abiding fellow citizens "at a time of terrible unemployment and economic distress."

Lawes perked up at this point, wondering if this was a veiled attack on the Jews.

Gurtner, mercifully, was concluding, promising prisoners "a right of complaint," which, while "far from the exaggerations of earlier times," still afforded "an absolute guarantee of protection from unjust treatment."

Lawes was skeptical. Talking afterward to a reporter for Hearst's *American*, he said, "I certainly disagree with the policy to make life more severe for criminals. I believe in rehabilitating criminals and not taking vengeance on them by being unhuman." Nevertheless, the Germans won the first round, getting the committee on sterilization to report in favor of asking all nations to commit to compulsory sterilization of the "unfit"—"in the interest of the individual, family, and society."

Lawes left appalled. The harsh theories propounded in Berlin, he told re-porters, "signalized in the Third Reich a return to methods we had long thought obsolete."

31

At home, there was more bad news. Pitts had not done well. After his tremendous struggle to enter professional baseball, he made his debut before nearly eight thousand fans in Albany in July 1935, going two for five at the plate and fielding flawlessly. He had also won a pregame race around the bases, coming in at under fourteen and a half seconds. But then he suffered a series of injuries. By the end of his first season with the Senators, he was batting just .233, with only three extra-base hits, and notwithstanding his great speed, he had stolen only three bases. He had also made eight errors, scoring worst among the league's outfielders in fielding.

Distraught, he explored a career in vaudeville with the ball club's ballad-singing manager. Lawes counseled him against pursuing it, not after all they had been through to establish his athletic bona fides. So when the Philadelphia Eagles beat out nineteen rivals to offer Pitts a football contract for fifteen hundred dollars, more money for seven games than he could earn in three months of baseball with the Senators, Lawes said he should take it, and he did.

He was benched for much of the season, but in a game against the Chicago Bears, fans began shouting, "We want Pitts! We want Pitts!" He was put in. He stymied one enemy touchdown and caught a long pass, but when it was over the Eagles had been quashed 39–0. At the end of the season, his luster tarnished, Pitts was offered a lesser contract with a pay cut, which he rejected while he pondered his options. Lawes was dismayed, but there was only so much he could do for someone. It was out of his hands.

It wasn't his only disappointment. His new magazine, *Prison Life Stories,* was foundering amid a whiff of scandal. The December issue was out with articles he had edited and flattering photographs of J. Edgar Hoover. But then, less than six months after startup, his chief publishing partner, Theodore Epstein, who also owned the track sheet *Daily Racing Tab*, was arrested for false advertising and "racetrack tipster racketeering." Deeply embarrassed, Lawes sought to portray himself as merely a contributor. Asked by the press if he wasn't also a 40 percent owner, Lawes didn't deny it but said he had yet to see a penny from the venture.

Things got worse. News accounts of the Sing Sing holiday show for the inmates had caught the eye of John Purdie, the private investigator who had flayed Lawes as a publicity-monger fifteen years before in his first year at Sing Sing. As he had before, Purdie complained about Lawes, this time to Governor Lehman. Then shortly after Christmas two cons had gone at each other, landing one in the hospital. The *Daily News* had reported the violence, catching Purdie's attention once again. As he had done before with Rattigan, Purdie wrote to the corrections commissioner, enclosing the clipping "accompanied by the inevitable picture of Warden Lawes." The information could not possibly have reached the press, Purdie contended, without the complicity of a publicity-hungry Lawes himself. No wonder criminals had such contempt for prison. "I firmly believe," Purdie said, "that a prison sentence is inflicted as a *punishment* for crime committed and that the rehabilitation is incidental and should begin with the individual." Moreover, what was a state official like Lawes doing writing books, going on the lecture circuit, and taking to the airwaves, "for all of which, presumably, he was paid?

"Before taking any further action along this line of thought," Purdie said ominously, "I await your opinion."

Lawes, shown Purdie's letter, was steaming. The old canard of coddling was back, at a time when Sing Sing was so overcrowded he was forced to house—though the word hardly seemed right—more than five hundred inmates in the medieval cellblock. The "hard-boiled, reactionary" Purdie had been a foe for sixteen years, Lawes reminded his superiors in a blistering response, as evidenced by the man's letters to three governors, two superintendents, and two commissioners. The accusation regarding the *Daily News* article was laughable, Lawes said; the piece had been occasioned not by him but by an anonymous tip from some guard or prisoner.

"Certainly I do not desire publicity of this character and you know that publicity is one of the terrific problems at Sing Sing." Publicity, he hardly needed to note, had brought down governors, commissioners, and wardens. "New York newspapers cover this institution twenty-four hours a day and it isn't a question of publicity or no publicity," he wrote. It was whether graft, inefficiency, and disorder or a constructive rehabilitation program held sway.

"America still happens to be a free country, despite the efforts of communists on one side and fascists on the other, to curtail our liberties. I am quite sure that an expression of opinion, whether in books or on the radio, is the right of any American citizen. Also, any citizen has the right to criticize, such as Mr. Purdie, but as Sing Sing receives prisoners from the Metropolitan district, which comprises, roughly, about seven million people, it is rather surprising that there are so few men who think as does Mr. Purdie."

It was time, Lawes thought, to go on the offensive.

Progressivism was an embattled cause, he told members of the General Federation of Women's Clubs. Severity was hardly the solution to crime. He was entirely opposed to corporal punishment, arguing that whipping brutalized the victim and the whipper, and eventually contaminated the entire community. "Punishments of that kind are like wars," he told the women. "The more you have of them, the more you have to have of them."

When asked if he held the same philosophy at home, Lawes laughed. He had three girls and had never found it necessary to beat them. The only perfect criminal, he added, was the babe in arms, and the rod didn't much help it develop a social conscience. He had met a few children he wanted to spank and a great many men "that a good punching in the nose might have helped." But apart from that, no, he did not believe in physical punishment. He belittled, too, the women's concern that a breakdown of the home was causing a sharp rise in juvenile delinquency, swamping the prisons. They were filled not with juvenile delinquents, he said, but with doctors and lawyers—"we have a lot of lawyers in Sing Sing, not enough, but a lot of them"—along with a good cross section of the community. Most of all, he told the women, they had to fight to keep politics out of the prison system.

He gave them a final piece of advice: "Don't expect to do the impossible. It is a slow work because civilization, if it is civilization we now have, is making very slow progress."

· · ·

Lawes would have little trouble, he thought, advancing the progressive agenda in the face of the Nazis and dolts like Purdie. But arguing against capital punishment was far more difficult when he was presented with cunning monsters like the droopy-faced and white-mustachioed sixty-five-year-old child murderer and cannibal now on death row.

A year before, in December 1934, the police had solved the mystifying 1928 disappearance of ten-year-old Grace Budd of Manhattan's West Fifteenth Street by arresting a stooped and grandfatherly Westchester housepainter, Albert Henry Fish. After a long investigation, Fish, a divorced father of six, led detectives to Wysteria Cottage, a decaying house in Irvington off the Saw Mill River Parkway, where a human rib and skull were found. Dr. Amos Squire, now county medical examiner, said they seemed to match the body of little Grace.

Fish then admitted that six years before, using a false name and posing as a gentleman farmer from Long Island, he had answered an advertisement placed in the *World* by Grace's sixteen-year-old brother Edward who was looking for a summer farm job. Fish purchased an ax, a meat cleaver, a saw, and a butcher knife, and intended to lure the boy and a chum to his suburban property upstate to be slaughtered and dismembered. Earlier, he had lured two other young boys to his apartment on East 110th Street, but they had found the weapons and fled, terrified.

A few days later, Fish wrapped the tools in canvas, deposited them at a newsstand, and went to visit the Budds. Edward wasn't there, but sickly little Grace was, and when she sat on his knee, Fish changed his plan.

"Something came over me," he told detectives. "I think it was connected with tales of cannibalism during famines in China written to me by my brother. I had a blood lust."

Detectives remained perplexed and asked why.

"It occurred to me," Fish said. "That's all I have to say."

He told the family he wanted to take Grace to a birthday party uptown that his sister was giving for one of her children, and Grace's mother agreed. "Oh, let her go," she said. "She never has much fun anyway."

Fish, retrieving his tools, took little Grace's trusting hand in his and escorted her on the elevated line to the Bronx, then took the railroad to Irvington. From there they walked a mile to the deserted house, where he stripped naked, to avoid bloodstains on his clothing, and strangled her as she cried, "I'll tell my mama." He then cut up her body and ate parts of it. Later he sent ghastly unsigned notes to the family, detailing their child's last moments and the disposal of the body.

In the investigation and trial, his history emerged. In 1903, two years before Lawes began his penal career, Fish had served time at Sing Sing for grand larceny. In 1930 he had been charged with sending obscene material through the mails and was sent to Bellevue, where he was eventually declared sane. Between Grace's murder and his arrest, he had been arrested six times on misdemeanor charges, and each time he was let go. He also confessed to the murders of several other missing children but then recanted.

His lawyer, James Dempsey Jr., argued that Fish was "an insane fiend," a Jekyll and Hyde character torn between devotion to his family and frenzied lust. Prison doctors then made a macabre discovery. Over the years, he had inserted some thirty sewing needles into his abdomen, in supposed expiation for earlier crimes. Somehow they had failed to pierce vital organs and still lay embedded in his flesh. "I caused others so much pain, I ought to suffer too" was Fish's only explanation.

The trial judge ruled out testimony about the needles. He also, over Dempsey's objections, allowed prosecutors to exhibit Grace's bones and skull to the jury. Fish's grown son and daughter testified, saying he was prone to religious hysteria and that "something snapped in his brain a few years ago." The daughter recounted that their mother frequently abused their father, who quietly withdrew to read the Bible. Then one day, while he was away, their mother gave the children money to go to the movies, during which time she ran off with a boarder, whom she subsequently brought back to the house and married.

Deliberating after a two-week trial, the jury agreed Fish had killed the girl, but some thought him out of his mind, saying he should not be put to death but placed in an asylum. They were swayed, however, by the majority who favored death.

At Sing Sing, Fish shocked prison officials with his twisted antics. He was interrupted in the process of trying to eviscerate himself with a pork chop bone he had gnawed to a cutting edge. He had incised a cross on his abdomen over the embedded sewing needles and was ready to slice through his flesh when a guard intervened. From then on, he received only strained food.

He entered the death chamber in January 1936, a tired old man with a stricken look, his droopy mustache trimmed short. "I don't know why I'm here," he blurted to his guards. "This is a sad day for me." He stared blankly at the witnesses and suddenly stopped in his tracks as if to speak, then sat down in the chair and sighed deeply.

He was dead in three minutes.

Talking to reporters afterward, Lawes shook his head over Fish. "He was above the average intelligence of death house prisoners," he said. He read the Bible regularly and wrote a good deal. Fish, he said, had told him: "I love children. I must have been out of my mind if I killed that little girl."

If any case cried out for vengeance, Lawes thought, this was it. But killing Fish didn't bring Grace back, and Fish, in the end, was a pathetic creature. What, Lawes wondered, did killing him accomplish?

It wasn't over. The death house was filling up with juveniles. As year's end approached, ten youths under twenty-one awaited execution, the highest such toll in Sing Sing history and probably, Lawes thought, in American history as well. Around Sing Sing, death row was being grimly called "the high school."

The forces of reaction were on the rise. The new state commissioner of correction, Edward Mulrooney, the former New York police commissioner who had led the final assault on the Manhattan hideout of Francis "Two-Gun" Crowley five years before, had set his sights on Sing Sing's football program. Why should spectators have to pay admission to support the team? he demanded. If the state backed the program, the state should pay.

Lawes saw through the ploy. The admission charge was the team's lifeblood, subsidizing equipment and the travel expenses of the visitors. Mulrooney wasn't explicitly outlawing football at Sing Sing, Lawes said, since he didn't have to. His ruling accomplished that. The legislature would never vote money for Sing Sing football. It was the end of the Black Sheep.

32

Lawes was a new grandfather. Their middle daughter, Crystal, had given birth to a daughter in the Ossining Hospital in December 1935. The Laweses, it seemed, produced only girls. Her parents named her Judith. Alabama Pitts, visiting the prison at the time, was pressed into service as an orderly for mother and child. If anyone did the math and calculated that the blessed event came seven months after the secretive wedding, it was not commented upon, and Lawes and Kathryn doted on their new grandchild. Kathryn's mother had known the joys of holding her great-granddaughter before she died at ninety-three in the Laweses' home.

Now with little Judith beginning to toddle, domestic life was blissful. The Laweses had happily settled into their luxurious new quarters outside the walls. There was plenty of extra spending money beyond the state's payments to Lawes of nine thousand dollars plus maintenance, a dividend of his speeches, articles, radio contracts, and film options. Whenever large expenses loomed, Lawes would wink at the adolescent Cherie and say, "Well, guess I'll have to go out and earn some money." And he did. His fourth book, *Cell 202—Sing Sing*, a fictionalized account of four prisoners who successively occupied a single cell from 1826 to 1911, and whose characters symbolized the march of the nation's history, met glowing reviews, even by the FBI, which prepared a summary for Hoover. The *New York Times* critic was beside himself with praise. "Warden Lawes's fiction has a gas-lit quality, recalling variously a George Bellows lithograph of a footpad relieving a top-hatted gentleman of his watch on a dark night, a Herbert Asbury 'that-was-New-York' excursion into the history of the Dead Rabbits Gang of the

Five Points, a ballad of the 'prisoners' song' variety, and the streets of Liverpool seen through a Mersey fog."

Lawes had contracted for the book as *The Four Prisoners* two years earlier, accepting a thousand-dollar advance and striking out a provision for a fifty-fifty split of movie rights with the publisher, Farrar and Rinehart. He wanted it all. He tried to sell the movie rights to Fox Films, but the span of time covered proved too much of a cinematic obstacle.

By 1937 Lawes had also renewed his radio contract for *20,000 Years in Sing Sing* with Sloan's Liniment at $1,300 a week for another twenty-six weeks plus $200 each for any rebroadcasts, all proceeds payable to the charitable Lawes Work Extension Fund. The half-hour crime show had bounced around the dial, from its original slot on NBC's Blue Network Sunday night at nine and then Wednesdays at nine, to Mondays at nine on the Red Network, and was soon to return to the Blue Network on Mondays at ten with a new name, *Behind Prison Bars*.

The same year Lawes also scaled another literary peak. He became a Broadway playwright.

His drama was called *Chalked Out*, prison slang for erased bad-conduct marks, and he had written it with Jonathan Finn, a screenwriter and former New York State assemblyman who, it was rumored, may have helped Lawes with *Cell 202* and earlier books. The plot was richly melodramatic. A young loser in love with his foster sister steals the gun of her cop boyfriend and gives it to a gangster for a robbery. The gangster kills his victim, and the police find the gun and trace it to the cop, who is sentenced to die in the chair. The gangster and the loser soon wind up in the same prison, with the conscience-stricken loser threatening to confess. He is drawn into an escape plot and shot, but finally tells the truth, just before the innocent cop walks the last mile. The script offered fireworks galore, particularly in the escape scene, where sirens wail and searchlights stab the darkened stage.

The play, directed by Antoinette Perry (later to be immortalized in the Tony Awards) was booked into the Morosco Theatre by producer Brock Pemberton, whose Broadway career began just after Lawes started at Sing Sing. Pemberton had doubts early on, ordering rewrites to make the script more commercial and reminding Lawes, "As far as I am concerned, any play that doesn't turn in profits belongs between book covers." But soon his doubts were allayed, and he assured Lawes, "I feel your play is Pulitzer Prize material." Lawes took care of many production details, securing the authentic gas gun, gas mask, rifles, and wooden model machine gun, as well as uniforms. He even hosted the entire cast of thirty at Sing Sing, to give the players a taste of real prison atmosphere. But he insisted that the name of Sing Sing be taken out of the script, fearing a lawsuit. Everyone would know it was Sing Sing anyway.

The show scored one preopening success. It rated an Al Hirschfeld drawing in the Sunday *Herald Tribune*. For the premiere in March 1937, Lawes asked for six free tickets and ordered twenty-four more at his own expense, rendering him an instant Broadway legend—a man who paid to see his own show. There was a tense moment early on when actor Charles Jordan, playing the gangster, fell ill. A rumor spread that he had died, and Pemberton was immediately alerted at the Algonquin Hotel. He waved it off. "It can't be true," he said. "He's got to give me two weeks' notice."

Reviews were mixed, calling the play realistic but less than convincingly dramatic. Walter Winchell took a swipe in his column, saying that "the jury found it guilty." It closed after twelve performances, but Lawes was philosophical, especially after he sold the film rights to Warner Brothers for $7,500 plus a share of the box office. Since the show had not run three weeks, Pemberton had no claim to any of the movie money, leaving Lawes and Finn to split it.

Then, to the delight of Lawes and Kathryn, Kathleen, their eldest, found a beau. A young man in the shirt business in St. Louis, Charles Miller, had met a friend of the Laweses' from Elmira and was taken to visit Lawes at Sing Sing. Lawes took a liking to Miller and invited him to a baseball game and then home to meet his family. Miller and Kathleen struck a spark, were soon courting, and then got engaged. There would be no elopement for them. Finally, Lawes and Kathryn thought, they would have their big wedding.

One late October Saturday, Kathryn left early to take a ride. Lawes thought little of it, since she often took the car to town to visit friends or drop off food packages to the needy. She couldn't pass an old person's house without asking, "What can I get you?" But by evening she had not returned, and a nervous anxiety gnawed at his gut. His blood pressure had been higher lately, and her absence did nothing to calm him. Kathryn was always home by dinnertime.

At 7 P.M. the phone rang. It was an attendant at the eastern end of the Bear Mountain Bridge on a crag over the Hudson twenty miles north of Ossining. Lawes's car was found parked there. The attendant had noticed it at ten that morning but had paid it no heed. When it was still there nine hours later, he checked the license plate, found it was registered at Sing Sing, and called the prison.

Panicked, Lawes telephoned Squire and then, grabbing Crystal's husband, commandeered a prison car and raced to the scene. His car was there, seemingly abandoned, and there was no sign of Kathryn. They peered down into the chasm where the river churned far below but saw nothing. They walked north from the bridge along a boardwalk and, looking down, saw a flash of color.

Scrambling down the embankment, they found Kathryn, a hundred feet below the bridge. She was still alive and conscious but incoherent. Her right leg was broken and she was in shock. She could say nothing. She seemed to have dragged herself back toward the car a hundred feet or more from where she had landed.

The three men cradled her body up the steep hill to the car and rushed her to Ossining Hospital, where she died three hours later. She was fifty-two.

State troopers retracing her steps thought she had fallen, or jumped, from the bridge. Later Squire found one of her high-heeled slippers wedged in a section of the boardwalk. He believed she had left the car, perhaps to pick flowers, caught her foot, tripped, and taken the fatal tumble.

Sixteen-year-old Cherie had been at dancing school, which, like piano lessons, her mother insisted on. After class, she had lunch with friends and went to a movie. When she got back, the house was in an uproar, and her father was at the hospital. She heard the terrible story, and a strange family tale flashed through her mind. Eight years before, her mother was visiting Elmira and went to see an eccentric aunt who read fortunes in playing cards. "Katy," she said, "you're not going home." Kathryn was incredulous. "What are you talking about?" she said, laughing. "Of course I am." Then she broke her ankle and had to stay for weeks. Cherie wondered whether the cards had predicted this, too.

The boys asked—*demanded*—to be allowed to say good-bye to the sainted mother of Sing Sing who liked to say she had three girls and two thousand boys. Speaking for his fellow inmates, Joseph Mallon petitioned Lawes: "We who knew her for her beneficence, her great personal sacrifices, her deep mother love, with always a lending hand to the downtrod [sic] can best appreciate her virtues." In short, Mallon pleaded, "the inmates have expressed a wish that they be permitted to view the funeral procession as it passes on its way to the church."

In fact, the prisoners wanted more. They wanted to join the procession. The route would take them past the principal keeper's house, around Chapin's birdhouse, out the south gate, and on to the church.

Lawes thought it over and agreed. He ordered the gate thrown open.

Principal Keeper Sheehy went first. Then the line formed up. Gunmen and gangsters and con men and forgers fell into place, filing out of the walls.

Lawes wasn't concerned. Anyone who would have tried to flee, he thought, would have been torn limb from limb long before the guards caught him. He was right. A thousand prisoners went out and a thousand returned.

Sheehy was incredulous. "I don't know how it was done," he kept repeating. "I can't believe it."

Lawes and his family and friends bade farewell to Kathryn at a funeral mass at the high-vaulted St. Augustine's Roman Catholic Church in Ossining. Lawes, not much of a churchgoer, thought Kathryn would have liked the service. Afterward, embalmed in a casket of solid copper under a quilted blanket covered with twelve hundred pink roses, sprays of lilies of the valley, and white sweet peas, she was borne in a cortege of twelve limousines and four flower cars to her final rest in Sleepy Hollow Cemetery.

Lawes was home with his grief when a stranger came to the door to offer his condolences. He said he owed the warden a favor and asked if there was anything he could do. And so it was that Lawes met again Mike the Rat Catcher from Hart Island and New Hampton, a teamster, noncommissioned officer in the Great War, devoted husband and father.

33

"I never knew that life could be so empty," Lawes wrote a friend. "It was all so sudden that I am still in a fog." He was left with the numbing paperwork of death. Kathryn had left no will, and her gross estate of just over $16,000—a considerable sum, representing her half share of their jointly held property—had to be apportioned between Lawes and their three girls. Days into the new year of 1938, his seventy-eight-year-old widowed mother, Sarah, suffered a stroke in Elmira. Lawes managed to get to her hospital bedside before she died. Then with what seemed like sympathetic timing by Uncle Sam, a check for $7,409 arrived from the United States Treasury, a refund for overpayment of income taxes.

Despondent and lonely, Lawes ventured out on the social scene at boîtes in New York. He was at the epicenter of café society at the fabled Stork Club one night when he literally bumped into Ernest Hemingway. They jostled each other and Lawes ended up on the floor. Club owner Sherman Billingsley was alarmed, worrying that it would look bad for the Stork. His public relations mastermind, Steve Hannagan, told him not to worry. One fight a year was good publicity, "providing the names of the fighters are big names."

Lawes sought solace in work. He was writing his fourth book, *Invisible Stripes*, dedicated to Kathryn. It started with an apology. As he began his thirty-fourth year in prison service, he was haunted by his unfulfilled hopes. The prisoner count was higher than ever. "There is no cessation in the march to Sing Sing. Crime still exists. The criminal swaggers on, practically unimpeded. The seeds of delinquency are being sown with careless profusion." And

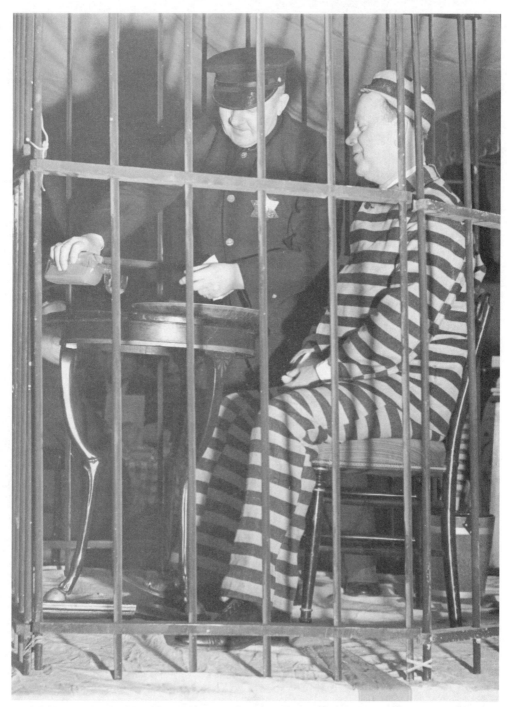

Lawes in mock cell for Saints and Sinners *show.* (COLLECTION OF RALPH BLUMENTHAL)

what had he done to change things? Clearly not enough. The first part of the
book took the form of a prisoner's diary as imagined by Lawes. He had himself
give a stern radio speech to the inmates after a fight in the yard and recorded
the reaction in prisoners' voices:

"That guy Lawes knows how to dish it out, all right."
"The guys that done it ought to stand up an' take their medicine."
"Yeah . . . Mussolini style, castor oil."
"Aw . . . that ain't legal."
"Hell, the only law in Sing Sing is Lawes."

The last remark, Lawes's fictional diarist wrote, "provoked general laughter all along the galleries."

The conceit gave Lawes a chance to show Sing Sing from a prisoner's per-
spective, after which Lawes provided a lengthy answer in his own voice,
tackling the familiar issues of recidivism and the failures of society, the family, and the education system that all ended up at his prison door. He had
said it before, but it seemed more cogent collected between covers.

He also wrote a three-hundred-word article on reformatories for the *Dic-
tionary of American History*. It paid only three dollars, a penny a word, but
money was not the point. It was something else to do. Clownishly, for charity's sake, he was inducted into the Dexter Fellows Tent of the Circus Saints
and Sinners of the Shriners, donning prison stripes and allowing himself to
be photographed in a mock cell being served a ration of water. He agreed to
a coast-to-coast broadcast on station WEAF with Dale Carnegie about how
to win friends and influence people. But when the crusading labor journalist
Victor Riesel of the liberal weekly *New Leader* asked him to do an article on
prisoner rehabilitation, suggesting that the magazine was looking for something "at variance with the psychology, if you can call it such, of men like
J. Edgar Hoover and his black-jack school of crime prevention," Lawes
begged off.

He continued making speeches, including an incisive talk on the role of
schools in preventing crime. Too many young people escaped school far too
early, Lawes said. Most of the prisoners at Sing Sing had never completed
sixth grade. Those who showed no proficiency in academics should be given
the opportunity to master a trade. Again, he saw the evidence at Sing Sing,

finding that an unusual number of inmates were adept in the factory shops. It was tragic that so many young men had to learn their trades in prison. Schools could combat crime in other ways, Lawes said. The home environment was a notorious breeder of antisocial conduct. Every school, Lawes said, "should have a group of trained social workers capable of diagnosing and correcting such difficulties." They should make frequent visits, inducing boys to join youth groups. "We should also remember," he said, "that social education is equally as important as acquiring knowledge."

Lawes wrote an article for *Harper's Monthly Magazine* defending parole. A New York paper had printed a cartoon of a fanged beast labeled "crime" clutching papers marked "parole." Once again, Lawes had to explain that parole was not something invented to coddle the criminal but for the protection of society, to ease a freed convict's return to the community, a path almost all would someday travel. Ideally, he wrote, there would be no set sentences. Those found guilty of crimes would appear before sentencing and parole commissions of penologists, psychologists, and psychiatrists that would study each individual and decide how long he should serve and when he might be eligible for supervised release.

Lawes couldn't resist a jab at Hoover's FBI for using fingerprint checks to expose old criminal records of ex-convicts seeking everyday jobs. What was there for the FBI to be so proud of? Lawes asked. Sure, some had sought jobs in law enforcement and should have been weeded out. But what of those who wanted to be taxi drivers or mechanics or plumbers? Were they to be denied livelihoods forever because they had once served time behind bars?

The article did not elude the Bureau, supersensitive to the slightest criticism. A special agent in Detroit wrote Hoover: "It would appear Mr. Lawes is badly informed." The agent was thanked for his vigilance. "It would seem that this is another illustration of the constant attempts to misinform the public concerning the position of the Federal Bureau of Investigation in connection with the maladministration of parole in so many of our States." The letters were put into Lawes's growing FBI file.

Lawes's movie career was also flourishing. He sold Warners yet a third prison story, called simply "Sing Sing," to star, once again, Humphrey Bogart, and he was working on selling to Hollywood his and Jonathan Finn's short-lived play, *Chalked Out*, and his new book, *Invisible Stripes*. In March 1938, three years after the deal for *Over the Wall* was closed, it opened at the

Strand on Broadway, with posters calling Lawes "Sing Sing's Fearless, Fighting Warden." The project had been hush-hush, Lawes insisting that it be
code-named "Evidence" until he approved the production, which he finally
did. The *Times* called the movie "the lightest stretch we ever did in a Warner
Brothers prison picture." There were, blessedly, no sirens, no searchlights,
no wall, and no Alabama Pitts, who had disappeared as a character.

In April the prison population was enriched by a new celebrity, Richard
Whitney, patrician ex-president of the New York Stock Exchange. He was
the biggest Wall Street mogul to journey up the river since embezzler Ferdinand Ward, who had ruined Ulysses S. Grant more than fifty years before.
Whitney, who had pleaded guilty to stealing hundreds of thousands of dollars
from the New York Yacht Club and from his father-in-law to cover cata-
strophic losses after the '29 crash, had been sentenced to five to ten years. He
arrived at Sing Sing shackled to two thugs and exchanged his polo coat and
double-breasted blue flannel suit for baggy gray prison shoddy. He also surrendered his gold cuff links and cash, settling in for labor at five cents a day.

Memorial Day that year was dedicated to Kathryn. A bronze tablet hon-
oring her had been put up on the side of the gymnasium that Harry Warner
had presented the prison for *20,000 Years in Sing Sing*. Frederick H. Mark,
a fifty-five-year-old master forger and one of the most erudite inmates, was
selected to deliver the tribute.

With Lawes and his family in front-row seats, Mark confessed to the trep-
idation with which he, "an outcast and an outlaw," approached the task. He
recalled past Memorial Days when their dear Mrs. Lawes would leave early
in the morning, her car overflowing with flowers for Sing Sing's friendless,
the robbers and thieves and victims of the chair, buried in pauper's graves.
He remembered how they all—those in keeper's blue and prisoner gray—
would brighten to see the warden's car passing by with the wave of a femi-
nine hand and a smile. "And I always think the smile was a little warmer and
the wave of the hand a little more cordial for the gray than it was for the
blue because our need of it was greater.

"To say that we loved her," he went on, "seems so pitifully inadequate. To
those of us who cannot remember our mothers she was the personification
of what we would have liked our mothers to be. To those who have never
known the joys of married life, she embodied every wifely virtue and trait we
would have longed for in our helpmates. Those of us who have daughters

cannot conceive for them a greater destiny than to grow up to resemble Mrs. Lawes in even a few of those characteristics which made her the ideal of everything that is fine and noble in womanhood."

All that she had ever demanded of any man was that he be true to himself and his conscience, Mark said as hardened inmates dabbed at their eyes. And if someone failed her once, twice, or however many times, "in the end she was as much their friend as she was before they disappointed her."

And so, he said, "I cannot speak for what you will do. For myself I have resolved that when my chance again comes, I will make of the rest of my life a monument which Mrs. Lawes would recognize as something worthy of her great spirit."

He called on Cherie to come up and join him. "From the day you were born amongst us to the day she left both you and us, you have shared your mother with us, and this degree of kinship gives us the courage to ask that you unveil this tablet for us."

Alone now with Cherie, Lawes threw himself into his work at Sing Sing. By midsummer, to his dismay, the prisoner count had climbed to 2,816, a record. Ninety-four men had to sleep in corridors. Much as he hated to do it, Lawes marked some of his boys for transfers upstate.

He needed a break. In July he went yachting with friends up the New England coast. But sailing off Nantucket he suffered severe sunburn and heat stroke and had to be rushed to Nantucket Hospital, and from there to the hospital in Newport, Rhode Island. Soon, however, he was well again and back at work, in time to attend rites for his patron and fellow reformer, Adolph Lewisohn, who died in August at eighty-nine. At the crowded service at Temple Emanu-El on Fifth Avenue, Lawes joined Mayor La Guardia and other public officials as an honorary pallbearer.

Invisible Stripes came out that fall, to respectful reviews—"a book which every American should read," said the *Times*—and a movie sale to Warners, which had in mind James Cagney and John Garfield for the leads. Not even a frightening Christmas tree blaze that nearly burned down the warden's residence a few days after New Year's, 1939, and the triple execution of three slum-bred youths who had killed a detective in a Second Avenue tearoom holdup, could shake Lawes's buoyant mood. He had a secret.

34

Lawes had found new love. She was Elise Chisholm, a vivacious southern belle and thirty-four-year-old Broadway press agent, born in 1905, the year Lawes started his prison career and courted Kathryn. Their paths had fatefully crossed in 1924 at the prison congress in Mississippi, her home state. Elise had been the young reporter for the *Jackson Daily News*, whose older cousin, B. Ogden Chisolm, had introduced her to Lawes at a chance meeting in the Edwards House. Lawes had been charmed then by the attractive young woman, although she insisted, when they met again years later in New York, that he could not possibly remember her. He said he remembered her brown eyes.

She came from Summit, seventy-five miles from Jackson, a doctor's daughter and seventh-generation southern girl with ancestral roots in the American Revolution. Her journalistic ambitions and wanderlust ran in the face of a tradition that expected her to stay home, marry, and rear an eighth generation of Dixie gentlefolk. She had always been a rebel, a contrary little blonde who scandalized the neighbors by being best friends with their black cook's daughter. With her father on his horse and buggy, she traveled on house calls to blacks and whites, but his hopes that his twelve-year-old daughter would follow him into the profession were shattered when he died suddenly at fifty-three, plunging the family into financial distress. She still managed to attend the University of Mississippi as its first co-ed, then drifted around until a family friend got her a job as a cub reporter at the *Jackson Daily News*. There, she was assigned to cover the 1925 American Prison Association Congress.

Years later, it was cousin Ogden who became the instrument of her reen-
counter with Lawes. He had persuaded her to leave Mississippi and come to
New York to help him in his work for the International Prison Commission.
By her mid-twenties she had gone on to do theatrical publicity for various pro-
ducers, one of whom, William A. Brady Jr., got to know her well enough to
spend time in a vacation cottage she had bought in Colt's Neck, New Jersey. In
September 1935, with Elise in New York and Brady's actress wife also away, he
apparently fell asleep while smoking and burned to death in the cottage. A li-
censed .45 automatic, which Brady carried to safeguard his payrolls, was found
near the body, but detectives discounted its significance in the case.

The awful episode behind her, Elise became acting president of the press
agents chapter of the Theatrical Managers, Agents and Treasurers Union
and once again met Lawes. She regarded him with awe, not imagining that
he might see anything in a gangly career girl with unruly hair and an aversion to glamour. That he did thrilled her beyond expression.

The widowed Lawes, still grappling with the loss of Kathryn but eager for
companionship, escorted her to restaurants, where, she was amazed to see,
he often could not prevail on the management to present a check. The
waiter would whisper in his ear: "This has been taken care of, sir, compli-
ments of the chef. He wants you to know he's getting along swell."

Taxi drivers refused his fare. "It's on me, boss," they would say. "I'm one of
the boys."

One afternoon, the day after an execution at Sing Sing, a morose Lawes
picked her up at her office. As they drove down Fifth Avenue at dusk he
seemed lost in thought. Then he took her hand and said: "I feel so much at
peace with you. You're like a pair of faithful, comfortable old slippers. I wish
I might have you with me always."

She told him she would need to think about it. She knew she loved him,
but to be the chatelaine of Sing Sing was something else. Her mother had
never taught her how to manage a home. She had never even cooked a meal
for anyone, she said. How could she ever run the domestic side of Sing Sing?
She had come to New York as an aspiring career girl surviving on twenty-
five dollars a week, but since then she had advanced considerably in the
ranks of theatrical press agentry and had acquired a fine apartment with a
housekeeper. She wasn't sure she could give up her serenity. Then, too, there
was the inescapable shadow of Kathryn.

She tried to explain her reservations. "We have a wonderful relationship. I'm fearful that the beauty of it will go if we marry and I fail you as a wife. Why can't we continue as we are?"

Lawes regarded her sadly. "No stray puppy ever came to our place and left. Won't you give us a trial?"

His disheartening analogy notwithstanding, she said yes, but on one condition. She had heard that prisoners, murderers even, staffed the mansion. She wanted civilians. She was sure the state budgeted for it.

Lawes begged her to reconsider. "Try it for two weeks. If you aren't satisfied, we'll make a change. *But give the boys a chance.*"

They married quietly in April but decided to withhold the announcement until June, when Kathleen and Charles Miller would wed. Lawes didn't want to overshadow his daughter's nuptials.

Lawes insisted on carrying Elise over the threshold of the warden's mansion. Inside, she was welcomed by a receiving line of six of the twenty-two prisoner servants—cooks, butler, housemen, tailor, launderer, gardeners— immaculate in white jackets and gray pants. Only two, she was assured, were actual murderers. They showed her the special dressing room they had made for her, with the sign: "Welcome to the Boss' New Boss. God Bless You Both." It was signed "The Boys."

Her first night in the house, Elise couldn't sleep. She lay awake listening to the wail of the trains slicing though the prison and then began to weep.

Lawes awoke, alarmed, asking why she was so unhappy.

She shook her head. "I'll try to do the best I can for you and the boys," she said.

Their first morning, he kissed her good-bye and started out for the prison. Half jokingly to cover her real nervousness, she asked him the question countless others had asked before. "Aren't you afraid to go off and leave your wife with a bunch of hardened criminals?"

"Afraid?" He laughed. "These men would protect you with their lives if necessary."

She soon fell into a routine, learning the location of the push buttons in each room that would quickly summon an attendant, and inspecting the cupboards and chests loaded with linens and china and silver, the flatware stamped with the crest of the state of New York. Shoes left outside the door were shined to mirrors, the official cars gleamingly polished. She now knew why, as Lawes had once ruefully admitted, even Al Smith had been taken aback on a visit to Sing Sing. "You really live like a king," he had told Lawes. "Maybe I should swap jobs with you."

Indeed, the boys strained to please, rushing to refill her coffee cup and whisking away her plate almost before she had put down the last forkful. They were, she saw, every bit as doting with Lawes, often broiling up a mess of bullheads freshly caught in the river and taking pains to toast his bread just so, buttered on both sides and browned the way his mother had made it, while always, in his view, falling just short of perfection.

They knew a lot about Lawes, advising her to stay away from him when he wore his brown suit. She was puzzled and asked what the suit had to do with anything.

Everyone in Sing Sing knew about the suit, they said. "Inside, we call it the 'mad suit,'" confided Frankie, the head butler, "and if the boss comes through the yard wearin' it, we starts walkin' the other way." When she asked Lawes about it, he laughed but refused to explain. Maybe, she thought, it was the suit he put on when he wanted to be left alone.

She called him Mistah. He loved the way her drawl inflected the word and the deference, if ever so slightly mocking, that it carried.

The boys looked out for her, once conspiratorially patching up the dented fender of a car she had damaged while Lawes was away on a business trip. It made her uneasy to see the effect she had on them, and she struggled, perversely, to please them. But the best thing she could do for them, she found, was to stay out of their way and let them run the household.

Serving on the warden's domestic staff was a highly coveted assignment, and applications from the prisoners kept pouring in. One had come from an affable Prohibition rumrunner who had been arrested with a machine gun under his bed. Now in the course of a long stretch in Sing Sing, he wrote Lawes asking for a job as houseman, adding, "I have had the job as butler outside and at one time I was a footman so I feel well qualified to work in your residence."

Lawes reviewed his record and responded. "I am in full knowledge of your background and crime. There is nothing whatsoever in this record that would in any way qualify you for such a position. If I were starting a revolution, I should very much like to have you on my side." Then he added: "Report for work at my residence at seven o'clock tomorrow morning."

• • •

Chalked Out, which Warners had renamed *You Can't Get Away with Murder*, opened at the Strand with Bogart as the gangster-killer. The *Times* was unimpressed, sneering in its review that Warners had indeed gotten away with murder.

Lawes shrugged it off. The checks cleared. *Invisible Stripes* was also in production, not with Cagney and Garfield as first envisioned, but with Bogart, George Raft, and William Holden. And Warners was preparing to remake *20,000 Years at Sing Sing* as *Years Without Days*—later renamed *Castle on the Hudson*—with John Garfield, Anne Sheridan, Pat O'Brien, and Burgess Meredith. To Hollywood, Lawes's Sing Sing was an inexhaustible quarry of prison scripts.

The inmates benefited from their warden's infatuation with the silver screen. Movie nights came twice a week. The boys had voted Shirley Temple their top marquee attraction, followed by Edward G. Robinson, Paul Muni, Clark Gable, Dorothy Lamour, Katharine Hepburn, Joan Blondell, and Ginger Rogers.

Lawes was also working on a sixth book, to be called *Meet the Murderer*, not, as could be expected given the way the world was going, an exposé of Adolf Hitler, but an anecdotal digest of Lawes's encounters with killers, who, he often said, made the best prisoners. It began with the first murderer he had ever spoken to, Old Chappleau at Clinton in 1905, who had counseled him to leave his club on the rack as "the emblem of authority, not the symbol of punishment." Lawes never forgot that wisdom.

As war clouds darkened over Europe, Lawes felt compelled to speak out. He particularly remembered his chilling encounter with Hitler's Germany, a nation that had dispensed with inconvenient penal laws and imprisoned people for what they *might* do against the general will, whatever that was. The analogy for Lawes was easy—Hitler was a criminal. Lawes had been dealing with criminals his whole life and knew one when he saw one. So when the *Jewish Advocate* of Boston, America's leading Jewish paper, asked him to contribute an article against anti-Semitism for a February 1939 issue, he was pleased to oblige.

"The Jewish peoples," he first wrote, "are a small, harmless minority, who ask little more than to be allowed to exist in peace." (Then, thinking he may have gone too far, he inserted an almost comical equivocation, calling the Jews "a small and on the whole a harmless minority.") He saw the Jews as a "race" that by hard work and ingenuity succeeded where others failed and were victimized by those they had bettered. "The crux of the anti-Semitic question is the world-old prodding of commercial jealousy." Unable to counter Jewish business competition, he theorized, rivals resorted to persecution. Why, said Lawes, should he even dignify the ravings of the anti-Semites by listing their grievances against the Jews? They were without substance. Persecution of minorities always betokened a civilization's decline, just as tolerance marked enlightenment. Anti-Semitism was repugnant to liberty-loving Americans, he said. Jews, then, had little to fear "from the mutterings of a fistful of disgruntled individuals whose violent attack upon Jewry would constitute an assault upon Americanism in general, since one form of persecution quickly leads to another." He did not like the term "Jewish-Americans." He did not like any hyphenated American label. Americans were Americans, he believed, and the Jewish people "needed no defense."

Even in that grave hour, Lawes was enough of a showman to accept George Jessel's offer to appear as a guest on his *Vitalis Program*, Wednesday nights at nine on WEAF in New York. It made for some snappy repartee.

> **Jessel:** How are George Raft and Jimmy Cagney getting along up in your institution?
> **Lawes:** You've been misinformed, George. Those two boys are doing time at Warner Brothers.
> **Jessel:** Every time *I* see them, they're up at your place.

Jessel had a confession to make, he told Lawes; he had a book overdue from the library for two or three months. Should he take it on the lam?

Lawes laughed. "Lots of people make mistakes. Once an old lady pointed me out to her grandson and said, 'Willy, there's a man to admire. Just think, he started out as inmate, and today he's head of the whole place!'"

Jessel asked about escapes and Lawes said, "You know something, George, I'd like to see every man in prison escape."

Jessel was taken aback. "How's that again, Warden?"

"I said I'd like to see every man in prison escape," Lawes repeated. "I mean, I'd like to see every man leave the prison when his term is finished, having escaped from any need to return to the poisonous influences which brought him there in the first place."

He offered another poignant apologia to the tournament director of the Minnesota State Checker Association, who had commended Lawes for his books and good works at Sing Sing.

I do not believe that I follow a philosophy of life in my work. I feel that I am just trying to do my job to the best of my ability, but I believe in doing it humanely. I have never believed in the "eye for an eye" principle, and feel that much more good can be accomplished by point [sic] out mistakes, and showing how to correct them, than by punishment.

Germany had attacked Poland and the war was on when *Coronet* magazine wrote Lawes with a macabre offer, asking him to follow H. G. Wells in contributing to a new series called "autobiographical obituaries." For the fee of $125, he would write about himself as if he had died. The charm of it escaped Lawes. "Perhaps," he responded, "there are a few people who would enjoy reading it," but he added, "I am afraid I am not big enough to attempt this and not small enough to try." His health was not the greatest, but they would have to be patient until he keeled over in earnest.

Lawes said he intended to stick to his post. As embattled 1941 marked the onset of his twenty-second year at Sing Sing, he told the papers, "This is no time for anyone to retire."

35

There was no immediate alarm, no shrill warning whistle to pierce the silence of a sleeping prison on the early morning of Monday, April 14, 1941. An ocean away the world was in flames, but in Sing Sing the only sounds came from the lapping of the waves and the whisper of springtime breezes.

On the third floor of the hospital building on the bluff overlooking the river, Joseph "Whitey" Riordan, a bulky, towheaded stevedore and ex–stickup man of the "Paper Bag Bandits," a gang notorious for carrying away its loot in bags, was in the infirmary complaining of an appendicitis-like pain in his stomach. That put him near one of his former Paper Bag cronies, John "Patches" Waters, a slight and balding thirty-year-old orderly working in the infirmary. Also present on sick call, complaining of a sprained back, was Charles McGale, a dark and wiry mechanic, master lock-picker, and prison trusty, at forty-five the old man of the three.

The night before, Waters had met Riordan and McGale in the bathroom and slipped them each a bundle in a towel.

Their rendezvous in the infirmary had been a year in the plotting. Waters had spotted a milk truck from Newburgh that made daily deliveries into the prison. He contacted a pal on the outside, Edward Kiernan, who started visiting Sing Sing pretending to be Waters's brother Thomas. In the visiting room, they laid their plans. Kiernan began tailing the milk truck, noting its route to Sing Sing. By March they were ready to act. Kiernan and a partner, William Wade, went to Newburgh with three guns and three sets of handcuffs tied up in a rag. When the truck backed up to a loading platform in Newburgh, Kiernan wriggled beneath the undercarriage and strapped the contraband to the crankshaft. When the truck reached Sing Sing, McGale, as a trusty with privileges, was waiting to relieve it of its illicit cargo. Meanwhile, he had made a set of keys that unlocked a series of doors from the cellar of the hospital to a utility tunnel of steam pipes, which in turn led to the New York Central Railroad tracks that bisected the prison between the hospital and the river. He crawled through the tunnel, nearly suffocating in the process, to the end, where an iron plate closed it off. He sawed the plate in half and carefully replaced it so it would not be noticed. From the icehouse he had taken a length of rope, which he hid under a steam pipe, and then he crawled back to the hospital.

Promptly at 2 A.M. that Monday, guard John Hartye, a fifty-five-year-old bachelor from the Bronx who had been at Sing Sing for more than eight years, began his patrol of the infirmary, unarmed, as was the practice for all but the guards on the walls, and telephoned his all-clear to the switchboard.

Suddenly, McGale, Waters, and Riordan leaped from their beds, snatched guns from the end tables, and fell upon Hartye. He struggled and went down with two bullets in his body. A prisoner in the infirmary with a heart condition saw the shooting and collapsed with a fatal heart attack. Another prisoner furtively picked up a phone to alert the switchboard, but when the operator came on, he panicked and, afraid of being fingered as a squealer, hung up.

The three prisoners, in gray trousers and white shirts, bolted into the corridor and encountered a trusty, awakened by the shots. Waters held a gun on him and marched him down to the basement. Upstairs, Riordan had surprised another guard and taken him hostage at gunpoint. "Take it easy, don't make any noise," he said. "This is a break. If you keep quiet you won't get hurt." The guard too was herded to the basement, where he and the trusty were shackled to a platform above the boiler pit. "Less noise, less killing, let's go," cautioned Riordan. They made their way to the tunnel, crawled through, and punched their way through the presliced plate. With the rope McGale had left, they lowered themselves thirty feet down to the railroad tracks. Then they ran a few hundred yards north along the tracks to the station plaza to meet Kiernan and Wade in their stolen getaway car.

Everything had gone smoothly—too smoothly. The three escapees were half an hour early. Kiernan and Wade, thinking they had time to kill until their cronies arrived, were still in a nearby bar, leaving behind two other accomplices who were to spirit Kiernan and Wade away in a separate car.

Just then Ossining patrolman James W. Fagan and his partner, William Nelson, drove through the depot plaza on routine patrol. Fagan, thirty-five, with seven years on the police force and a wife and nineteen-month-old son at home, carried shield number 13. He had often been kidded about it but insisted he was not superstitious.

Nelson spotted the two loiterers waiting for Kiernan and Wade and got out of the car to look them over. He had no warning of any danger, for the prison alarm whistle had not yet sounded.

Fagan, at the wheel, then noticed Riordan, Waters, and McGale, who were wandering around in search of their getaway drivers Kiernan and Wade. He called them over. The answer was a shot through the windshield that pierced a button on his uniform and lodged in his heart. He staggered out of the car and emptied his weapon at the fugitives, missing wildly, before collapsing dead.

Nelson heard the shots and ran back toward the car, firing from two hundred feet away and managing to drill Waters through the forehead, killing him instantly. He radioed frantically for aid while Riordan and McGale fled.

The two accomplices also fled, stranding Kiernan and Wade, who had heard the gunfire from the bar. They waited until it seemed quiet and then ventured out to a taxi office, where they jumped into a waiting cab and told the driver to take them to White Plains. The cabbie had heard something about a policeman being shot and was suspicious. He delayed, going through the motions of seeking clearance from his dispatcher, until another police car appeared in the plaza. The taxi driver beckoned it over and the two men were ordered out at gunpoint.

They insisted they had come to Ossining with a couple of pickups, "Betty" and "Peggy," who had rebuffed a pass and marooned them there. They were taken in for questioning. The stolen getaway car, a 1939 two-door Plymouth sedan with a submachine gun on the backseat, was soon found nearby.

A short distance away, at Holden's Dock on the Hudson, Charles Rohr Jr., a sad-faced shad fisherman, was packing his catch for delivery to the Fulton Fish Market when two men shoved guns in his stomach. "Is that your boat?" one demanded. Rohr said it was. "Get going," he was told. "We just killed a cop." Rohr wasn't about to argue. "Take the boat," he said. One of the gun-men motioned him to move. "You're rowing. Get going."

He sat in the bow of the little sixteen-footer and for an hour and a half in the inky darkness rowed them the three miles across the Hudson, one of them in the stern and the other in the middle seat, both of them covering him with their guns and whispering.

On a sandy beach on the western shore near Rockland Lake, he let them off. They seemed ready to shoot him.

Rohr thought fast. "That won't do you no good," he said. "Everybody around here knows my boat and if they find it you will be in a tough spot. It'll be better for you to let me row back to Ossining and then nobody will know where you landed."

The two exchanged hurried whispers, then turned and plunged into the woods, leaving Rohr to row his way tremblingly back across the river in a pouring rainstorm.

By this time, Sing Sing's whistle had sounded. Nelson's calls for aid had brought hundreds of police officers flooding in from surrounding towns and an army of newspapermen and photographers streaming in on rumors of a mass breakout from Sing Sing. The railroad put a yard engine at the disposal of the police, who rode up and down the tracks with flashlights probing the darkness.

On the streets, the early editions were already blaring the news.

By dawn more than a thousand lawmen—state troopers with blood-hounds, local officers, and Coast Guardsmen in a seaplane, two launches, and two cutters—had joined the manhunt. Fishermen who had seen Rohr depart so stealthily alerted the police, and when Rohr got back he was able to report where he had dropped the two.

The posses found footprints leading off the beach, and dogs picked up the scent. The searchers were tracking the fugitives up the wooded slopes of Hook Mountain in Palisades Interstate Park when they spotted the pair, poorly disguised in suede jackets they had found somewhere. A trooper called, "Come out or we'll let you have it!" Riordan and McGale meekly sur-rendered, handing over their loaded .38-caliber pistols. Roughly cuffed to-gether, they were slapped around and put aboard a Coast Guard cutter for the trip back to Ossining and police headquarters.

DAILY NEWS

Average net paid circulation
for March exceeded
Daily---1,925,000
Sunday-3,700,000

Copr. 1941 by News Syndicate Co. Inc. NEW YORK'S PICTURE NEWSPAPER   Trade Mark Reg. U. S. Pat. Off.

FINAL

Vol. 22. No. 251   New York Monday April 14, 1941*   40 Pages   2 Cents IN CITY LIMITS | 3 CENTS Elsewhere

3 DIE IN BREAK AT SING SING; GANG AT LARGE

Story on Page 2

Easter Parade a Big Hit. What you see here is one of the largest Easter Sunday crowds in the memory of some aged Easter Sunday experts, gathered outside St. Patrick's Cathedral. If you didn't get up to look over the city's annual fashion event, you can read the story on pages 4 and 6 and see what the notables were wearing by turning to the center fold.

Headline from 1941 escape. (© NEW YORK DAILY NEWS, L.P. REPRINTED WITH PERMISSION)

In the station, the two were questioned by police officials and by Lawes, who demanded details of the worst breakout in Sing Sing's 116-year history. Riordan and McGale put the blame on Waters, conveniently dead.

Lawes's most pressing question went unanswered. *Why? After all he had done, or tried to do, at Sing Sing? Why?*

With two law officers dead, the fury of the police was unleashed on the shackled prisoners, who were beaten so brazenly that news photographers were able to show them being punched, knocked down, and yanked around by the hair. One photo showed a jackbooted officer astride the two men on the floor of the station house, a frightened-looking Riordan trying to shield his body, and a battered-looking McGale clutching his crotch. Out of sight of the photographers it was worse. Between interrogations by the prosecutor, Riordan and McGale, cuffed together, were brutalized by troopers and detectives for hours at a time. The assaults stopped briefly when someone called out that the prosecutor was coming, and resumed after he left. Riordan's bridgework was knocked loose, and he nearly choked to death on his false teeth. His pleas for water were ignored while in front of his eyes an open faucet gushed tantalizingly.

Lawes was devastated. Was this where it all led? A career of progressive penal policy and now this? *Treat a man like a dog and you will make a dog of him.* But what if you treated a man like a man, he wondered, and he made a dog of you?

In the days that followed, Corrections Commissioner John J. Lyons demanded answers, reminding Lawes of his worst times with Rattigan. Feebly, Lawes complained of inadequate resources. Sing Sing had long been a medium-security facility given the task of serving as a maxium-security one. But his pleas for more state funding had been consistently rebuffed.

Albany loosed a barrage of angry questions. Why had it taken an hour and a half to sound the whistle? How did all those guns get into the prison, and how had they escaped detection? Why hadn't the rope stolen from the icehouse been missed? How had McGale managed to make all those keys to open all those locks? Where was Lawes in all this? Writing his books and screenplays? Wasn't anyone paying attention down there? And just what steps was Lawes taking to safeguard Sing Sing against a repetition of the unprecedented violence?

And then came the inevitable question he most dreaded: Was prisoner coddling to blame? Lawes's humanitarian approach was well known. Is this what came of it?

Lawes was at a loss to respond, having too many questions of his own.

As Lyons descended on Sing Sing for his inquiry, refusing to speak to reporters, Lawes wearily took their questions.

Clearly, he said, the "machinery" of the prison had failed. "Something went wrong. Just what that was is being investigated and the proper corrections will be made." The tunnel, he said, was not sealed off because the steel doors had seemed to provide adequate security and repairmen needed ready access. McGale's privileged position at the powerhouse had given him the opportunity to betray that trust. Unquestionably, delivery trucks coming into the prison should have been combed for guns and other contraband, but fifteen to thirty trucks passed through the gates daily. The siren was not immediately sounded because Lawes and his deputies assumed, wrongly, that the escapees had to be holed up in the basement. Missing inmates were often recaptured on the grounds.

After his discussions with Lyons, Lawes announced that an illuminated pit would be dug at the prison service entrance over which all trucks would have to pass for undercarriage inspection. The tunnel system, also too late perhaps, would be reviewed.

The crusading district attorney of New York County, Thomas E. Dewey, deepened Lawes's anguish by proclaiming the dangerousness of the escapees. Dewey called Riordan and Waters "two of the worst criminals ever prosecuted by this office" and said, "In the light of what these escaped men might have done while at liberty, their capture was an excellent and very important job."

The night after the breakout, at midnight, the Sing Sing whistle erupted in seven alarming shrieks that blasted the inmates awake and sent Ossining police officers with riot guns charging to the prison. Guards rushed to the gates with machine guns and sawed-off shotguns. Lawes raced over from his house. Ossining's telephone lines were jammed with calls.

A guard had checked the night's count in cellblock A and come up with 669. There were supposed to be 670. One short. He alerted Lawes and sounded the whistle.

Postcard view of Sing Sing about the time of Lawes's arrival in 1919. (COLLECTION OF RALPH BLUMENTHAL)

Hundreds of frantic policemen, guards, and armed citizens ringed Sing Sing as crowds of curiosity seekers pressed in. Guards, fingering their weapons, held the mob at bay, warning, "There is likely to be shooting here any minute."

A plane full of newsmen circled over the prison. Radio stations broke into their programs broadcasting bulletins that two more heavily armed killers had escaped.

Then the word came down. Miscount. No one was missing. Everyone could stand down. Shaking guards reshouldered their shotguns.

Lawes suppressed a nervous smile. To the clamoring press he said: "If the people here want the whistle blown when there is trouble or an escape, we will blow it."

As the Westchester district attorney convened a grand jury with Lawes to be the leadoff witness, the next day was given over to funerals. In Ossining, Patrolman Fagan was memorialized in St. Augustine's Roman Catholic Church before the biggest crowd ever to honor a police officer in Westchester. Nine hundred mourners, including Elise, filled the pews while a larger number waited outside. Afterward, the Post Road was closed as five hundred police officers escorted their comrade to his final rest.

Lawes was in the Bronx, attending the funeral of guard John Hartye.

Those who knew the warden in the olden days might not have recognized him. He was dapper as ever in a dark suit, white shirt, and tie, double-breasted chesterfield, fedora, and kidskin gloves, but his eyes were sunken in their sockets and his gaunt form was accentuated by thinning hair combed over a vast expanse of forehead.

The funerals were only the beginning. Ahead, Lawes knew, lay a painful inquest, if not an inquisition, and a protracted trial at the end of which lurked—with dreadful certainty—the chair.

36

The breakout was still a raw wound when Lawes suffered another blow. Alabama Pitts was dead. The last Lawes had heard, his star halfback and fielder who had assisted at the birth of his granddaughter, Judith, had moved to Valdese, North Carolina, where he was coaching sports at the high school and making ends meet by working as a knitter in a hosiery mill. Pitts had married and had a child. The details were sparse, but news reports said that on a June night in 1941 he was at a Valdese roadhouse. A band was playing by the swimming pool, and when he tried to cut in on a dancing couple, the girl's escort stabbed him. He died minutes later from a severed shoulder artery. He was thirty years old. Lawes mourned in seclusion.

The ghastly trial of Riordan and McGale and their accused accomplices Kiernan and Wade followed, forcing Lawes to relive the murderous escape, along with a grotesque new element. The two defendants charged that they had been savagely beaten to coerce their admissions, although they insisted that the dead Waters had masterminded the scheme.

The prosecutor, in his opening to the jury, conceded that Riordan had been "knocked down" by an Ossining police officer, and that a Sing Sing guard "took a swing" at McGale, but he insisted it was no third degree. The defense cited medical evidence of beatings: one month after his arrest, Wade still bore bruises.

When the defendants took the stand to challenge their confessions, a gruesome picture emerged. State troopers had mauled McGale, joking that by the time they were done, he "would admit he killed Lincoln." Wade estimated he had been struck a total of fourteen *hundred* times and strung up by his wrists fifteen times. He testified that a state police inspector had cautioned his men not to disfigure the prisoner's face. Yet, he said, they battered him all over, and when he started to scream, the inspector had given an order: "Gag that bum—he's disturbing the DA."

The jury, initially deadlocked, soon reached a predictable verdict. Guilty. Riordan and McGale were to die in the chair. Accomplices Kiernan and Wade got life.

Lawes had little sympathy for the killers, but he was sickened by the beatings. He remembered Squire's sordid tales of police savagery and kept thinking of Riordan on the stand with his broken English and hopeless profanity, and of McGale, who testified that in five years in Sing Sing he had received but a single visitor, a lawyer asking if he wanted to contest a family will.

With the trial over, Lawes knew what he wanted to do. No one had thought he would last twenty-one months at Sing Sing, much less twenty-one years. But now the time was at hand. He was fifty-seven years old. He had spent more than thirty-six of his years in service to the state, behind prison walls. Now he and Elise had bought a small farm in Garrison, a pretty riverside bluff a few miles up the Hudson across from West Point. In July 1941 he resigned, quietly putting in his papers. Commissioner Lyons promptly accepted them. When bulletins began rocketing out of Sing Sing four days later, reporters asked about the boys. "They don't know it yet," Lawes told them. "Some of them will probably feel bad. A great many of them have been here a long time, men who have been saved from the chair and sentenced to life. Some of them have been very valuable, very fine men and, I might say, very fine friends." Due a pension of six thousand dollars a year, he would write, lecture, and devote himself to his causes, he said.

The day he left, the prison whistle blew at 2 P.M. Work stopped in the shops. All Sing Sing came to a standstill. In the administration building, Lawes said farewell to two hundred employees and accepted their gift of a silver service inscribed with a tribute:

To Warden Lewis E. Lawes,
in sincere appreciation of your humane leadership.
1920–1942
From the employees of Sing Sing.

From there Lawes moved on to the chapel, jammed with 2,400 prisoners, all but those on death row and in disciplinary confinement.

As his farewell speech neared its end, the chapel rocked with stamping feet, applause, and whistles, a clamor that swallowed up the rest of Lawes's remarks. The prisoners heard him proclaim, "God bless you," and they surged forward, engulfing him in a huddle of bear hugs and fervid hand-shakes. It was all the secretary of the Mutual Welfare League could do to break through to present him with a testimonial scroll from the boys. Lawes accepted it with reverence.

There was a final round of hand-shaking. Lawes stopped to bid farewell to financial wizard Richard Whitney, who was set to follow him out the gate shortly, having won parole after three years and almost four months. He had lost $11 million on Wall Street but had made a profit in Sing Sing, which owed him workshop earnings of $181.01.

Word of Lawes's retirement shot around the country. Walter Winchell flashed it on his radio show. W. Colston Leigh, king of the lecture circuit, of-fered to book Lawes on lucrative speaking tours. Letters poured in, and even Lyons signed a tribute from the State Commission of Correction that called Lawes's retirement "well earned" and praised him as "an executive of ability, intelligence, common sense, and human sympathy." Burdette Lewis, the for-mer penal commissioner who had first encountered the twenty-eight-year-old Lawes at Columbia and was now an education official in the federal security agency, wrote to say, "I hope you didn't get mad and quit too soon." Sing Sing, he confided, was a "picnic" compared to the bloodletting going on in Washington. Roosevelt's confidant James A. Farley also sent best wishes.

The Osborne Association hailed him for keeping the reformer's torch lit and compared him to a lifer released at last. The American League to Abol-ish Capital Punishment looked forward now to his fuller attention. A Syra-cuse woman wrote, "I likened you to a shepherd watching over their flock." She couldn't afford to buy Meet the Murderer, she said, but had borrowed it from the library and loved it. From Geneva, Nebraska, a Congregational pastor thanked Lawes for his opposition to capital punishment. Lawes had not always succeeded, but, the minister said, "neither did Jesus."

A judge in Pittsburgh recalled happy days officiating at football games at Sing Sing. "In a way it was an inspiration, and gave me a keen insight into the results that can be obtained when a penal institution is properly administered." A California man wrote: "You have proven one thing to me, that a man can be big even though he spends his life among many who are not." The labor secretary of a New York bakers' union said Lawes's radio shows had inspired him to buy books and send them to the Sing Sing library "as a matter of making my small contribution to the voice of humanity." Lawes's old pal in the insurance business, Monroe Flegenheimer, reminded Lawes how he had considered giving up penology for an insurance job fifteen years before and said encouragingly, "I am inclined to think that you made no mistake in turning it down." And his old collaborator Jonathan Finn said he was trying to revive interest in a movie of *Cell 202* and thought that Lawes should throw himself into filmmaking.

That, of all prospects, sounded the most intriguing to Lawes, especially after Finn cabled him from Los Angeles:

CAN ARRANGE DEAL WITH MAJOR STUDIO
FOR DEVELOPING PRISON STORY IDEA.
PRICE FIFTY THOUSAND DOLLARS.

Lawes got back to him in a hurry. Earlier, Finn had proposed writing a biography of Lawes, but flattering as that was, Lawes had put him off, saying, "There's plenty of time for that." Now the two pitched Warners a biographical feature, to be "supervised" by Lawes. They overplayed their hand. "We do not deem it necessary to discuss the dramatic possibilities of such a picture. We believe Mr. Lawes, as an authority, would be in the best position to evaluate its dramatic possibilities. It is intended that Mr. Lawes would have complete control over the script, its authenticity and production. Should he desire to appear in the picture it would be in the dignified role of Commentator." Lawes would get $15,000 upon signing, then additional payments of $10,000 and $17,500 as production progressed. Hollywood was mum.

August brought welcome news. Three and a half months after the deadly Sing Sing break, Commissioner Lyons vindicated Lawes, finding "no maladministration" but "some weaknesses" that he addressed with tight new regulations under the new warden, Robert J. Kirby, who had been principal keeper at Attica Prison. Henceforth, Lyons directed, all visitors would be fingerprinted. Common-law wives could not visit except with his express

permission. Additional fencing would ring the prison, and guards would patrol around the hospital all night.

While he waited for Hollywood to call back, Lawes sought to rouse the na-
tion to prepare for war. On a rainy summer night in August 1941, he joined
Rear Admiral Richard E. Byrd, poet Carl Sandburg, and Associate Justice
Owen J. Roberts of the United States Supreme Court at the rostrum of an
antifascist rally in a flag-bedecked Madison Square Garden that rang with
hisses and boos for appeasers like Charles Lindbergh. They cheered for
Lawes, known for championing a strong American role in the war against
Hitler and for abolishing the Neutrality Act that kept America from aiding
embattled England and Russia.

When a wild beast stalked an African village, Lawes began, the populace
closed ranks and destroyed the marauder. So it should be with the democra-
cies, he urged. "You and I meet in this hall tonight faced by the greatest
menace that has ever stalked the earth. And like our African cousins, we
must plot the destruction of our enemy. For only the blind or the insane will
ask us to ignore the world's most dreadful scourge—Nazism."

He denounced merchants eager to preserve their commerce with Germany for failing to see that Hitler had targeted America as well. And Hitler,
in Lawes's vernacular, was "the world's most notorious gangster," who adver-
tised his schemes in his "criminal handbook," Mein Kampf. It was there for
all to see in the sad histories of Spain, Austria, Czechoslovakia, Poland, Belgium, and Holland. It had never been their fight either, Lawes warned, until
one by one they fell. "This must not happen to America." Now Russia alone
blocked Hitler's way to England and the West. This was no time for petty
quarreling with allies; America had to arm England, Russia, and China.

He knew, he said, he might be labeled a warmonger, but he could imagine
worse insults. He could actually relish the title "if I acquire it while rallying
my countrymen to oppose the greatest warmonger of all time." Nazi spies,
traitors, saboteurs, and propagandists were everywhere, Lawes warned, and
America fought with hands tied by the Neutrality Act. It had to be repealed
so that America's merchant fleet could be armed and escorted to repel the
Nazi raiders of the seas.

And who were those, he asked, who hid behind the magic word "peace"?
Who could not be for peace? But what kind of peace? And on whose terms?

Here, he said, the appeasers fell silent. He knew about peace, he said. There could even be peace in a prison. "I ought to know," he said, to a ripple of laughter. "I headed one for a while." There could be peace—a monstrous peace—in the vast prison house Hitler had made of Europe. And so, he warned, a domestic fascism was afoot in America, fomented by traitors backing Hitler who called him invincible, worth doing business with, sentiments that meant only one thing, Lawes said: *They wanted him to win.*

He reached back to his Sing Sing days to recall an old slogan reminding criminals that crime didn't pay: "You can't win." Today, he said, that slogan was being used against the American people, but he would reply: "We can win, if we are united!" The Garden thundered its approval.

In November he spoke over radio station WOR for the New York Fight for Freedom Committee to Defend America. Hitler was being called many things, Lawes said, madman, monster, butcher, tyrant. But above all, he said, speaking from experience, Hitler was a criminal akin to Dillinger and Capone, only it was not money he sought but power. Lawes cited the rogue's gallery of Hitler's henchmen: "Göring, the elephantine racketeer"; Reich finance minister Friesler, who had served three terms for embezzlement; the "twisted" Goebbels; Rudolph Hess, "the beetle-browed trigger man"; and Himmler, "the führer's favorite stool pigeon, whose Gestapo are the eyes and ears of the mob."

Just imagine, Lawes went on, if Capone's criminal sway had extended over not just the nation's bootlegging industry but the entire American economy. Well, he went on, "fascism is simply gangsterism legally entrenched."

And then he said, reaching for a new vocabulary that would prove prescient, "the holocaust that is Hitler is not the problem of one country alone." Hitler was a master criminal who had broken the laws of twenty nations. "Therefore, an international gangster such as he must be exterminated through the combined efforts of all these nations."

Warners finally responded. It had tinkered with a Lawes-centered biographical story line, with little success because, as producer Bob Lord confessed, "I knew practically nothing about the facts of your life, or your personality." Instead, writers concocted another prison melodrama that sent Lawes into apoplexy. Lord backed down, saying they were rethinking it and would take the matter up with Hal Wallis, "the High Chief Muck-a-Muck here." In mid-November, Lawes and Elise took the train to Los Angeles at Warners' expense to discuss it.

Nothing was decided, and they had just got back when the Japanese attacked Pearl Harbor. His project swept off the table, Lawes petulantly made out his expense statement, billing Warners $351.96 for out-of-pocket expenses including $4.48 to express ship his clipping scrapbooks to California. In his grievous disappointment, he wrote Lord, now Major Lord: "Looks as if the Japs put a nasty, but effective, one over on us. You are in a great spot for action. I suppose that you are now likely to be called to the Army."

Among the casualties of the attack, Lord told Finn, were prospects for their movie. "I personally do not think that it is the proper type of picture to make these days." Still, he said, it would be up to Jack Warner and Hal Wallis.

Lawes reminded Finn that it was Warners that had come to him in the first place and that out of affection for Harry Warner, he had signed with Warners rather than two other studios that had offered more money. Blinded by his hurt, he complained, "I did not start the present war" and said he expected Warners to live up to its contract. "Everyone will be getting enough war without filming war pictures, which must be censored and directed by the Government. People are jittery now and there is a great deal of confusion. We are in for a hell of a time but entertainment is essential to keep up the morale. Of course comedies will be plentiful, but if we are going to remain a democracy, we must keep the democratic way of life before the people of this country."

With no prospect of a quick resolution, Lawes booked a busy speaking tour that would shuttle him, in two weeks, to Indianapolis, Memphis, Salt Lake City, Seattle, Spokane, and San Diego to talk about the death penalty, penal reform, and, of course, Hitler as archcriminal.

And then, to his happy surprise, Warners got back to him. They liked his suggestions. A revised script would be sent shortly. Lawes, excited, forwarded his itinerary. The script could be sent to any of his stops.

And then silence. His letters to Lord went unanswered.

While he waited impatiently, Riordan and McGale, on death row for their murderous breakout, ran through their final appeals. After their conviction for killing Keeper Hartye, the state had not bothered to try them for the murder of Officer Fagan. They could be electrocuted only once. In a final bid to Governor Lehman for clemency, Riordan's lawyer had claimed his client had talked Waters out of killing the second guard and trusty taken captive. The guard had supported the story, saying Riordan had intervened to save their lives. Lehman was unmoved. On a June night in 1942, fourteen months after the deadly escape, the two men went to the chair. Riordan went first and died in the last hour of his twenty-seventh birthday.

Four months after his last contact with Warners, Lawes finally heard from the studio that Lord had gone into active service with the army, and the script had been turned over to a new producer, thirty-eight-year-old Mark Hellinger. Lawes could not have hoped for a more engaged collaborator, a popular Broadway columnist who had enlivened the *Daily News* with the lore and gore of the Prohibition underworld before going on to write short stories and movie scripts. After joining Warners as an associate producer in 1937, he made *The Roaring Twenties*, *They Drive by Night*, and *High Sierra*, among other hits.

Hellinger wrote Lawes promptly. "I am definitely enthused about the property," he said, "and I hold the feeling that it is shaping into a thoroughly human and very exciting story." He expected to have a shooting script to send Lawes shortly, and he promised it would be "a very heart-warming document."

It arrived in August, and Lawes read it with distaste. The writers had taken great liberties, overdramatizing some episodes and leaving out large segments of his story. The facts were wrong, Lawes stipulated in voluminous notes, and they would all have to be corrected.

Hellinger had had enough. "Obviously our viewpoints clash on a number of items—some unimportant, some so important that a new script would have to be written in order to correct them." He offered Lawes a short course in screenwriting. "I'm certain we both recognize the blunt truism that, in searching for popular and commercial success, it is almost an impossibility to adhere precisely to strict fact. I do not question your facts, sir; your splendid career speaks for itself. But I do question the popularity of these facts when projected, without a bit of pulse-quickening coloration, in motion picture form." He had turned over Lawes's letter to Harry Warner, Hellinger concluded ominously, "and I know you will be hearing from him."

The letter came not from his old friend Harry but Jacob Wilk, Warners' longtime acquisitions chief, whose first job in New York in the 1910s, as it happened, was as press agent for the father of producer William Brady Jr., who had burned to death in Elise's cottage seven years before. Wilk addressed the letter rather formally to "Dear Lewis Lawes" and broke the bad news that "the studio advises so many changes would have to be made in the existing script as to make the job too great to undertake at this time." And so, he concluded, cruelly dashing Lawes's hopes for new fame on the silver screen, "they prefer to let the matter ride for the time being."

37

American trains were crowded and dusty as they clanked their way across the country in the war year of 1943, old rattletraps, moving on ingenuity and hope. Every bit of steel plate that the mills could turn out went for ships and tanks and guns. Trains had no priority. Day after day, week after week, Lawes sat in the stale and drafty cars, his increasingly threadbare suits flecked with grit and his white shirts, grayish now, smudged by smokestack filth as he crisscrossed the country for the prison industries branch of the War Production Board.

From stops along the way he dropped letters to his beloved Elise, asking about Cherie in college and despairing of the struggle overseas. "I am also fearful that our army is one hell of a mess and it will take time to cure it. I hope the cost will not be too great." He signed himself "Mistah" and she addressed her mail to him the same way. Occasionally he managed to get off a telegram.

A WORLD OF LOVE TO THE
SWEETEST GIRL ON EARTH THIS
ST. VALENTINE'S DAY. MISTAH.

She, in turn, filled him in on the comforting minutiae of life in Garrison, the chowchow she had made, and the mincemeat and chili. She had stayed up late playing cards at Crystal's. She was worried about him. "Try to remember not to eat too fast and eat a green vegetable or salad each day."

That January he had presented himself at the board's regional office on

East Forty-second Street to be fingerprinted—he relished the irony—and pressed into service as a government consultant. With his prison experience, Lawes would see if prisoners could help raise more of their own food, taking a burden off the wartime economy and perhaps providing some extra for their hard-pressed allies England and Russia. Lawes would also try to hasten the rehabilitation of convicts so they could take their place in the war effort. The fingerprinting ceremony, as expected, drew the press—Lawes was still catnip for the camera boys. But when reporters asked him about his new job, he was uncharacteristically silent. He would not be able to issue a statement, he said, until he had done some work.

After the spotlight of Sing Sing and the bright lights of Broadway and Hollywood, Lawes could now be found at state penitentiaries from Trenton, New Jersey, to Columbus, Ohio, presenting awards and banners to the patriotic inmates for their output of shoes and other supplies for the army, and hearing in return: "There isn't any one of us who wouldn't be glad to exchange the stripe on our trousers for one on our sleeve."

He was still in demand as a speaker, appearing at the New York University Faculty Club in Greenwich Village to discuss the chief civilian preoccupation of the time, anxiety over a postwar crime wave. Juvenile delinquency was a potent threat, Lawes said, urging special schools for parents of delinquents. "Problem children usually come from problem parents," he asserted. In contrast, prisoners were an inspiration to the nation, displaying "unquestionable patriotism" in their tireless manufacture of wartime provisions.

When he finally made it home, Elise suddenly had to leave. A family emergency drew her back to Jackson in the spring of 1944. Now it was her turn to suffer the wretched trains and understand his miserable lot. The strains took their toll on both of them and tense words sparked a painful spat. But then Lawes managed to get a telephone call through, and her dulcet voice soothed the pain and loosed again their pent-up love. Their talk, Lawes assured her afterward, "clarified many things and made us close together as we have always been."

On borrowed government stationery he scratched her out a note, writing in the "subject" line: "mutual interests—5th anniversary." He had managed to buy her some earrings and was sending them airmail and promised to send a wire as well, as soon as he could make up some military-sounding jargon that would get the cable through restrictions on civilian traffic.

Alone, he was disconsolate. "With you away, I am like a ship without an anchor, though you lift me up rather than weigh me down." A friend invited him to Floyd Bennett Field with Jack Dempsey to see a full ticket of boxing. In the old days nothing would have pleased him more—fast-fisted gladiators, a roaring crowd, and cigar smoke. But now he begged off.

Back home again, with Lawes once again away on the road, Elise found New York bleak, the stores empty. She had gotten a gift certificate to John David on Fifth Avenue and hoped to buy some gabardine, but there was none to be had. She had ordered Lawes some ties from Saks, but they had never arrived.

He struggled against pessimism. "I am convinced," he wrote her, "that if anyone thinks that money is the only value in life, that ruthlessness and not ability is the most desirable trait to possess, one shudders for the future, but if we have the farm and each other we will get by."

Home again for a visit in October 1944, Lawes was excitedly back in his old element, addressing the American Prison Association's Seventy-Fourth Annual Congress of Correction at the Pennsylvania Hotel across from Pennsylvania Station. To the thousand delegates who packed the hall one question was uppermost: With all the war-hardened, depression-era young men streaming home after victory in Europe and the Pacific, would there be a postwar crime wave?

This was red meat to Lawes, and he pounced on it. "If there are no jobs there will be an upsurge in robbery and burglary," he declared. "There must be jobs, and by jobs I mean jobs that pay sufficiently to enable Americans to maintain a decent standard of living."

As for whether there would be a crime wave, he said that depended. "Will we eliminate after the war other causes of crime so well known by now: slum areas and the like? And will we intelligently cope with another crop of potential criminals, today's juvenile delinquents?"

The question was whether society could undo all the recent damage caused by the war: schools closed for lack of teachers, recreational facilities shuttered, children lured to factory workbenches instead of classrooms, and labor laws ignored. Lawes had his doubts. But he had no fear that veterans would return as murderers. There was no mass urge to kill, he said. That would disappear with the war.

The trains were worse than ever. With gasoline rationed, the whole country was trying to move on rails. He had trouble getting a ticket from Chicago to Los Angeles and sometimes was forced to take freight trains to visit his prisons. He had long thought that there was nothing worse than the Northern Pacific, he wrote Elise. Well, he found out, there was.

She tried to distract him with cozy reports from the home front. "We have to have a bearing fixed in the lawn mover." Ho Ping, their faithful cook and former tong warrior who had stayed with them after his release from Sing Sing, was having problems with immigration.

Lawes's health was deteriorating. His teeth and gums, neglected too long, were in terrible shape. He went for hour after hour of treatment, suffering painful extractions and the tortures of what felt like a pile driver pounding into his gums. The bill was painful too, Lawes complained to Elise—$150, with the bridgework yet to come.

His world was collapsing. Al Smith, who had given Lawes his reluctant start at Sing Sing a quarter century before, had died at seventy. One hundred sixty thousand mourners, from the lowliest denizens of the sidewalks of New York to Governor Thomas E. Dewey and Eleanor Roosevelt, streamed through St. Patrick's Cathedral. Lawes wished he could have been among them, but he was on the road.

He was in St. Louis for a speaking engagement and had stopped to visit Kathleen and Charles when his right side went numb. They rushed him to the hospital, where doctors diagnosed a stroke—he had recently turned sixty-one—and treated him with phenobarbital and bed rest. He was recovering well when he came down with pleurisy and pneumonitis in his right lung. Doctors treated him with large doses of sulfadiazine and he recovered quickly. All his functions had returned after the mild stroke, and he was soon released to get back on the train and ride home.

He was on the road once again when the Prison Association of New York marked its hundredth anniversary at a lunch at the Biltmore Hotel. Lawes put together his thoughts and sent a message to be read for him. The big problem facing society, he warned yet again, was juvenile delinquency. It was not just petty crime and mischief. Around the country, he had found youth infected by the intolerance and hatred that had turned Nazi Europe into an inferno. In America too they were attacking Jews and defacing synagogues. "These youngsters were indoctrinated—and still are—by adult demagogues as vicious and dangerous as our enemies abroad," Lawes declared.

Lawes circa 1930s.
(JOAN L. JACOBSEN)

"To counteract the influence of these home-grown Fascists—and I fear that their numbers may increase—the schools must lay greater emphasis on the tenets of our democracy, and we must wage constant war against racial and religious bigotry."

Casting aside fears of ridicule, the former prison boss joined the board of directors of the National Kindergarten Association, then advocating a bill to extend preschool education across America. As he wrote the group: "I was in the prison game about thirty-seven years and at Sing Sing, as Warden, for nearly twenty-five years. At that time I firmly came to the conclusion that preventive measures, such as education, were much preferable to punishment or rehabilitation. Recently, I have rather come to the conclusion that, among other things, the establishment of kindergartens is essential and important."

When the war ended, Lawes remained in his post, summing up his work for the War Production Board's Prison War Programs Office. He had visited forty-five of the forty-eight states and talked to hundreds of inmates, correction

officials, and governors. Not in forty years of penal work had he seen such a patriotic outpouring as the prisons evidenced in the years following Pearl Harbor. In the goods they had turned out, the war bonds they had bought, the
blood they had donated—even in the selfless guinea-pig experiments they had
voluntarily endured for research in lifesaving medicines—prisoners had contributed far more comparatively within their means than those outside the
walls. It proved what he had always said, Lawes proudly wrote to the Office of
War Mobilization and Reconversion, which was planning the return to a civilian economy: everyone deserved a second chance. Men who had been trained
in prison workshops and released when their time was served performed
valiantly in war plants. And by and large they did not return to prison. In fact,
Lawes noted, America's prisons during the war operated at about 50 percent of
capacity—"thank God!"

Now, with peace, he said, it was likely that the prisons would refill. A
hundred thousand convicted felons had served honorably in the armed
forces, but some now would undoubtedly return to old ways and lives behind
bars. But society need not throw up its hands. Something could be done.
Surplus products could be turned over to prisons for vocational training of
inmates. Most of all, the Prison War Programs Office should be perpetuated,
as the American Prison Association urged. "I realize the tremendous problems of reconversion," Lawes concluded, "but it is so easy for busy people to
think of prisons as simply jails where men are locked up. Prisons are really
communities populated by human beings. A little foresight now will prevent
the needless ruin of many lives in the future."

By November 1945, his work done, Lawes resigned his consultancy and
returned home. He had, once again, joined the ranks of the unemployed.
Within a year, however, he signed up to do a new radio series tentatively entitled *Behind Prison Bars* and scheduled to run for an astonishing 260 weeks
starting in October 1946. He would be paid $750 a weekly episode for the
first year, $900 for the second, and by the 1950–51 season, $1,650. By the
time it premiered on the Mutual Network, sponsored by Clipper Craft
Clothes, it was being called *Crime Cases of Warden Lawes*. The formula was
familiar—more dramatized tales from the seemingly inexhaustible files of
America's best known and most beloved warden. Listeners loved it.

Four days before Christmas, 1946, amid a raging sleet storm, Lawes
stood at the altar of a small Roman Catholic church in nearby Cold

Spring, New York, and gave away his baby daughter. Cherie—known now by her proper name, Joan Marie—was marrying her high school sweetheart, Henry A. Jacobsen, a department store manager in New York. They had met at the Scarborough School when she was sixteen, and now, nine years later, after her college years at Pembroke and Rollins and after many tearful breakups and makeups, they had decided after all that they were made for each other. After the nuptials, the newlyweds, Lawes and Elise and their families, and a hundred guests made their perilous way through the storm to a restored 1761 tavern and stage stop, the Bird & Bottle Inn. Through the mullioned windows soft candle glow fell on the celebrants gathered around the crackling hearths as Lawes held forth with toasts and stories, jokes and oratory polished in a lifetime of addresses to penal conclaves and convict audiences.

The following spring, Lawes sat in his study in Garrison and composed a difficult letter to his friend Harry Warner. The war years had taken their toll on him, he said. "I have had two strokes since I last saw you plus a seige [sic] of pneumonia and arthiritis [sic]. Although I have made a wonderful recovery, I have to take it very easy which is pretty hard on someone as active as I have always been." What was on his mind, he continued, was the story of his life that Warners had bought when he retired. For one reason or another, it had never been made.

"As it now stands my contract restricts and prohibits me from doing many things which have been offered me and which would bring me remuneration I sorely need. Since the studio has not made the picture during these years, I thought and hoped that you and I might come to some satisfactory arrangement whereby you would release to me the contract provided, of course, I recompensed you for the money you have paid me. I would then be in a position, without too much effort on my part, to earn some money to take care of me in my remaining years." He begged Harry to think it over and get back to him.

There was no immediate reply. Lawes found that Harry too had been sick, and wrote him again after a few weeks, having himself suffered a relapse that confined him to his room. "I have long been a victim of hypertension (high blood pressure to us laymen)," Lawes wrote, "and am now afflicted with 'word aphasia' which causes me a slight difficulty with my speech. However, I am taking it easy on my farm here and hope soon to be up and around again."

Harry himself answered two days later. He had just gotten back to business, he told Lawes, and had discussed the matter with his brother Jack. They had invested exactly $64,118.56, he wrote. He suggested that Lawes see another studio executive who knew the situation "and I am sure he will work out something to your satisfaction."

If Lawes had hoped he might prod Warners into finally doing the movie, he was disappointed. "We cannot at this time undertake to make this story," Harry said.

Another Warners executive who had worked with Lawes before wrote him sympathetically a few days later. He would have called, he said, but for a telephone strike. Now, he offered to drive to Garrison to discuss a favorable settlement. He was sorry to hear about Lawes's ailments and assured him that he and Warner had "every desire to cooperate with you to meet your wishes in this matter and to make things comfortable for you, insofar as it is within our power."

Lawes never saw the letter. Given his frail condition, Elise withheld his business mail. She opened it, though, and responded with thanks. He kept asking if Harry had answered yet.

A week later, on April 13, 1947, Lawes, at sixty-three, suffered a cerebral hemorrhage at home. He clung to life, refusing to succumb. He had recently managed to finish a survey of the Massachusetts State Prison at Charlestown for the governor, but he still had a full schedule of radio talks to deliver. His broadcasting contract had four and a half years to run.

Ten days later, with Elise, Crystal, and Cherie at his bedside and Kathleen on her way from St Louis, Lawes died.

Five hundred mourners jammed the small Roman Catholic church of St. Theresa for Lawes's funeral service. Father McCaffrey—now Monsignor McCaffrey—was there, as was the faithful Squire, his mournful eyes pouchy and his off-center-parted hair sparse on his balding pate. There were fellow wardens and corrections commissioners and some of the boys, but only those who were out now, for this time, under a new warden, Sing Sing did not throw open its gates. The pallbearers were former aides from Sing Sing who accompanied the boss on his final journey to Sleepy Hollow Cemetery, where Kathryn lay waiting for him.

The papers were filled with tributes, which Lawes would have been delighted to clip for his scrapbooks. The State Commission of Correction, which had so often thwarted him, now rushed, if somewhat awkwardly, to canonize him.

"His administration was marked by considered humaneness, honesty, resistance to outside pressure and an unceasing faith in the worthwhileness of striving to upbuild broken and sullied lives to a level of decency and self-respect. He often stated that his efforts were based on a straight course between coddling prisoners on one hand and brutality on the other. His administration was free of scandal. He was sometimes accused of being soft with prisoners; yet no one denied that he knew and understood them. Those who knew him well regarded him as a man's man and not at all a sentimentalist."

The National Kindergarten Association mourned its newfound friend and the loss his death signified for the young and helpless. The Prison Association of New York proudly recalled its role in educating Lawes at Columbia's School of Philanthropy and bringing the ambitious young guard to the attention of Katharine Bement Davis. Burdette Lewis wrote to the *Times* from Tokyo, where he was chief of the prison branch of the U.S. occupation authority. Lawes, he said, "had a quality obviously telepathic, which gave him power instantaneously to get in tune with those inner harmonies of a prisoner in punishment or on the fields of sport and parade." It took, he said, "only a word out of the side of the mouth to an angry would-be prison rioter in a punishment cell with a bandaged head at Hart Island which would cause the angry one to come forward ready to tell his inner secrets. Or it would be a pat on the shoulder to 'Mike the rat catcher' conveyed by telephone from my office in the Municipal Building to the latter in the old hay barn at New Hampton Farms, New York, which would cause 200 boisterous 'kids' from the streets of New York to behave and go to work." One of the greatest days of all, Lewis recalled fondly, was when Lawes armed the entire inmate population as Mexican soldiers and U.S. Cavalrymen and sent them into battle for the Biograph silent feature *The Brand of Cowardice*. Who but Lawes would ever have risked that? And what was it all for? A motion-picture projector so the boys could watch their own movies. Oh where, Lewis asked, would society ever find such a man again?

Perhaps the finest tribute came, not from any public official, but from just another of the boys who were standing in the yard of the Massachusetts State Prison at Charlestown when word came over the loudspeaker that Lawes had died. There was a moment of stunned silence. Then the inmate said, to no one in particular, "There was a right guy."

AFTERWORD

The Lawes story was over but it did not end. Elise picked up the pieces and tried anew, in vain, to get Warners or another studio to make the biographical picture that was his last crusade. She also tried print. With her initial encouragement, Emile Gauvreau, the facile and soigné Roaring Twenties tabloidist who had been a fan of Lawes's since buying *Life and Death in Sing Sing* for excerpt in the *Daily Mirror*, completed a manuscript about Lawes that he called "Thou Shalt Not Kill," but his liberties with the story triggered an ugly legal struggle with Elise and the Lawes daughters, who thwarted the publication. Elise wrote her own book, called variously "Lawes of Sing Sing" and "I Married Sing Sing," but it was universally rejected. Scribner's turned it down even though, it said, "Lawes sounds like a very nice person." In desperation, her lawyer, James Dempsey Jr.—who, strangely enough, had defended the cannibal child murderer Albert Fish more than a dozen years before—said he would try his writing hand, but he fared no better.

Lawes's legacy was already in danger, Elise feared. In 1949 the state correction department's official magazine, *Correction,* managed to put out an entire issue devoted to the history of Sing Sing in the twentieth century without ever once mentioning Lawes. It could only have been a deliberate slight by his enemies.

In 1971 Elise collected all of her husband's letters and papers and scrapbooks, framed photographs, signed baseballs, and other memorabilia—more than fifty cartonfuls in all—for sale to a suitable institution. New York University, Colgate, and Michigan State made bids, but the prize went to the most ardent suitor, Howard Washburn, librarian of the John Jay College of Criminal Justice of the City University of New York, the nation's premier institution educating penologists of the future, for seven thousand dollars.

Then, nine years later, after Washburn had left, something very peculiar happened, something very *Lawes*—as if he, perhaps, from wherever he was, was enjoying a last cosmic joke.

A bookseller in upstate Greenwich, New York, wrote to the John Jay College library offering to sell, on behalf of an unnamed owner, "the private papers, photographs, mss's, etc of Warden Lawes of Sing Sing to your institution before going public with the sale." An attached list cited hundreds of items, including a large plaster bust of Lawes. The price was ten thousand dollars.

The chief librarian wrote back, puzzled. The college already held "a very similar collection acquired by Washburn." It would be delighted, of course, to add the new material, but resources were meager. If, however, they could come to terms, it would certainly enhance the collection.

There was no further response.

Three years passed. Then, in 1983, the librarian received a call from another bookshop, in Albany. The bookseller knew that John Jay College held a large Lawes archive and she, too, offered to sell a collection of Lawes papers and photographs, this time for $12,000. Intrigued now, and thoroughly mystified, the librarian inspected the materials. There were dozens of boxes along with a large plaster bust of Lawes, suggesting strongly that the materials being peddled were the same as those that had been offered by the Greenwich bookseller in 1980. This time John Jay came back with a counteroffer: $3,500 for the files, scrapbooks, and letters. The bookseller could keep the photos and the plaster bust. It was quickly accepted.

Later, as the librarian was sorting through the purchase, she came across Howard Washburn's address book.

The librarian scratched her head. Clearly her predecessor Washburn had known about this second set of papers and had been through them. The only plausible conclusion was that after the John Jay library had bought and received Elise's archive, Washburn had removed a large part of it, perhaps for personal resale. It had wound up in Albany, and now the college had bought the same thing twice. The librarian shrugged it off. A little larceny was hardly out of place among the Lawes papers at the John Jay College of

Criminal Justice. Besides, the Lawes collection was back together and John
Jay had it.

The collection, cataloged in two admittedly artificial sections—the original archive from 1971 and the supplemental papers of 1983—is indispensable to anyone researching the career of the man who made Sing Sing sing,
and I am deeply indebted, most of all, to the John Simon Guggenheim
Memorial Foundation for granting me a fellowship in 2001 that enabled me
to take time from my duties at the New York Times to exploit this treasure
house for my book. I am deeply indebted, too, to Dr. Larry E. Sullivan, chief
librarian and professor of criminal justice at John Jay, for guiding me through
the Lawes material and offering wise guidance. My thanks also go to present
and former library staff, Ellen Sexton, Eileen Rowland, and Nicole Demerin.
Scott Christianson, author and curator of the chilling exhibition and book,
Condemned: Inside the Sing Sing Death House, documenting the executions in
the electric chair, freely shared his extensive research and insights.

Warden Lawes's sole surviving kin, his youngest daughter, Joan Marie
Jacobsen—Cherie of the Sing Sing marching band—generously contributed
her invaluable family recollections in lengthy interviews and made available
her private scrapbooks and photographs. Kathleen's widower, Charles Miller,
also graciously filled in parts of the family story, as did Willard Gwilliam, who
had been married to Crystal's daughter, Judith. I was privileged, too, to gain
access to the voluminous files of the Ossining Historical Society under its
ever gracious fount of information, Roberta Armenio. Sing Sing's Superintendent Brian Fisher opened the gate to an indelible visit that enabled me to
envision the prison as it was in Lawes's time. Bob Globerman regaled me with
tales of growing up at his family's restaurant at Ossining's depot square, site of
the shootout in the deadly 1941 Sing Sing escape. Tony DeAngelis told me
about the great day he snared the baseball Babe Ruth blasted six hundred feet
or more out of Sing Sing in 1929 and that he then got Ruth and Lou Gehrig
to sign, and I'm really sorry his mother threw it out. Fred Starler provided a
living link to Lawes's Sing Sing—he shared stories of having started as a
guard there in 1939. Another Ossining old-timer, William Brady, recounted
tales of the Lawes family. Stanley Katz added an intriguing element by showing me a copy of Lawes's 20,000 Years in Sing Sing in which his uncle, Jacob
Katz, a rabbi at the prison, had marked a passage that he claimed to have

written. A similarly elusive tale came from Robert Gold, who bravely tracked down the story of his father, Harry N. Gold, who did a stretch for robbery in Sing Sing and had befriended another prisoner, "Jules," who claimed to have ghosted Lawes's book. Joan Shalleck, of Ossining's arts community, contributed insights into movies and sports at Sing Sing. Jeff Roth, the *Times's* indefatigable researcher, crime maven, and boulevardier, was, as usual, indispensable in unearthing obscure but vital facts. Chapin's biographer, James McGrath Morris, generously shared information.

My thanks go, too, to my astute editors, Webster Younce at Picador and Charles Spicer at St. Martin's Press, and my supportive agents, Anne Sibbald of Janklow & Nesbit Associates and Brian Siberell of CAA.

A family's loyalty and love can never be repaid, but I hope this work is some testament to the sacrifices of my dear wife, Deborah, and our daughters, Anna and Sophie.

I suppose I might add a word on how this all came to be. As a young man, I myself was in Sing Sing. Yes, it's true. My father, Hans, had a dental supplies business in Westchester, and Sing Sing was one of his clients. Starting in the late 1950s, I made deliveries for him inside the walls, each time with pounding heart as the heavy gate rose up for me and then clanged shut behind me as I unloaded the car. In 1966, as a young *Times* correspondent in Westchester, I went back to Sing Sing to interview Warden Wilfred Louis Denno as he retired after sixteen years of running, as I wrote, "the tightest ship on the Hudson." In the course of the article I cited Lawes as one of his distinguished predecessors. But I thought no more about Lawes until thirty years later, when I was going through the notes of café society impresario Sherman Billingsley for a book on his Stork Club and came across this account in Billingsley's own hand: "Ernest Hemmingway gave Warden Laws of Sing Sing a push one night. Laws fell down, that's all that happened, but the press played it up big. I asked Steve if this kind of publicity was good or bad for me. Steve said one fight a year is good publicity providing the names of the fighters are big names like Hemmingway and Laws."

I knew who "Hemmingway" was. But who was this "Laws" whose name I couldn't recall ever hearing before? Once I got the name right, I found out.

A NOTE ON SOURCES

As explained in the Afterword, much of this book is based on letters, speeches, scripts, manuscripts, and news clippings in hundreds of files of the Lewis E. Lawes Collection of the library of the John Jay College of Criminal Justice of the City University of New York. Rather than encumber the reader with voluminous citations, I would direct anyone with detailed interest in Lawes to this prize archive. In particular, I would like to acknowledge a debt to an authoritative source of information in the Lawes Collection, the unpublished autobiography of Lawes's second wife, Elise, which is, at the same time, a biography of Lawes. While unfinished and fragmentary in places, the work, variously titled "I Married Sing Sing" and "Lawes of Sing Sing," offers details about Lawes's family, childhood, and domestic life that are not available elsewhere. Also valuable for its colorful evocation of Lawes and his era is another manuscript in the Lawes Collection that I drew upon, Emile Gauvreau's "Thou Shalt Not Kill." Not included in the collection but rewarding for its history of Sing Sing is a 1999 doctoral thesis (and forthcoming Harvard University publication), "Citizens and Criminals: The Rise of the American Carceral State 1890–1935," by a Columbia University Ph.D. candidate, Rebecca Mary McLennan.

BIBLIOGRAPHY

Brockway, Zebulon Reed. *Fifty Years of Prison Service*. 1912 Reprint, Montclair, N.J.: Patterson Smith, 1969.

Chapin, Charles E. *Charles E. Chapin's Story: Written in Sing Sing*. New York: G. P. Putnam's Sons, Knickerbocker Press, 1920.

Christianson, Scott. *Condemned: Inside the Sing Sing Death House*. New York: New York University Press, 2000.

———. *With Liberty for Some: 500 Years of Imprisonment in America*. Boston: Northeastern University Press, 1998.

Churchill, Allen. *Park Row*. New York: Rinehart & Company, 1958.

Cobb, Irvin S. *Alias Ben Alibi*. New York: George H. Doran Company, 1925.

Conover, Ted. *New Jack: Guarding Sing Sing*. New York: Vintage Books, 2001.

Darrow, Clarence. *The Story of My Life*. New York: Charles Scribner's Sons, 1934.

Douglas, Susan J. *Listening In*. New York: Times Books, Random House, 1999.

Early, Eleanor, and Constance, eds. *The Constance Letters of Charles Chapin*. New York: Simon & Schuster, 1931.

Fitzpatrick, Ellen F. *Endless Crusade: Women Social Scientists and Progressive Reform*. New York: Oxford University Press, 1990.

Gauvreau, Emile. *Hot News*. New York: Macauley Company, 1931.

———. *My Last Million Readers*. New York: E. P. Dutton & Company, 1941.

———. *The Scandal Monger*. New York: Macauley Company, 1932.

———. "Thou Shalt Not Kill." Manuscript, Special Collections, Library of City University's John Jay College of Criminal Justice.

Irene, Viola, ed. *The Uncensored Letters of Charles Chapin*. New York: Rudolph Gold, 1931.

Kahn, E. J. *The World of Swope*. New York: Simon & Schuster, 1965.

Kroeger, Brooke. *Nellie Bly: Daredevil, Reporter, Feminist*. New York: Times Books, Random House, 1994.

Lawes, Elise Chisholm. "Lawes of Sing Sing" (also called "I Married Sing Sing"). Manuscript, Special Collections, Library of City University's John Jay College of Criminal Justice.

Lawes, Lewis E. *Cell 202—Sing Sing*. New York: Farrar & Rinehart, 1935.

————. *Invisible Stripes*. New York: Farrar & Rinehart, 1938.

————. *Life and Death in Sing Sing*. Garden City, N.Y.: Garden City Publishing Company, 1928.

————. *Man's Judgment of Death*. New York: G. P. Putnam's Sons, Knickerbocker Press, 1924.

————. *Meet the Murderer*. New York: Harper & Brothers Publishers, 1940.

————. *Sing Sing*. Privately printed, author's collection, 1933.

————. *Strange Stories from Sing Sing*. Privately printed, author's collection, 1934.

————. *20,000 Years in Sing Sing*. New York: Blue Ribbon Books, 1932.

Lowrie, Donald. *My Life in Prison*. New York: Mitchell Kennerley, 1912.

Macfadden, Mary, and Emile Gauvreau. *Dumbbells and Carrot Strips: The Story of Bernarr Macfadden*. New York: Henry Holt & Company, 1953.

McGrath, Edward F. *I Was Condemned to the Chair*. New York: Frederick A. Stokes Company, 1934.

McLennan, Rebecca Mary. "Citizens and Criminals: The Rise of the American Carceral State, 1890–1935." Ph.D. dissertation, Columbia University, 1999.

Morris, James McGrath. *Jailhouse Journalism: The Fourth Estate Behind Bars*. New Brunswick, N.J.: Transaction Publishers, 2002.

————. *The Rose Man of Sing Sing: A True Tale of Life, Murder, and Redemption*. New York: Fordham University Press, 2003.

Osborne, Thomas Mott. *Within Prison Walls*. New York: D. Appleton & Company, 1914.

Piscotta, Alexander A. *Benevolent Repression: Social Control and the American Reformatory-Prison Movement*. New York: New York University Press, 1994.

Rafter, Nicole Hahn. *Creating Born Criminals*. Urbana: University of Illinois Press, 1997.

Reynolds, Quentin. *I, Willie Sutton*. New York: Farrar, Straus & Young, 1953.

Squire, Amos O. *Sing Sing Doctor*. Garden City, N.Y.: Garden City Publishing Company, 1937.

Sullivan, Florence J. *Sing Sing Capital Punishment and "Honest Graft."* New York: Connolly Press, 1927.

Sutton, Willie, with Edward Linn. *Where the Money Was*. New York: Viking Press, 1976.

Tannenbaum, Frank. *Osborne of Sing Sing*. Chapel Hill: University of North Carolina Press, 1933.

INDEX

Illustration pages are *italicized*.